PUBLIC MEN AND EVENTS.

PUBLIC MEN AND EVENTS

FROM THE COMMENCEMENT OF

MR. MONROE'S ADMINISTRATION, IN 1817,

TO THE CLOSE OF

MR. FILLMORE'S ADMINISTRATION, IN 1853.

BY

NATHAN SARGENT,

LATE COMMISSIONER OF CUSTOMS (FORMERLY KNOWN AS A POLITICAL WRITER UNDER THE NOM DE PLUME OF "OLIVER OLDSCHOOL").

VOL. I.

PHILADELPHIA:
J. B. LIPPINCOTT & CO.
1875.

TO

THE ENLIGHTENED CONDUCTORS OF THE PRESS,

THE ARCHIMEDEAN LEVER BY WHICH, STANDING UPON THE FIRM BASIS OF CHRISTIANITY, EDUCATION, AND THE RIGHTS OF MAN, AND AIDED BY SCIENCE, THEY ARE MOVING THE WORLD,

This Work is Respectfully Inscribed

BY ONE WHO, FOR MANY YEARS, WAS PROUD TO BE NUMBERED AS ONE OF THEIR FRATERNITY.

INTRODUCTION.

It is well known to the people of the United States generally, and to the public men of the country especially, that from 1825 to 1853, and even eight years later, was a period of very exciting political conflicts, during which many great questions of public policy, and important measures involving the vital interests of the nation, came before Congress and underwent searching, able, and not unfrequently acrimonious discussion in the Senate and House of Representatives. And the names of prominent men of that day in whose hands were the destinies of the nation—John Quincy Adams, Andrew Jackson, Henry Clay, Daniel Webster, John C. Calhoun, Martin Van Buren, Thomas H. Benton, Horace Binney, John Sergeant, John Davis, John M. Clayton, Thomas Ewing, Lewis Cass, James Buchanan, Silas Wright, George McDuffie, James K. Polk, William L. Marcy, and a hundred others—are even now familiar as household words to the American people.

But precisely what those great questions and measures were, how they arose, what were the principles involved, and the parts taken by the leaders of the two parties contending against each other, very few now upon the stage of action have any very definite idea.

During the period named, party spirit ran high, and party contests were carried on with great virulence. To read the full debates of that day, on any of the important measures which were discussed in Congress and the public press, would require more time than any man can afford to give to the past in these "fast" times, when one can hardly keep up with the current events of the day. And yet there are many who may be glad to obtain some just notion of the questions which then agitated the community, how they were disposed of, and the parts acted, respectively, by the leading men whom I have named. Others, too, who were themselves participants in these scenes, will no doubt be gratified to have a brief retrospective view of them presented, whereby they can refresh their memories and retrace the paths they long ago trod in the heat of conflict with companions long since gone to their rest.

My purpose in preparing this work has been to give, in as brief a manner as possible, an account of the sayings and doings of that day,—of the various questions which came before the nation, and the spirit of the debates in Congress, keeping up, at the same time, a continuity of narrative of important events as they occurred,—interspersing the whole with interesting incidents, anecdotes, and descriptions of the appearance and characteristics of the public men, with many of whom it was my lot to be brought in personal association.

During the period to which I have confined myself took place the animated discussion on the Panama question, on which the opposition to Mr. J. Q. Adams's administration first arrayed themselves in solid phalanx; the celebrated debate between Mr. Webster and Colonel Hayne; the debate on the tariffs of 1828 and 1832, and on the compromise tariff of 1833; on the bill to re-charter the United States Bank, and on the veto of that bill; on the Force bill, and the bill to distribute the proceeds of the public lands; on the removal of the public deposits from the United States Bank, and on Mr. Clay's resolutions censuring the President for that act, followed by that on the

President's protest against these resolutions, and on the proposition of Colonel Benton, finally carried, to "expunge" one of them from the journal of the Senate; on the exposition, by a select committee of the House, of the astounding defalcations of Federal officers; on the nomination of Martin Van Buren as minister to England; on the annexation of Texas, the war with Mexico, the acquisition and admission of California, Utah, and New Mexico, and, finally, the long-protracted debates on Mr. Clay's Compromise measures, in 1850, including the Fugitive Slave Law.

It was during this period that "Nullification" first raised its hideous front, and was crushed out by General Jackson's proclamation and energetic measures; that the presentation of Abolition petitions in the House produced great irritation, and those intensely exciting and tumultuous scenes in that body in which Mr. Adams was ever the champion of the right of petition, and Mr. Wise, Mr. Rhett, Mr. Gilmer, Waddy Thompson, and other Southern gentlemen opposed with much eloquence and fiery zeal the reception of these petitions.

From 1829 to 1837 there was at the head of the government a man of indomitable will and implacable temper, who, impatient of opposition from any quarter, required implicit acquiescence on the part of his friends and partisans. These personal qualities of the President gave character to his party and to the political contests of the day, which, as I have said, were carried on with unusual spirit and acrimony.

From the commencement of Mr. Monroe's administration, in 1817, to the close of the year 1825, tranquillity pervaded the country like the placid calm of an "Indian summer." From 1820 to 1832, excepting the commercial revulsion of 1825, the nation enjoyed, generally, a rare degree of prosperity; but from the commencement of the war upon the United States Bank, the veto of the bill re-chartering it, the removal of the public deposits to what were termed "pet banks," and other measures of the government more or less affecting the business relations and commercial operations of the country,—measures then styled "experiments upon the currency,"—all was changed; and in May, 1837, these "experiments" culminated in a stoppage of specie payments by every bank in the United States, and in a financial panic which paralyzed every industrial interest in the nation.

During the period covered by these recollections, namely, from 1817 to 1853, and indeed to a later date, I took a warm interest in politics and public affairs, being for a considerable portion of the time connected with the press, which necessarily brought me in association with many of the leading men of the country. From 1841 to 1846, inclusive, I was the Washington correspondent of the Philadelphia "United States Gazette," writing over the signature of "OLIVER OLDSCHOOL;" and on the meeting of the Thirtieth Congress, December, 1847, I was elected Sergeant-at-arms of the House, and held the office during that and a portion of the Thirty-first Congress, and of course had official relations with every member of the House of those two Congresses.

It may be supposed I have had some experience in organizing parties and carrying on political campaigns. I have also held important offices in the Treasury Department,—Register of the Treasury and Commissioner of Customs,—and know from a tolerably long experience something of official life and of public men at Washington.

Many partial friends, knowing the experience I have had in public affairs, and my associations with many of the leading characters of the past, have, for several years, urged me to write out my recollections of the men and incidents of my time;

but other avocations, a disinclination to undertake so arduous a task, and a distrust of my ability to produce a work that would commend itself to the public, deterred me from complying with their requests; probably I should never have given way to them but for the fact that on my retirement from the office of Commissioner of Customs, in 1871, which I had held for ten years, I became restless for want of occupation. My regular habits being broken up, my mind, like the first dove sent out from the ark, could find no resting-place. "To rest is to rust," as Mr. Seward justly said of himself after leaving the office of Secretary of State; and I must therefore seek new employment, for employment was as necessary to my mind as food for my body. The kindly suggestion of a friend at that moment turned me to the occupation—which I have by no means found irksome, but quite the contrary—the fruit of which is this work. It has occupied me a little over two years, which time I have spent agreeably with the men and in the scenes of by-gone years; though the pleasure I have enjoyed has been deeply tinged with sadness by the reflection that almost to a man they have passed away.

In recording my recollections of these, it will readily be seen that I occupy the stand-point of "an old line Whig," such as I was, and as such I cannot pretend to have related past events with exact impartiality. Time, it is true, softens the asperities, removes many of the prejudices, and corrects some of the errors inseparable from a participation in party strife, and especially does it assuage those rancorous feelings which violent party contests engender. But time does not entirely divest us of the feelings—prejudices, perhaps—which then governed us, nor wholly, if at all, change our views in regard to the characters of the men and the merits of the measures which divided parties. Of these, generally, I have spoken with freedom, and sometimes, perhaps, with a little of the old feeling. Yet I trust I have done no one injustice, having intended to make no statement not warranted by undeniable facts.

I have closed with the end of Mr. Fillmore's administration, 1853; not being disposed to enter upon that tempestuous Kansas-Nebraska period which immediately followed and continued during the administrations of General Pierce and Mr. Buchanan, finally ending in the great Rebellion and the utter extinction of slavery.

N. SARGENT.

May 5, 1874.

CONTENTS.

CHAPTER I.

CHAPTER II.

CHAPTER III.

CHAPTER IV.

PUBLIC MEN AND EVENTS.

CHAPTER I.

General Remarks.—The Rise of Parties.—Federal and Republican, or Democratic.—Opposition to the War of 1812 fatal to the Federal Party.—Mr. Monroe nominated for President by the Democratic Caucus.—His Competitor Wm. H. Crawford.—Rufus King the Federal Candidate.—Monroe elected.—His Cabinet.—His Long Journey East and North.—The Era of "Good Feeling."—Creek and Seminole War.—Jackson enters Florida.—Executes Arbuthnot and Ambrister.—The Subject before Congress.—Florida acquired from Spain.—Duel between Commodore Barron and Commodore Decatur.—William Lowndes, of South Carolina.—William Pinckney.—Candidates for President, 1824.—General Jackson.—Nominated for President by the State Federal Convention of Pennsylvania; also by the Democratic State Convention.—Mr. Calhoun nominated by the same Convention for Vice-President.—Washington Society.—Intrigues to make General Jackson President.—His Coleman Letter.—His Monroe Letters.—The Presidential Vote of 1824.—The Plot to destroy Mr. Clay.—He is charged with Bargain and Corruption.—Proceedings in the House thereon.—George Kremer assumes the Responsibility, but refuses to appear before the Committee and substantiate his Charge.—Election of Mr. Adams by the House of Representatives.—How this was effected on the First Ballot.—The Scene in the House.—Mr. Adams inaugurated.—Congratulated by Mr. Monroe and General Jackson.

POLITICAL parties are the natural product of free government. Wherever there is freedom of speech and freedom of the press, discussions and conflicts will arise; and where the people rule or elect their rulers, there will be clashing of opinions in regard to public affairs, the fitness of candidates for office, and a rivalry growing out of personal interests. Thus parties spring up and sometimes run to such extremes and become so infuriated as to set all law and authority at defiance, ending in bloody, savage, and remorseless massacres.

Our own country has never been entirely free from parties:

before the Revolution they existed in the different colonies, based on local questions and interests, and in some of them were characterized by great heat and asperity. But the great controversy between the colonies and the mother country, which culminated in our independence, absorbed and overrode all minor and local questions, dividing the people into new parties, denominated *Whig* and *Tory*.

The formation of the Constitution gave rise to conflicts of opinions as to the powers that should be conferred on the national government or reserved by the several States; and these adverse opinions soon originated new parties, which divided the nation for many years after. These were at first designated *Federal* and *anti-Federal*, afterwards *Federal* and *Republican*, or *Democratic*. Though not regularly organized during General Washington's administration, they were, nevertheless, exceedingly hostile to and abusive of each other. The vituperation poured out upon General Washington, who was known to be a *Federalist*, can scarcely be conceived by those in whose minds he is the canonized patriot and father of his country. The political history of that period is painfully interesting.

It was not until the Presidential contest between John Adams and Thomas Jefferson, in 1800, that the two parties came into the field arrayed against each other; but from that time down to 1817, when Mr. Monroe was elected President, party animosity raged with great fury,—far beyond anything since witnessed, except, perhaps, during the two terms of General Jackson's administration.

Opposition to the War of 1812 proved fatal to the Federal party, which ceased to exist as a national party with the close of Mr. Madison's administration. Not only did the odium of opposing the war tend to annihilate that party, but the questions upon which the two parties differed were, in a great measure, settled or disposed of by the war; others, relating to the general interests of the country, such as a tariff, internal improvements, the chartering of a national bank, erecting fortifications, etc., taking their place, and finding advocates and opponents in both the old parties.

Candidates for President and Vice-President were then selected by the respective parties by what was termed a Congressional caucus. Mr. Monroe was placed in nomination for President by a caucus of the Republican members of Congress, Daniel D. Tompkins, of New York, being nominated by the same caucus for Vice-President. Mr. Crawford, of Georgia, was Mr. Monroe's competitor, and fell but few votes behind him in the caucus.

Rufus King was the candidate of the Federal party, or what there was left of it, against Mr. Monroe. The latter received one hundred and eighty-three electoral votes, the former thirty-four.

No President ever encountered less opposition during his four or eight years' service than Mr. Monroe. Parties and the country seemed to be tired of contention, and desirous to enjoy repose. A most able cabinet was selected, consisting of Mr. J. Q. Adams as Secretary of State; William H. Crawford, Secretary of the Treasury; John C. Calhoun, Secretary of War; Smith Thompson, Secretary of the Navy; and William Wirt, Attorney-General. For long and eminent public services, great and tried abilities, and patriotic devotion to the free institutions of the country, this cabinet might proudly challenge a comparison with any one whose members have since filled their places.

Before the cabinet was formed, General Jackson addressed a letter to Mr. Monroe, which was brought out and made public during the Presidential contest in 1824, when Jackson himself was a candidate, urging him in selecting his cabinet to disregard party. "In every instance," General Jackson says, "party and party feelings should be avoided. Now is the time to exterminate that monster called party spirit. By selecting characters most conspicuous for probity, virtue, capacity, and firmness, without regard to party, you will go far to, if not entirely, eradicate those feelings which, on former occasions, threw so many obstacles in the way of government, and perhaps have the pleasure and honor of uniting a people heretofore politically divided. The chief magistrate of a great and powerful nation should never indulge in party feelings." . . . Patriotic sentiments, truly. But who would have then supposed that entering upon the duties of President twelve years later, he would cast these sentiments to the winds, and adopt the most proscriptive, thoroughly *party* system of making removals and appointments ever known in the government?

Soon after Mr. Monroe entered upon the duties of his high office he started on a tour to the East, North, and West, accompanied only by his private secretary, Mr. Mason, and General Swift, Chief of the Corps of Engineers; the latter for the purpose of making observations for works of defense along the seaboard.

In all the cities, towns, and villages through which the President passed he was received with great demonstrations of respect, the people striving to do him all the honor due to the chief magistrate of the nation,—all uniting in these demonstrations without distinction of party. In Boston, especially, the head-quarters of Federalism, the Federalists vied with their political opponents in their demonstrations and in the honors shown him. Addresses poured in upon him, not only from the citizens, corporations, etc., of the cities and towns through which he passed and sojourned, but from distant cities, towns, and counties. Such was the exuberance of good feeling manifested towards the President by all classes of the people on and near the route he traveled,—in every part of New England and New York, indeed,—that it was termed "the era of good feeling," and this was applied to the whole eight years of his administration. His journey seemed to have annihilated or "exterminated that monster called party spirit."

The President proceeded as far east as Portland, Me., which he reached on the 15th of July, six weeks after leaving Washington! Thence he went to Burlington, Vt., and from thence to Plattsburg. From Plattsburg to Sackett's Harbor his route was through a wilderness called the Chateaugay Woods. From Sackett's Harbor the President proceeded by the lake to the mouth of the Niagara River, visited the Falls and some of the principal scenes of military operations on that frontier during the war, went to Buffalo, from thence to Detroit, thence through Ohio to Pittsburg, where he arrived on the 5th of September, and at Washington on the 18th, having been absent from the seat of government three and a half months, performing a tour which could now be traveled in, possibly, a little more than a week, including the necessary stoppages to hear and answer congratulatory addresses. The appearance of the President of the United States among the people far distant from the seat of government was a novel, and therefore great, occasion, and made a great sensation. Nobody had ever seen a President, and all who could must see him. The road was lined with people as he passed, and he found every village and hamlet in his way, or where he rested overnight, crowded with the eager inhabitants of the surrounding country, who had left the plow in the furrow, the cream in the churn, and the clothes in the tub, to see what had never before been seen there, the President of the United States.

CREEK AND SEMINOLE WAR.

Soon after Mr. Monroe became President, hostilities broke out with the Creek and Seminole Indians, occupying a part of Georgia and Florida. As commander of the Southern military district, General Jackson was ordered to take the field against the hostile red-skins; and as many of them took refuge in Florida, where they were believed to be countenanced, if not aided, by the Spaniards, the general deemed it his duty to enter Florida with his army and take possession of St. Mark's and Pensacola. He also seized, and had tried by court-martial, two Englishmen, Arbuthnot and Ambrister, who were charged with aiding and inciting the Indians in their depredations upon our people. They were both found guilty and hung.

These proceedings caused the President great anxiety. They were considered in cabinet council, and condemned and disavowed by every member except Mr. Adams. A paper was drawn up and made public, declaring that in entering Florida and taking possession of St. Mark's and Pensacola, General Jackson had acted without authority and upon his own responsibility; and it was decided that the places taken should be immediately evacuated. As the general claimed to have authority from the Secretary of War for what he had done, this condemnation of his course, mild as it was, roused his fiery temper, which found expression in some of his peculiarly emphatic expletives.

The arrest, trial, condemnation, and execution of the two Englishmen in a foreign country was alleged to be a palpable and gross violation of international law, and the military occupation of the Floridas an act of war upon Spain, involving our government in serious difficulties with a friendly nation.

Negotiations had been for some time pending between Spain and the United States for the cession of Florida to the latter, but were interrupted by the proceedings of General Jackson. The Spanish government and minister were in a towering rage; but Mr. Adams, who had in cabinet council refused to join in censuring General Jackson, or to draw up the letter the council determined should be transmitted to him, prepared a masterly defense of the general, in which his proceedings were unequivocally justified; and ere long the negotiations for the acquisition of Florida were resumed, and in the end brought to a favorable result,—a treaty of cession.

Meantime, however, the subject of the invasion of Florida was brought before Congress by Mr. Cobb, the personal friend of Mr. Crawford, who introduced a resolution in the House of Representatives condemning General Jackson's proceedings, upon which arose a very acrimonious, irritating, and prolonged debate. It was referred to the committee on military affairs,—seven members,—a majority of whom made a report severely censuring General Jackson, while the minority reported that, instead of condemnation, General Jackson deserved the thanks of the country. Upon a final vote the general's conduct was approved,—100 to 70.

In the Senate the papers relating to the Seminole war, which were communicated by the President to both houses of Congress, were referred to a committee of five,—Messrs. Burrill, Lacock, Eppes, King, of New York, and Eaton, of Tennessee. Of these, the first three made a report severely condemning General Jackson's proceedings, while the minority justified them. No vote was taken upon the report in the Senate.

The result was, on the whole, pretty nearly a drawn game between General Jackson and those who condemned him. But the debates and proceedings in Congress had caused great irritation and animosity among members (including Senators) and in the city of Washington during the whole session; General Jackson and his hot-headed young friends indulging very freely in denunciatory language towards those opposed to him; and the latter, perhaps, giving no less license to their condemnation of what they termed his lawless proceedings in Florida.

General Jackson being delayed at Winchester, Va., on his way to Washington, and being fêted by the prominent citizens, gave as a toast, "John C. Calhoun,—an honest man is the noblest work of God." Eleven years after, he discovered that Mr. Calhoun was the member of Mr. Monroe's cabinet who proposed to censure him for his invasion of Florida, as was now attempted by a portion of Congress.

Some very important public events—one of which, at least, caused great excitement and sectional irritation—illustrated Mr. Monroe's administration; but, as the interest they then excited has long since passed away, I shall content myself with a mere mention of them. The admission of Missouri as a State, with what is known as the "Missouri Compromise," was the measure or question upon which the North and the South were then arrayed against each other as distinct sections, slavery being the bone of contention. The next very important public measure was the acquisition of the Floridas by a treaty with Spain, signed the 22d February, 1819. The treaty was promptly ratified by the Senate; but the King of Spain haggled, procrastinated, and endeavored to get us to make new stipulations, trifling with us, until the President deemed it necessary to present the subject to Congress, when an act was passed, just at the heel of the session, authorizing him to take possession of the ceded provinces and establish a temporary government over them. These measures brought the king to his senses and to terms forthwith.

By "the Florida Treaty," so called, the United States relinquished their claim to that portion of Texas lying east of the Nueces, which Mr. Adams, Mr. Clay, and many other of our statesmen contended belonged to us, as being a part of Louisiana, purchased by Mr. Jefferson. Both the gentlemen named were very unwilling to surrender this portion of Texas; but

Mr. Monroe and his cabinet, all except Mr. Adams, so determined. Mr. Clay was strongly opposed to this surrender, and became for a time a quasi opponent of the administration.

MILITARY POSTS ESTABLISHED IN THE FAR WEST. THE YELLOWSTONE EXPEDITION.

To overawe and keep peace with the Indians of the Plains and the Rocky Mountains, encourage the extension of white settlements, command the fur trade of the Rocky Mountains, which was exceedingly profitable, and prevent the Hudson Bay Company from establishing trading-posts and extending their trade towards the sources of the Missouri, it was deemed proper to establish military posts farther into the Indian country than had heretofore been done. A military post was therefore established on the Mississippi River a little below the Falls of St. Anthony, which was known as Fort Snelling; another at the Mandan villages on the Missouri; and a third at the mouth of the Yellowstone River, eighteen hundred miles above St. Louis. In establishing these military posts, especially the two last, Mr. Calhoun, Secretary of War, thought it would be good policy to make a deep and lasting impression upon the wild tribes of Indians, who knew nothing of the power of the United States. To do this, a steamboat was built in the form of a great water-snake, which, dashing forward against the strong current of the river, should emit volumes of smoke through the mouth of what appeared to be some huge monster. To heighten the impression of awe and wonder which this apparent monster must create, heavy guns were occasionally fired, whose reverberations along the river-banks and through the wilderness might be taken by the wandering savages for the bellowing of this strange animal.

The boat proceeded the first season to Council Bluffs, twelve hundred miles above St. Louis, where the expedition wintered, 1819–20, preparing to proceed to the Yellowstone the next season; but for some reason or other the expedition was abandoned. The experiment of frightening the Indians did not prove very successful, for they soon discovered that this huge-looking creature was only the work of the white man, and not the creation of the Great Spirit. These advanced military posts, however, afforded protection to our fur-traders, hunters, and trappers, and checked the further encroachments of the Hudson Bay Company.

MR. CALHOUN.

The Secretary of War was at this time a young, enterprising, and far-seeing statesman, animated by a patriotic desire to promote the greatness and prosperity of the nation. His views were then limited by no State lines, but expanded to the uttermost bounds of the United States.

The question in regard to internal improvements by national means had been considered by Congress and by the Executive, the former favoring such improvements, the latter questioning the power of the general government to make them. The House of Representatives having passed a resolution at the first session of the Fifteenth Congress, directing the Secretary of War to report "a plan for the application of such means as are within the power of Congress, for the purpose of opening and constructing such roads and canals as may deserve and require the aid of government, with a view to military operations in the time of war, the transportation of munitions of war, and also a statement of the works of that nature which have been commenced," the Secretary, Mr. Calhoun, at the second session of that Congress, presented an elaborate report to the House, stating that, in his opinion, "a judicious system of roads and canals, constructed for the convenience of commerce and the transportation of the mail only, without reference to military operations, is itself among the most efficient means of defense, as the same roads and canals, with few exceptions, would be required for the operations of war. Such a system, by consolidating the Union, increasing its wealth and fiscal capacity, adds greatly to the resources of war."

"There is no country," says the Secretary, "to which a good system of roads and canals is more indispensable than the United States. Great as is the military capacity of the country compared with the number of people, yet, when considered in relation to its vast extent, it must be obvious that it is difficult for the government to afford adequate protection to every part. This difficulty is in a great measure overcome by a good system of military roads and canals."

Mr. Calhoun was at this time enthusiastically in favor of "connecting the various portions of the country by A JUDICIOUS SYSTEM OF INTERNAL IMPROVEMENTS." I first became acquainted with him in June, 1824. I then visited Washington on business, bearing a letter of introduction to him from an old personal friend of his, and a former neighbor in South Carolina. On presenting the letter to him at the War Department I was very cordially received. He made many inquiries in regard to old friends and neighbors who had emigrated to Alabama, and many also in regard to that new but rapidly-settling State. He soon spoke of a national road he had projected, or had in contemplation, from Washington to New Orleans, via Abingdon, Va., Knoxville, Tenn., thence through Alabama, passing near Cahawba, and so on to New Orleans. But this was only one of many great national improvements he had projected and spoke of accomplishing in the most confident and earnest manner. He soon had his table and floor covered with maps of these various improvements, by which he expected to make Washington City the great commercial emporium of the nation, as well as its political capital.

Among the projected improvements to be accomplished by national means, chiefly or in part, I recollect, were the following: the opening of an inland sloop navigation from New York to Savannah by a canal from New York to Philadelphia, a canal uniting the Delaware and Susquehanna Rivers, a canal from Chesapeake Bay to the Potomac at Washington, the Dismal Swamp Canal uniting Chesapeake Bay with Albemarle Sound, and so on to Savannah; the Chesapeake and Ohio Canal, as a channel of commerce for the great West; many other canals, the routes of which I cannot now recollect; and, finally, a national road from Washington to Buffalo.

Mr. Calhoun spoke of his projected improvements and the great benefits that the country would derive from them with a warmth, earnestness, and enthusiasm which indicated that his whole soul was in "the system" he had projected. That he continued to hold the views expressed in his report to the House as late as 1825 appears from the following extract from a speech delivered by him to his constituents at a public dinner given him by his neighbors at Abbeville, S.C., on the — day of June, 1825, for which see "Niles's Register," *passim.* Addressing them, he said,—

. . . "Not doubting the necessity of an enlightened system of measures for the security of the country and the advancement of its true interests, nor your disposition to make the necessary sacrifices to sustain it, I gave my zealous efforts in favor of all such measures: the gradual increase of the navy, a moderate military establishment, properly organized and instructed, a system of fortifications for the defense of the coast, the restoration of specie currency, A DUE PROTECTION OF MANUFACTURES OF THE COUNTRY, which had taken root during the period of war and restrictions,* and, finally, a system of connecting the various portions of the country by A JUDICIOUS SYSTEM OF INTERNAL IMPROVEMENTS.

. . . "You nobly sustained all these measures. Soon after the adoption by Congress of this SYSTEM OF MEASURES, which grew out of the experience of the late war, I was transferred to preside over the Department of War. . . . In this new position my principles of action remained unchanged."

In this speech Mr. Calhoun said, "No man would reprobate more pointedly than myself any concerted union between States for interested or sectional objects. Such concert would be against the spirit of our Constitution, which was intended to bind all the States in one common bond of union and friendship."

This reads strangely in the light of subsequent events,—events, too, which took place but a few years after these patriotic words were uttered.

At a dinner given to him at Pendleton, his own home, during this visit, one of the toasts was the following, embodying, in a few words, his views in regard to internal improvements at that time, and fully in accord with his speech at Abbeville on that subject:

* Embargoes, non-intercourse, etc.

"*Internal improvements:* Guided by the wisdom and energy of its able advocates, it cannot fail to strengthen and perpetuate our bond of union."

Strange that in one or two years from this time internal improvements were pronounced *unconstitutional* by Mr. Calhoun and all his followers, and not a man in South Carolina could be found who had the courage to reiterate the above sentiment!

Mr. Calhoun was a graduate of Yale College, New Haven, and while there developed the peculiar characteristics which so distinguished him in after-life. Dr. Dwight, president of the college at that time, predicted that, if his life should be spared, he would run a splendid public career, as he saw that his mind was bent on a political life and the attainment of political honors; that his ambition was boundless, and his capacity equal to any position under the government.

From the time he left college he took a warm interest in public affairs, though, as has been, or will be, shown, his principles were not very firmly fixed; at least they were easily abandoned for others.

FATAL DUEL BETWEEN COMMODORE BARRON AND COMMODORE DECATUR.

A tragic event occurred at Washington, in March, 1820, which produced intense excitement not only there but in every part of the country: namely, a duel between Commodore Barron and Commodore Decatur, in which the latter was killed and the former received a wound which, for some time, was expected to prove mortal.

Commodore Decatur stood at the head of his profession; had signalized himself by daring feats of bravery in the Tunisian war, and by eminent services in the late war with England. He was one of that gallant band of officers whose skill, bravery, and daring had raised the character of our navy and made it the pride of the nation. It is hardly necessary to say that he was a great favorite at the capital, and one of the ornaments of its social circles.

That he had been imperious and overbearing towards Commodore Barron, and had opposed his being placed in command of the Columbus, seventy-four, there was no doubt. His feeling towards him may be seen at the close of his last letter of the correspondence which preceded the duel: "your jeopardizing your life depends on yourself, and not on me, and is done with a view of fighting your character up; I shall pay no further attention to any communication you may make to me other than a direct call to the field." This was supercilious, and left Commodore Barron no other course than to "call him to the field."

A challenge followed, and the duel took place at Bladensburg, March 22, 1820. Captain Jesse D. Elliott was the second of Barron, and Commodore Bainbridge of Decatur; the distance but eight paces, making it morally certain that one or both must fall; and that Barron expected both would may be inferred from what he said to Decatur while the seconds were loading the pistols: "I hope, Decatur, that when we meet in another world we shall be better friends than we have been in this." To which Decatur replied, "I have never been your enemy, sir."

The word being given, both fired so near together that there was but one report, and both fell, each wounded in the hip, and believed to be mortally. Both were placed in carriages and conveyed as rapidly as possible to their respective homes,—Decatur to the house he built and then occupied, on the corner of H and Sixteenth Streets, diagonally opposite W. W. Corcoran's, still known as the Decatur House. He lived but a few hours. Barron, quite unexpectedly, recovered.

It may be satisfactory to the reader, too young to be familiar with the events of that day, to know the causes which led to this famous duel. They were of a date as early as 1806, and grew out of the more famous affair of the Chesapeake and Leopard. The latter, a British ship of war, far superior to the Chesapeake and well prepared for action, threatening an attack on the former, on account of her having, as was alleged, British seamen on board, Commodore Barron, being in command of the Chesapeake, and wholly unprepared for action, declined it, and suffered the men thus claimed to be taken on board the Leopard. This was a circumstance mortifying to the whole nation, roused a bitter feeling towards England, and called forth loud condemnation of Commodore Barron.

A court of inquiry was held, which condemned the commodore. A court-martial was then ordered, of which Commodore Decatur, who had strongly condemned the conduct of Barron, was a member. This court decided that Commodore Barron was guilty, not of cowardice or want of firmness, but of neglect of duty and unofficer-like conduct in not clearing his ship for action on the probability of an engagement, and sentenced him to be suspended from all command in the navy and from all pay and emoluments for the term of five years from the 8th of February, 1808; which sentence was approved by the President. This excluded him from the navy during the war with England. The severity of this sentence he attributed to Decatur, whose hostility to him was undisguised. Upon the expiration of his suspension he claimed his rank and employment, and the command of the Columbus, seventy-four, in which, as before stated, he was opposed by Decatur.

I became acquainted with Commodore Barron in 1837, when he resided in Philadelphia, and a more estimable, kind-hearted, Christian gentleman I have seldom met, esteemed and beloved by all who knew him.

It was said that a reconciliation took place while both lay on the field supposed to be mortally wounded. Said Decatur, "Why didn't you come home, Barron [he was in France], and help us in the war?" "Because," answered Barron, "I had no money, and could not." "If you had only let me know your situation, I would have sent you the money."

There was a high-toned generosity about Decatur, while Barron was destitute of all malice. Could these gallant officers have come together in a friendly spirit and given and taken explanations from each other, it is not at all probable that this unfortunate and fatal duel would ever have taken place.

Outrages upon our merchantmen similar to that perpetrated by the Leopard on the Chesapeake, namely, impressing our seamen by British cruisers, were among the causes which finally led to the War of 1812, during which our gallant little navy performed marvelous feats of daring bravery and successful manœuvring, and fought itself into public favor, which it has retained to the present day. Humbling indeed was it to British pride to see ship after ship surrender, after a short but murderous action, to the heretofore despised Yankees; but it was a humiliation they were compelled to undergo.

The tragic death of Decatur, who was universally admired, and of whom the nation as well as the city was justly proud, produced a most profound sensation, and spread gloom like a pall over the metropolis. A levee at the Presidential mansion and other social parties were postponed, everybody feeling the sadness of the occasion. The funeral was attended by the President and his cabinet, the judges of the Supreme Court, Senators and members of the House of Representatives, and an immense concourse of people. The occasion was long vividly remembered, and there are a few, a very few, now living who still remember it.

Subsequently, on the occasion of the death of Mr. Cilley, in the duel with Graves, the judges declined attending the funeral, wishing thereby to show their repugnance to duels.

WILLIAM LOWNDES, OF SOUTH CAROLINA.

Fame reports Mr. Lowndes, of South Carolina, to have been one of the wisest, most prudent and judicious legislators who had occupied a seat in Congress. Such was the testimony borne of him by Mr. Clay, who served many years in Congress with him; and thus spoke of him Mr. Webster and other contemporaries. Colonel Benton speaks of him as "one of those members, rare in all assemblies, who, when he spoke, had a cluster around him, not of friends, but of the House,—members quitting their distant seats and gathering up close about him, and showing by their attention that one would feel it a personal loss to have missed a word he said. It was the attention of affectionate confidence. He imparted to others the harmony of his own feelings, and was the moderator as well as the leader of the House, and was followed by its sentiment in all cases in which inexorable party feeling or some powerful interest did not rule the action of the members, and even then he was courteously and deferentially treated." This accords with the testimony of others. Mr. Lowndes was always spoken of with profound respect and affectionate regard by those members whom I knew and who had served in Congress with him.

He was a very Saul in stature; of a plain, winning countenance, bland manners, and equable temper, of which he never lost control. He had, consequently, a strong hold of the members of his own party,—the Republican,—and exercised great influence also with his political opponents on all questions and measures which did not involve party politics. He was the leading advocate of the Tariff bill of 1816, which adopted the principle of *protection* to American manufactures, and was ably sustained by his colleague, Mr. Calhoun, and by Mr. Clay.

Such was the estimate of him by his friends that his elevation to the Presidency was looked for at no distant day.* But, his health failing, he resigned his seat in Congress in 1821, and, taking a voyage to Europe by the advice of his physician, in 1822, he died at sea.

> "Only the memory of the just
> Smells sweet and blossoms in the dust."

It may not be out of place to indulge a little speculation here as to what would or would not have occurred in South Carolina from 1821 to 1831 and subsequent years, had Mr. Lowndes lived and preserved his health. He was a very firm, consistent, conservative statesman, always acting on views and opinions well matured. His influence in South Carolina was supreme, and elsewhere at the South very great. He was the father of the *Protective* bill of 1816, and favored internal improvements by national means; and it was not in his nature to be changing and whiffling about like a weathercock. Had he been living, therefore, in 1825, it is not likely that Mr. Calhoun, who stood under his shadow, would have faced to the right-about, as he did, on the questions of protection and internal improvements, and denounced those measures as *unconstitutional* which he had but a few months before advocated with the zeal of an enthu-

* Mr. Lowndes was the first to remark that the Presidency was an office too high to be either sought or declined. General Jackson reiterated the sentiment to some effect, and has been considered its author.

siast, and the earnestness of one thoroughly convinced that he was right.

We shall generally, if not at all times, find the springs of history in the dark recesses of the human heart. Men control nations, and are themselves controlled by their ambitions, rivalries, jealousies, revenges, hopes, and fears. Few public men are governed by the sole desire to promote the true interest of the country; and many deceive themselves by supposing that they are thus governed, when, in truth, self-interest sways the needle from the true pole. How Mr. Calhoun could have honestly entertained such diametrically opposite opinions on the great questions mentioned, in 1824 and 1826, it would be idle to undertake to explain upon the supposition that his motives in changing were entirely disinterested and had no reference to his future career. It is quite certain, I think, that, had Mr. Lowndes lived, we should never have heard of nullification or secession, and possibly History would have been spared the painful task of writing the dark pages of a four years' bloody rebellion.

WILLIAM PINCKNEY.

The most eloquent and distinguished man of his day in the United States, if we may credit his contemporaries, was Mr. Pinckney, of Maryland. His fame has descended to us in its fullness of glory as an orator, statesman, and advocate.

He was, at the time of his sudden and premature death, a member of the United States Senate, and admitted to be there unrivaled in the power and beauty of his forensic efforts. But he spoke rarely in that body, only on some important occasion or question, and then only after the most laborious and thorough preparation, not merely in regard to the arguments and illustrations, but in the general construction of his speech, and especially in the preparation of those passages, including the peroration, which were intended to electrify his audience.

That Mr. Pinckney ranked as first at the bar of the Supreme Court, composed of such distinguished lawyers as David B. Ogden, John Wells, Josiah Ogden Hoffman, and Thomas Addis Emmet, of New York, Daniel Webster, of Massachusetts, Chapman Johnson, of Virginia, William Wirt and General Walter Jones, of Washington, and others of similar calibre, is sufficient evidence of his great ability as a jurist and his extraordinary powers as a speaker. His arguments before that tribunal where sat a Story, a Johnson, a Livingston, and a Washington, presided over by a Marshall, were learned, logical, compact, and strong; but, not content with strength and solidity, he took infinite pains to make them attractive and more effective by the most elaborate ornamentation. He well knew the effect of glowing passages of eloquence, even in a solid legal argument,—diamonds set in gold,—upon a promiscuous, or even a select, intelligent, and refined audience. Nor did he undervalue those echoes of admiration which his electric oratory sometimes, indeed, almost invariably, called forth: they were delicious music to his ear.

It is related of Mr. Pinckney that he was very desirous that the splendid passages in his speeches, which he took so much pains to prepare, should be thought to be the impromptu inspirations of his genius, and not the studied productions of midnight toil; and that to give the appearance of this, he would sometimes resort to the *ruse*, on the morning of the day he was to speak in the Senate or Supreme Court, of mounting a horse, riding some miles into the country, returning and entering the Senate or court, whip in hand, booted and spurred, with the appearance of haste, just at the moment he was expected to rise and speak, as if he had forgotten that he was to occupy the floor and had come wholly unprepared, and at once go on with his splendid display of oratorical power fragrant with the oil of the midnight lamp.

On the great Missouri question, Mr. Pinckney took the lead in the Senate in favor of the Compromise, opposed to Rufus King, who led the opposition to the admission of Missouri as a slave State. His speech on that occasion was one of the greatest efforts of his legislative life; but another, which he made many years before, denouncing slavery and slave-holders for maintaining it, was the best answer to it.

Mr. Pinckney had a very extensive and lucrative business before the Supreme Court,—greater than that of any other member of that bar,—which demanded so much of his time and labor that he had little to spare for the Senate. And this was somewhat singular, as he had spent many years, from 1796 to 1811, as minister, at different times, to England, and in 1818 to Russia and Naples.

His biographer and nephew speaks of the "punctilious and studious attention to dress, which he acquired in foreign courts, and which he retained to the close of his life." He was not less distinguished for his exquisite taste in dress, the faultless cut of his garments, the delicate tint of his gloves, the gossamer fineness of his ruffles and pocket-handkerchiefs,—in short, for the high fashion and fine material of his costume,—than he was as an eminent lawyer, able statesman, and refined gentleman.

His death was startlingly sudden; but, in the words of his biographer, "he fell in his might, before the tribunal he delighted to address, and on the arena he most loved to tread."

CANDIDATES FOR THE PRESIDENCY.

The caucus system of nominating candidates for the Presidency having been denounced and abandoned, it was left to the friends of any aspirant to present his name or announce him as a candidate for that high office; and this was done, except that Mr. Crawford had received the nomination by a quasi caucus. Mr. Adams, Mr. Clay, General Jackson, and Mr. Calhoun were severally announced as such. With the exception of General Jackson, each was announced without any sort of clap-trap or attempt to forestall public opinion. General Jackson was first nominated by the Legislature of Tennessee; then by public meetings of the citizens of Carlisle and of Dauphin County, Pa.; and again by the citizens of Blount County, Tenn.

GENERAL JACKSON.

General Jackson was a man of a noble and commanding presence,—tall, straight, with a military air and mien that made a strong and favorable impression upon every one at first sight. In any promiscuous assembly of a thousand men he would have been pointed out above all others as the man "born to command," and who would, in any dangerous emergency, be at once placed in command. Ordinarily, he had the peculiar, rough, independent, free-and-easy ways of the backwoodsman; but at the same time he had, whenever the occasion required, and especially when in the society of ladies, very urbane and graceful manners.

But, though extremely affable when it was his humor, he was, when he chose to be, haughty and overbearing, impatient of restraint and irascible in temper; opposition in any shape aroused his anger, which was fierce and unrelenting. He who crossed his path, thwarted his purposes, or held opinions in opposition to his own, though honest and sincere in those opinions, and opposing him under a high sense of duty and not from personal feelings, was looked upon as an enemy, however warm had been his previous friendship. He never forgave: implicit and unreasoning acquiescence in his opinions and purposes was the price of his friendship, and to such friends he knit himself with hooks of steel; there was no service in his power he would not render them. Hence the strong hold he had of his friends, and the zeal with which they served him.

His affectionate regard and devotedness to his wife, and his ready submission to her soothing voice, even when in his most excited and revengeful moods, were beautiful and commendable traits in his character. And it is strong proof of her excellent judgment, self-control, mild temper, and ardent affection for him, that she had such a controlling influence over him.

He had crowned himself with glory by his splendid victory at New Orleans. His proceedings subsequent to that event, —in entering the Floridas at the head of his army, taking St. Mark's and Pensacola, and hanging Arbuthnot and Ambrister,— together with the investigation of his proceedings in Congress, and the long and acrimonious debate which ensued, had made his name as familiar as household words to every American citizen; and probably every one "had formed and expressed an opinion" in regard to him, of condemnation or approbation.

With the frank bearing and apparent guilelessness of a rough soldier, the general possessed in a high degree the tact and shrewdness of an adroit politician. He knew as well as Alcibiades the importance of keeping himself constantly before the people and of being talked about, and to this end seized every favorable opportunity to utter some emphatic or striking sentiment or expression that should "tickle the ears of the groundlings." No one understood this art better than himself, or practiced it more successfully. His reply to the letter addressed to him by the committee of the Dauphin County meeting which nominated him, is a model for an aspiring politician. This reply is dated New Orleans, February 23, 1823, and in it, among other things,—for this letter was by no means a brief one,—he says,—

"For the services which I may have rendered, and which, it is hoped, proved in a degree beneficial to my country, I have nothing to ask. They are richly repaid with the confidence and good opinion of the virtuous and well-deserving part of the community. I have only essayed to discharge a debt which every man owes his country when her rights are invaded; and if twelve years' exposure to fatigue and numerous privations can warrant the assertion, I may venture to assert that my portion of public service has been performed, and that with this impression I have retired from the busy scenes of public life with a desire to be a spectator merely of passing events.

"The office of chief magistrate of the Union is one of great responsibility. As it should not be sought by any one individual of the republic, so it cannot with propriety be declined when offered by those who have the power of selection. It is interesting to the American people alone, and in the election they should exercise their free and unbiased judgment. It was with these impressions, I presume, and without any consultation with me, that the members of the Legislature of the State of Tennessee, as an additional testimony of their confidence in me, thought proper to present my name to the American community. My political creed prompts me to leave the affair, uninfluenced by any expression on my part, to the free will of those who have alone the right to decide.

"Your obedient, etc.,

"ANDREW JACKSON.

"The Committee of Dauphin County."

For adroit insinuation, apparent guilelessness and absence of all ambition or desire to be President, commend us to this epistle. It was generally published, and called forth much comment. The first part of the last paragraph took wonderfully with the people: "The office of chief magistrate of the Union is one of great responsibility, and should not be sought by any one individual of the republic." It expressed exactly the idea of that portion of the American people whom the general flatteringly denominated "the virtuous and well-deserving;" that is, that no man ought to have an office, and especially the Presidency, who sought it.

But General Jackson took the precaution to say that though the office of chief magistrate should not be sought, neither should it be *declined* "when offered by those who have the power of selection," thereby intimating that if nominated by the *people*, instead of by a *caucus*, he should not decline the honor. He was at this time, and ever after, hostile to the "caucus," which had already nominated Mr. Crawford.

As all the candidates now presented to the country for the high office of President, except General Jackson, were necessarily residing at Washington, or were called there for a time during the sessions of Congress in the discharge of important public duties, it is not improbable that the friends of the general deemed it important to his success that he should be placed on public duty there, where Presidents had been and might again be made; where he could play a part in the great game, or watch the manœuvres of his rivals. Luckily for him and his special friends, the term for which Colonel John Williams, of East Tennessee, had been elected had expired on the 3d of March, 1823.

Colonel John Williams had long served his State as United States Senator in the most acceptable manner. He was a man of high-toned honor and principle, and of ability far above the ordinary standard, but he was known to be partial to Mr. Crawford. This, and the desire to place General Jackson where he could look after his own interests and stand prominently before the public, induced the Legislature to elect him over Colonel Williams to the Senate of the United States, and he took his seat at the session of Congress of 1823–4.

But in elevating him to the Senate of the United States it was deemed necessary to do it in a manner that should attract attention and produce dramatic effect. His formal consent to serve the State in the high position of Senator was to be obtained; and in seeking this his declaration to the Dauphin County committee,—that "office should be neither sought nor declined,"—which had so pleased the people, could be reiterated so that it might not be forgotten, and he could be furnished with an opportunity to write another letter for the public eye, to be read by "the virtuous and well-deserving," whose good opinion he was very laudably desirous to win.

The following letter was on this occasion addressed to him:

"MURFREESBOROUGH, September 20, 1823.

"DEAR GENERAL,—I am particularly requested, by many friends of yours, to inquire if you are willing to serve in the Senate of the United States. The general wish here is that you may assent to what your friends earnestly desire, and enter upon a service which, though at war with your individual interest, is yet one which it is hoped you will not decline. Indeed, looking to the declaration made by you to the committee of the State of Pennsylvania, 'that office should be neither sought for nor declined,' a strong disposition was entertained to venture your name for the proposed appointment without inquiring of you aught about it; but, considering that you are at a convenient distance, I have thought proper, at the desire of several of the members, to propose it in confidence to you.

* * * * * * * *

All we want is a belief that you will permit your name to be used.

"I am, with very great respect, your most obedient,

"ABRAM MAURY.

"GENERAL ANDREW JACKSON."

To which General Jackson returned the following reply:

"HERMITAGE, 21st September, 1823.

"DEAR SIR,—Your letter of yesterday has reached me, stating it to be the desire of many members of the Legislature that my name may be proposed for the appointment of Senator to Congress. It is very true, as you remark, that I have not only said, but have, I believe, through life acted upon the principle, that office, in a republican government like ours, should not be solicited, nor yet, when conferred, declined; still, I would suggest to my friends whether they ought not to excuse me from accepting the appointment they have proposed. There are many better qualified to meet the fatigues of the journey than myself, and on whose services a reliance for a time to come, with a prospect of becoming better as they advance, might be safely reposed: whereas, from health impaired and advancing age, neither the one nor the other could be calculated on from me; and, besides, it might be thought, nay, would be said, that my State had conferred it upon me with a view to other objects and for other purposes, which are at present pending before the nation. I have, therefore, earnestly to request my friends, and beg of you, not to press me to an acceptance of the appointment. If appointed, I could not decline; and yet, in accepting, I should do great violence to my wishes and to my feelings. The length of time I have passed in public service authorizes me to make this request, which with my friends, I trust, will be considered reasonable and proper.

"With great regard, I am very respectfully yours,

"ANDREW JACKSON.

"MAJOR ABRAM MAURY, member of the House of Representatives."

This letter is also a model one. What maiden-like coyness and *sincere* excuses! "It is true I have through life acted on the principle that *office should not be solicited*, nor yet, *when conferred, declined.* But I would suggest to my friends whether they ought not to excuse me. There are others better qualified to meet the fatigues of the journey,—impaired health, advancing age. I beg you, therefore, not to press me to accept the appointment. If appointed, I could not decline; but in accepting, should do great violence to my wishes and feelings." The tenor of the letter was well understood by those to whom it was addressed, and who acted in accordance with the known wishes of the general in electing him. He was, of course, not excused.

Meantime, the tide of his popularity was steadily rising; the halo which surrounded "the hero of New Orleans" was enlarging and brightening, and attracted more and more the attention of the common people, especially in Pennsylvania and some of the Southern and Southwestern States.

GENERAL JACKSON NOMINATED FOR PRESIDENT BY THE STATE CONVENTION OF FEDERALISTS OF PENNSYLVANIA.

Though the Federal party, as a national party, had long ceased to exist, it still maintained its organization in Pennsylvania,—Mr. Buchanan having been elected to the Eighteenth Congress as a *Federalist*, in opposition to his *Democratic* competitor. That party held a State convention at Harrisburg, February 22, 1824, and nominated Andrew Gregg for Governor. They also nominated General Jackson for President, under the impression that they could carry the State by the force of his military popularity.

Mr. Calhoun was popular in Pennsylvania, from the fact that he was the advocate of protection to domestic manufactures and internal improvements,—Pennsylvania's favorite measures. At a meeting of the citizens of Carlisle a resolution was offered expressing their preference for him for President, which was amended by striking out his name and inserting that of Andrew Jackson, the amendment being carried by acclamation. Similar indications of a preference of the people of that State for General Jackson over all others were made manifest.

Soon after this, on the 18th of February, a large Democratic meeting was held in Philadelphia to select delegates to the State convention to be held at Harrisburg on the 4th of March, 1824. At this Philadelphia meeting Mr. George M. Dallas, the well-known friend of Mr. Calhoun, rose and said that in deference to what seemed to be the preference of the people of Pennsylvania he withdrew the name of John C. Calhoun as a candidate for the Presidency, and proposed the nomination of Andrew Jackson for President and Mr. Calhoun for Vice-President, and that these nominations be recommended to the State convention. The proposition was carried without opposition. After nominating Andrew Shultz for Governor, the State convention nominated Jackson and Calhoun for President and Vice-President, though not without strong opposition. An attempt was made to get the convention to confirm the nomination already made by the Congressional caucus,—Mr. Crawford for President and Mr. Gallatin for Vice-President,—but this most signally failed, the Democrats no longer recognizing the authority of a Congressional caucus, and that which had nominated Mr. Crawford having been recognized and attended by very few members.

The nomination of General Jackson by the State convention greatly incensed the Crawford men, or *Radical* Democrats, as they were called, who condemned it as an act of political treason, since he was at this time denounced by all the leading Democratic papers in the cities and different parts of the country, in unmeasured terms, as "no Republican," "unfit to be President," "whose election would be a curse to the country," etc. The Democrats *par excellence*—Crawford men, or "Radicals" —called and held a convention at Harrisburg on the 9th of August, and in the most energetic terms repudiated the nomination of General Jackson and resolved to adhere to "the true Democratic candidate, Mr. Crawford." But the general having been nominated by the regular conventions of both parties, no opposition could check his overwhelming popularity in the Keystone State. He was the idol of the German population, some of whom, it used to be ironically said, continued to vote for him long after he was laid in his grave. His Dauphin letter, and his letter to Mr. Maury, consenting, with maiden coyness and modesty, to accept an election to the United States Senate, delighted the people and gave him a popularity wholly unprecedented.

The withdrawal of Mr. Calhoun as a candidate for President by his personal friend Mr. Dallas, and his nomination as Vice-President with Jackson as President, created some surprise, inasmuch as it was no secret that he had all along preferred the election of Mr. Adams above all others. But it was soon known that he "accepted the situation." How far this committed him to the support of General Jackson was not then known. He was popular in New England, Mr. Adams's stronghold, and received nearly every electoral vote of that section, except that of Connecticut, and enough elsewhere to give him one hundred and eighty-two out of two hundred and sixty-one electoral votes.

WASHINGTON SOCIETY, 1817–25.

In looking back to the customs, modes, manners, ceremonies, and dress of our first and early Presidents and those who constituted the best society of those days, or, as some have styled the society at the national capital, "The Republican Court," which is by no means an uninteresting review, we must bear in mind the circumstances by which they were surrounded, their early education, training, social position, and wealth. They had mostly been born and reared under a monarchical government, of which aristocracy was one of the main pillars.

As in the mother country, so in the colonies, there was a broad distinction between the upper and the lower classes; yet there was a middle class in England then, as now, and also in all the colonies, consisting of landed proprietors, eminent and successful merchants, bankers, lawyers, physicians, etc. In the colonies, these constituted the leading men of the country, and their families the social circles. Many of the professional men, especially lawyers, and many also of the Southern planters, were educated at our own colleges, or, either in whole or in part, in England, where they mingled in the best society of the mother country. Some, if not many of them, had relatives there belonging to the aristocracy of title, rank, or wealth. Of course the forms, usages, and fashions of that class in England were those of the best and most refined society in the colonies. Such, and so educated, were our Washingtons, Adamses, Hancocks, Jeffersons, Madisons, Hamiltons, Otises, Quincys, Cabots, Sedgwicks, Jays, Randolphs, Pendletons, Pinckneys, Kings, Shermans, Shippens, Carrolls, Gerrys, Binghams, Willingses, Clintons, Winthrops, Chews, Ogles, Taylors, Lees, Izards, Ellsworths, Edwardses, Wolcotts, Goodriches, and thousands of others, whose names have now become obscured or blotted out altogether.

General Washington being commander-in-chief of the armies of the Revolution, and subordinate to him not only American generals of high reputation and self-appreciation, such as Lee and Gates, but French and other foreign generals of high rank and social position in their own respective countries, it was necessary for him to assume and maintain the dignity and command the respect due to him as chief. That he preserved that dignity and inspired that respect we all know.

When he became President of the United States, he considered himself, in his official capacity, as the representative and embodiment of the NATION, and felt it incumbent on him to maintain in his own person the dignity of a free and independent people; and this was to be done by observing, in some measure, the forms, ceremonies, and etiquette of foreign courts. In carrying out this idea, he undoubtedly conformed to the general opinion of those by whom he was surrounded, and who at that time, to a considerable extent, formed and controlled public opinion.

There was, therefore, under Washington much official ceremony and formality. He received company at his levees with a dress-sword by his side, bowed to them as they came up and passed on, but never shook hands with any one, or relaxed his dignity and formality so far as to speak familiarly to any one, while thus receiving, as the embodied nation, the homage or salutations of all. From the President, the company passed on and were presented to Mrs. Washington, who received them with grace and dignified affability.

All this stateliness and ceremony would be out of place now, and might excite ridicule and denunciation; but the present usages would have been as abhorrent to our forefathers as theirs could possibly be to us. They were governed by the usages they had been accustomed to; so are we.

Mr. Adams had not the commanding presence and stately dignity of Washington, nor the moral impression which the latter produced upon all who approached him. But the usages and etiquette established by the first President were kept up by the second, except in regard to equipage. General Washington was fond of horses, and prided himself on his stud of full-bloods, six of which were attached to his carriage on state occasions.

Mr. Jefferson, though accustomed, in early life at least, to aristocratic society, came into the Presidency as a democrat and the apostle of democracy, and upon entering the White House discarded all forms and ceremonies, adopting a rather ostentatious plainness of living and receiving company,—all being free to come and go at all times.

Under Mr. Madison's reign, former customs and modes were partially resumed by Mrs. Madison, who presided at the White House with great *éclat*, winning golden opinions and admiration from all. No material change took place during Mr. Monroe's eight- or Mr. J. Q. Adams's four-years' administration; but a great change was perceptible under General Jackson, and from that time to the present it has been going on.

With these preliminary remarks, I come to the society in Washington from 1817 to the close of Mr. J. Q. Adams's administration.

Among the eminent and distinguished men who constituted and adorned "Washington society" at that time—Senators, members of the House of Representatives, Judges of the Supreme Court, officers of the army and navy, besides the five candidates for the Presidency, Adams, Crawford, Jackson, Clay, Calhoun—were the venerable and learned Marshall; the vivacious, witty, and profound Story; the sage yet chivalric Johnson, of South Carolina; the two "model gentlemen" of the old school, of small-clothes and courtly manners, Senators Rufus King and Gaillard, of South Carolina; the two Lloyds, Senators from Massachusetts and Maryland; the heroic Brown, Scott, Gaines, Ripley, Macomb, Jessup, Towson, Gibson, Decatur, Bainbridge, Hull, Stewart, Tingey, McDonough, and Chauncey; besides a constellation of lesser, but equally brave and heroic, military and naval stars; the eloquent "model gentleman," Pinckney; the accomplished Wirt; the massive Webster; the mellifluous Storrs; the grave James, and the metaphysical Philip P. Barbour; the poetic and universally admired Wilde; the logical, clear-headed Sergeant; the indefatigable, dogmatic, and imperious Benton; the impassioned McDuffie; the historian of "the Six Nations," Colden; the witty and facetious John Holmes; the smooth-tongued Van Buren; the bland Lewis McLane; the upright and honest John McLean; the modest but fearless Governor Metcalf; the brave, noble-hearted General Vance; the pioneer patriots Governors McArthur and Morrow; the humorous Letcher; the erratic genius Barton; the gallant Hotspur, Hamilton, of South Carolina: in short,—for I could treble this list,—here assembled the very *élite* of those in any way connected with the government, in Congress, in the army and navy, and in the civil service. And here, too, were those of the other sex, worthy companions of the first in the land, together forming a brilliant and harmonious whole rarely met with elsewhere.

At no period since the government was removed to its *permanent* seat has the society of Washington been more refined and brilliant than when its hospitalities were dispensed by Mr. Madison, Mr. Monroe, Mr. Adams, Mr. Calhoun, Mr. Wirt, Mr. Rush, Mr. Southard, General Scott, General Macomb, and other Americans, and Mr. Vaughan, Don Onis, Hyde de Neuville, Mr. Serrurier, Baron Krudener, Count de Menu, and other foreign ministers.

The various drawing-rooms were not then filled to suffocation by a motley crowd generally unknown to each other and hardly known to the host and hostess. A large portion of those who constituted "the society of Washington" were personal acquaintances; their social intercourse was more frequent, genial, and agreeable, and especially free from that stiff reserve and lack of conversation which must characterize a company made up mostly of those who are unknown to each other, and especially of those but little accustomed to refined society.

There were no railroads in those days; consequently the number of persons, especially ladies, sojourning here during the sessions of Congress was very small compared to the present time. Besides, it was less the custom then for heads of families, and even unmarried men and women, to leave their homes and spend the summer at one place and the winter at another, seeking that happiness which, if not found at home, can be found nowhere.

There was less wealth in those days, but not less refinement and happiness. It might be considered invidious or cynical were I to say that both men and women had something to do at home, and were not driven away by idleness and ennui, the most insupportable of all companions.

It was customary to go to parties about eight o'clock* and leave from ten to eleven. Dancing at parties was usual,—invariable, I believe, at large parties. The rooms, however, were furnished in a far less costly manner than at present. Hair-seated mahogany chairs and sofas were the most fashionable and expensive then used; nor did all even well-to-do people have these.

The custom in Washington then was, at every large evening party, to set tables for those gentlemen who preferred to amuse themselves with cards; and there were often several parties thus engaged. Whist was the game, and the stakes were generally high. Mr. Vaughan, British Minister, and afterwards his successor, Mr. Fox, nephew of Charles James, Baron Krudener, Russian Minister, and his successor, Mr. Bodisco,—indeed, nearly all the foreign ministers,—Mr. Clay, General Scott, General Cass, Mr. Forsyth, Mr. Poindexter, and many others whom I might name, were usually seen thus amusing themselves. Mr. Fox had his uncle's passion for play, and it was generally believed lost pretty large sums.

When a candidate for the Presidency, Mr. Clay was denounced as "a gambler." He was no more "a gambler" than was almost every Southern and Southwestern gentleman of that day. Play was a passion with them; it was a social enjoyment; they loved its excitement, and they played whenever and wherever they met; not for the purpose of winning money of one another,—which is the gambler's motive,—but for the pleasure it gave them. They bet high as a matter of pride and to give interest to the game.

Of Washington society in 1824 we have pleasant glimpses furnished by letters written by Mr. Carter, editor of the New York "Statesman," who was in the city that winter as a correspondent of his own paper, and furnished graphic sketches of it; also by verses written by John T. Agg, descriptive of a "reception" or ball given by Mrs. Adams, the accomplished lady

* This would be a very unfashionable hour to appear at a large party now.

of the Secretary of State, on the evening of the 8th of January, 1824, in honor of General Jackson and the anniversary of the battle of New Orleans.

Mr. Carter gives us a pleasant account of the "levee" held by President Monroe on the evening of the 1st of January, 1824, and of the celebrities, male and female, there present.

This reception at the White House by the venerable President, which Mr. Carter so graphically described, may be remembered by some who "still live;" but the party given by Mrs. J. Q. Adams, one week later, became almost historical from its brilliancy and the circumstances attending it. From the elaborate and lively description of it given by Mr. Carter, who seems to have been the Jenkins of the day, in a letter to the "Statesman," I have made the following brief extract, not only as an admirable exhibit of the high-toned society of Washington nearly fifty years ago, but as showing the friendly and social relations existing between Mr. Adams and General Jackson one year previous to the election of the former and the defeat of the latter. As the party was given in honor of the "hero" and "the victory of New Orleans," General Jackson was "the star of the evening," "the observed of all observers;" and it must be admitted that he honored the assembly which honored him.

After describing the reception-rooms and their decorations, and giving us glimpses of the brilliant assemblage, Mr. Carter proceeds:

"At nine o'clock General Jackson entered the room, and with great dignity and gracefulness of manner conducted Mrs. Adams through the apartments. He was in a plain citizen's dress, and appeared remarkably well, saluting and receiving the congratulations of his friends with his usual urbanity and affability.

"Mrs. Adams was elegantly but not gorgeously dressed. Her head-dress and plumes were tastefully arranged. In her manners she unites dignity with an unusual share of ease and elegance; and I never saw her appear to greater advantage than when promenading the rooms, winding her way through the multitude by the side of the gallant general. At the approach of such a couple the crowd involuntarily gave way as far as practicable and saluted them as they passed.

"Mr. Adams, who is known to be proverbially plain, unassuming, and unostentatious in his manners, received his guests with his usual cordiality and unaffected politeness.

* * * * * * * *

"At about ten o'clock* the doors of a spacious apartment were flung open, and a table presented itself to view loaded with refreshments of every description, served up in elegant style, of which the company were invited to partake without ceremony.

"Conviviality and pleasure reigned throughout the evening, and I never saw so many persons together where there was apparently so much unmingled happiness."

The description of this brilliant assemblage, which included all the celebrities of Washington, Georgetown, and Alexandria, as well as large numbers from Baltimore and Richmond, Va., would hardly be complete without the well-remembered verses of Mr. John F. Agg, by which he duly celebrated the occasion in advance, and which have done much to hand down its celebrity to posterity.

These lines appeared in the "National Intelligencer" on the morning of the 8th of January, and created a lively sensation.

"MRS. ADAMS' BALL.

"Wend you with the world to-night?
Brown and fair, and wise and witty,
Eyes that float in seas of light,
Laughing mouths, and dimples pretty,
Belles and matrons, maids and madams,
All are gone to Mrs. Adams'.
There the mist of the future, the gloom of the past,
All melt into light at the warm glance of pleasure,
And the only regret is, lest, melting too fast,
Mammas should move off in the midst of a measure.

"Wend you with the world to-night?
Sixty gray, and giddy twenty,

* Supper at ten o'clock! What very *un*fashionable people!

Flirts that court, and prudes that slight,
State coquettes, and spinsters plenty.
Mrs. Sullivan is there,
With all the charms that nature lent her;
Gay McKim, with city air;
And winning Gales and Vandeventer;
Forsyth, with her group of graces;
Both the Crowninshields, in blue;
The Pierces, with their heavenly faces,
And eyes like suns that dazzle through.
Belles and matrons, maids and madams,
All are gone to Mrs. Adams'.

"Wend you with the world to-night?
East and West, and South and North,
Form a constellation bright,
And pour a blended brilliance forth.
See the tide of fashion flowing;
'Tis the noon of beauty's reign.
Webster, Hamiltons are going,
Eastern Lloyd, and Southern Hayne;
Western Thomas, gayly smiling,
Borland, nature's protégée,
Young De Wolfe, all hearts beguiling,
Morgan, Benton, Brown, and Lee.
Belles and matrons, maids and madams,
All are gone to Mrs. Adams'.

"Wend you with the world to-night?
Where blue eyes are brightly glancing,
While to measures of delight
Fairy feet are deftly dancing;
Where the young Euphrosyne
Reigns the mistress of the scene,
Chasing gloom, and courting glee,
With the merry tambourine.
Many a form of fairy birth,
Many a Hebe, yet unwon,
Wirt, a gem of purest worth,
Lively, laughing Pleasanton,
Vails and Tayloe will be there,
Gay Monroe, so debonair,
Hellen, pleasure's harbinger,
Ramsay, Cottringers, and Kerr.
Belles and matrons, maids and madams,
All are gone to Mrs. Adams'.

"Wend you with the world to-night?
  Juno in her court presides,
Mirth and melody invite,
  Fashion points, and pleasure guides!
Haste away, then, seize the hour,
Shun the thorn, and pluck the flower.
Youth, in all its spring-time blooming,
Age, the guise of youth assuming,
Wit through all its circles gleaming,
Glittering wealth and beauty beaming,
Belles and matrons, maids and madams,
All are gone to Mrs. Adams'."

Mr. Carter, of whose letters I have availed myself, spent several winters in Washington as a correspondent for the New York "Statesman," of which he was editor and proprietor. His letters were highly attractive, and greatly extended the circulation of his paper. He afterwards went to Europe, and wrote letters from there to the "Statesman," which were published in a volume entitled "Letters from Europe." He was a pleasant writer, and his letters were very generally read.

I first saw Washington City in June, 1824, coming here from New York, not flying through with the speed of the wind, while one is taking a pleasure-excursion into dream-land,—surrendering himself into the soft arms of Morpheus at Newark, and rising gently therefrom, invigorated and ready for the toils of the day, in Washington,—but in a take-things-easy manner, as if one did not wish to hurry through the world and get to the end too soon.

I took the steamboat from New York to New Brunswick; there found splendid stages, and equally splendid horses,—usually nine stages, each drawn by four horses, and carrying nine passengers inside and two on the seat with the driver. From the boat the baggage was transferred to the stages,—a trunk or valise to each passenger, with an allowance of a bandbox to a lady; a pest and annoyance to gentlemen when, as was often the case, the bandbox was an inside passenger. The trunks of that day! why, a lady's trunk of the present would easily contain half a dozen of those diminutive things invariably covered with untanned calf-, horse-, or cow-hide with the hair on, nailed on with an abundance of brass nails, and able to stand for long years the wear and tear of travel by stage-coaches, outlasting a dozen trunks of the present day and the present custom of banging them in and out of baggage-cars. The bandbox, the invariable accompaniment of a lady, was the receptacle of the bonnet and sundry small articles frequently needed on the journey, and which are now carried in that far more convenient article, the satchel.

Well, the passengers being all seated, and the baggage, to the last trunk, being well packed in the "boot" behind the stage, and strapped down so as to be made sure, the drivers, proud of their teams and their coaches, as well they might be, cracked their whips, and away went the nine (sometimes more) stages: if in dry weather, throwing up a cloud of dust that soon made the outside garment of each passenger, hat and all, the same color and the color of the red-clay soil over which we were whirling.

The steamboat from Philadelphia came up to Trenton when the state of the river permitted; but when the water was too low for this, it stopped at a landing some miles below, and at very low stages of the water at Bristol. But to whatever point the boat came, there the stages met her and transferred their passengers and baggage. Thence to Philadelphia was by boat, the passengers dining aboard, and reaching the city about six o'clock P.M. Fare from New York to Philadelphia, two dollars and fifty cents. Here we rested over-night. Next morning, at six o'clock, left Philadelphia for Baltimore; namely, by boat to New Castle, Del., stages from thence to Frenchtown, head of Chesapeake Bay, and boat, under command of Admiral Chater, from thence to Baltimore, dining aboard the boat, and arriving at Beltshoover's about six o'clock P.M. Fare from Philadelphia to Baltimore, six dollars. Next morning took the stage at Beltshoover's tavern for Washington; dine at Waterloo, the half-way house, famous for all sorts of rare live birds and pet animals; arrive at Washington about four o'clock P.M.; stop at the "Indian Queen," now the "Metropolitan," designated by an appropriately-painted sign of an "Indian queen" swinging near the house, kept by the prince of landlords, Mr. Jesse Brown, or drive on to Gadsby's, then on the Avenue west of

Twenty-first Street, beyond "the seven buildings," whose abundant table was always adorned, as was the general custom in those days, with decanters of brandy, rum, gin, and other liquors, stationed at short intervals, from the head to the foot of the table, along its centre; and for all this, and excellent attendance, one dollar and a quarter per day! Fare from Baltimore to Washington, four dollars; dinner on the way, fifty cents.

This, in spring, summer, and autumn; but when the Chesapeake Bay and the Delaware River became closed, or so blocked with ice that the boats could not run, then the poor member of Congress, or other traveler, might exclaim,—

"Hic labor, hoc opus est."

The journey was often, in the winter, of two days' and one night's length between Philadelphia and Baltimore by stage.

For many years after this, the "Indian Queen" swung and creaked invitingly to arriving weary travelers, many of whom, especially those from the West and South, came on horseback, and some with a colored servant on another horse, and a pack-horse besides, Mr. Brown being prepared to furnish "food and lodging for man and horse." The next time I visited Washington, Mr. Gadsby had built and occupied his new hotel, the present "National." This he conducted in a sort of military style, and especially was this observed at his long dinner-table. The guests being all seated, and an army of colored servants standing behind the chairs, Mr. Gadsby, a short, stout gentleman, standing at the head of the table, the guests silent with expectation, the word was given, "Remove covers!" when all the servants moved like automata, each at the same moment placing his hand upon the handle of a cover, each at the same instant lifting it, stepping back in line and facing to the head of the table, and, at a sign from Mr. Gadsby, all marching and keeping regular step to the place of depositing the covers, and then back, to commence waiting on the guests.

Who, of the hundreds of thousands who in these good old cheap times—only a dollar and a quarter a day—enjoyed the hospitalities of this gentlemanly and most liberal Boniface, can forget his urbane manner, his careful attention to his guests, his well-ordered house, his fine old wines, and the princely manner in which he would send his bottle of choice Madeira to some old friend or favored guest at the table?

Washington, in 1824, was the most "straggling" city on the continent. The buildings, from the Navy Yard to Rock Creek, were standing here and there, on the Avenue, with wide spaces between, like the teeth of some superannuated crone, giving rise to the sarcasm that it was "a city of magnificent distances," and, as some added, "splendid expectations." For the depth and adhesiveness of its mud in wet weather, and the quantity of its dust in dry, few cities could vie with it, even within a very late period; and as for lights, if the pedestrian did not provide and carry his own, he was in danger of discovering every mud-hole in his route and sounding its depths.

Thanks to Congress and our very *economical* Board of Public Works,* there are now comparatively few streets through which a sturdy pedestrian may not make his way in any one of the twenty-four hours.

Gadsby and Brown, though of a past generation, like Gales and Seaton, were, in their day, essential parts of Washington; and, though they have gone the way of all flesh, they have left pleasant memories behind them, and monuments of their good judgment, enterprise, and industry, in the "National" and "Metropolitan."

At the time I speak of—1824—there were a few good houses in the vicinity of the White House, and some on Capitol Hill, especially on North A Street and Jersey Avenue South; but, with the exception of these, and some west of the White House, the whole eastern, southeastern, and northeastern portions of the city were inclosed fields or common pastures. On the north side of the city, east of Fourteenth, the population had only in a very few instances advanced north of F Street. From the Post-Office, on E Street, all north was common pasture, except the great number of brick-yards, then making brick for the Capitol. On these common pastures were hundreds of

* Now blown sky-high by Congress.

cows, owned by the citizens, every family then having one or more, no milk being carried around for sale or to supply families, as now. Where the Smithsonian building and grounds now are were innumerable quagmires in the fall, spring, and winter. Great numbers of the clerks in the departments and general Post-Office rode to and from their places of business on horseback. There were extensive stables for the use of these and the horses of members of Congress, many of whom came on horseback from their lodgings—not a few from Georgetown.

The last regular horseback member whom I knew was R. Barnwell Rhett, of South Carolina, who always boarded or lived in Georgetown, and galloped to and from the Capitol to his residence, his horse, while he was at the Capitol, being kept in the government stable.

During the summer of 1824, William H. Crawford, Secretary of the Treasury, being in bad health, retired to a mansion *in the country*, to wit, the Clement Hill mansion, still standing, but improved, on the northwest corner of Fourteenth Street and Massachusetts Avenue. It was then far in the country, very retired.

Living, in Washington, at that day, and for twenty or twenty-five years after, was very cheap. Best pieces of beef,—sirloin,—eight to twelve and a half cents per pound; mutton, six to eight; oysters, twenty-five to thirty-five cents a bushel in the shell; turkeys, fifty to seventy-five cents each; partridges and other game-birds abundant in their season, and shad, rock, and other fish plenty and cheap; flour, five to six dollars a barrel; wood, four to five dollars a cord; servant-hire, four dollars a month; rents of genteel houses, from one hundred and fifty to three hundred dollars a year; large mansions, from five hundred to eight hundred dollars a year. But most people owned the houses they lived in.

Heads of bureaus and clerks in the departments, House of Representatives, and Senate were then *at home* here, and felt no apprehension of being turned into the street with their families, some cold, stormy night, to make way for some lady's friend or cousin, or to punish them for entertaining and expressing a political opinion not acceptable to the powers that be

The statesmen of that day, down to the 4th of March, 1829, were "old fogies;" "modern improvements" had not reached them; they were simple enough to think that if a man performed his duties *honestly* and *faithfully*, it was all the government should require of him; his political principles were no more a subject of inquiry than his religious opinions. Clerks and other officers of the government were not then expected to take an active part in politics. Quite the contrary: they were expected and enjoined to leave such matters to others. It followed that they were neither taxed to carry on a political campaign, nor required to return to their respective States and vote at elections. Such a practice was never heard of until, under General Jackson's *reign*, it was assumed that the public offices were "the spoils of the victors," to be seized and distributed as rewards to faithful partisans, whether competent to perform the duties or not. Like fiefs under the old feudal system, they were the rewards of service, but to be held only on the continual rendition of service; and thus the federal officers became a standing army of political mercenaries! Is it any wonder that, after this demoralizing system has been in operation forty-three years, a reform should be loudly called for?

INTRIGUES TO MAKE GENERAL JACKSON PRESIDENT.—HIS COLEMAN LETTER.

It was the general opinion of the people of the United States, in 1823–4, that General Jackson was a calm and passive if not an indifferent observer of public events, and especially of what *appeared* to be the spontaneous movement of the people in his favor. The machinery which was industriously put in operation behind the scenes to effect the actual results brought about was unperceived and unsuspected. But it will be shown that he was no such indifferent observer as he was supposed to be. He had a corps of friends around him who were as skillful as they were indefatigable tacticians in political management.

They had established or secured the use and influence of a paper in Philadelphia, the "Columbian Observer," Stephen Simpson, editor, and it will be seen they kept him well advised in regard to their movements, and well instructed as to the course he was to pursue,—whom he was to assail and whom to flatter or mollify.

Major John H. Eaton, General Jackson's colleague in the United States Senate, and William B. Lewis, of Nashville, were at this time the general's most confidential friends. It was supposed, in 1824, that Mr. Crawford was the candidate most formidable to the general; it was, therefore, the policy of his friends to endeavor to depreciate him in the public estimation: hence they represented Mr. Crawford as "a GIANT OF INTRIGUE," and as being engaged in various intrigues with prominent men with a view to secure his election as President.

On the 7th of April, 1824, Major Eaton addressed the following letter to Mr. Simpson, editor of the "Columbian Observer:"

"DEAR SIR,—I believe, as I all along expressed myself, that our Presidential contest will result in but one way. The leading men say that long practice and established usage is in favor of the caucus system. To sustain the principle,—for they profess to act on principle,—the caucus candidate will be pressed through every possible channel and by every possible means that policy and ingenuity can suggest. MR. CRAWFORD IS THIS MAN.

"In opposition to that and him stands the *people's* candidate, based on the ground that caucus dictation is illegitimate, and that the people are sovereign and should bear sway. On whom is this sentiment *to be made* to rally? Not on Mr. Adams,—he cannot fasten here, nor is he, nor can he be, the caucus favorite. Jackson, I say, is the only man on whom the feeling of the nation and the people can be rallied. *He and Crawford are to make the race.* If so, policy dictates that nothing on the part of *Jackson's friends* should be said or done to excite or drive to *the Crawford banner* the friends of Mr. Adams."

In a similar strain wrote Wm. B. Lewis to Simpson on the 6th of September, 1824. Mr. Lewis says,—

"I have just been informed, by a gentleman of laudable veracity, . . . that the friends of Crawford and Clay have agreed to unite their forces in favor of the former, and in that way secure his election. . . . The scheme in the western section of the Union is, that the name of Mr. Clay shall be kept up with a view of getting as many of the electoral votes as possible, which, before they proceed to elect the President and Vice-President, are to be turned over to Crawford. . . .

"I have also been informed, by a gentleman who, I know, is in the confidence of the Radicals [Crawford men], that if Mr. Crawford shall be elected Clay is to be his Secretary of State, and that Mr. Cheves is to be made Secretary of the Treasury. . . . The same gentleman informed me that Webster is to be made Secretary of the Navy. When I look at the conduct of these gentlemen, I cannot doubt the correctness of the information; and I trust in God that the people will rise in the majesty of their power and arrest this GIANT OF INTRIGUE [William H. Crawford] in his career before it is too late.

". . . Permit me to suggest *the propriety of not being too severe on* ADAMS *and his friends.* I have no doubt, if Adams cannot be elected himself, that he would prefer the election of General Jackson to that of any other person. I am somewhat fearful that if Adams should be broken down altogether, the New England States will go for Crawford if he should get the State of New York. Therefore let us take care and not lose Adams and his friends."

Mr. Lewis adds, "I have thought proper to advise you of these things in order that you may understand the movements of these electioneering, intriguing, and unprincipled gentry."

No machinations, no political scheming, no intrigue here! Mr. Crawford, who, according to Mr. Eaton, was to make the race with Jackson, is denounced as "*a Giant of Intrigue*," and an intrigue is manufactured for him which comprehended himself, Mr. Clay, Mr. Cheves, and Mr. Webster, of which neither of those gentlemen knew aught, and which existed only in the scheming brains of these intriguing friends of General Jackson.

Was General Jackson privy to this intrigue going on with a view to the securing of his election? It is not probable that he was entirely ignorant of it; and this supposition is sustained by the following letter written by himself to Mr. Simpson:

"HERMITAGE, NEAR NASHVILLE, August 18, 1824.

"S. SIMPSON, ESQ.:

"DEAR SIR,—This will be handed you by *John H. Lewis, Esq.*, of Albany, to whom I beg leave to introduce you. Mr. Lewis is on a tour of observation upon the western and eastern sections of the United States, and will be thankful for any civilities which you may extend to him. I recommend him to your notice as a gentleman of good standing and respectability, and who will justly appreciate the attentions which are bestowed upon him.

"With great respect, sir, I am your very obedient servant,

"ANDREW JACKSON."

"On a tour of observation"—of what? Why, to see how Jackson was taking with the people, and to ascertain which of the other candidates stood most in his way; what must be done to conciliate the friends of this or charge the friends of that candidate with bargain and intrigue.

Though Mr. Calhoun had been nominated as Vice-President by the same convention in Pennsylvania that nominated General Jackson for President, Mr. Simpson had expressed distrust of him and his friends, which called out a letter from Major Eaton to him, dated 13th December, 1824.

He says, "In your paper, received to-day, I perceive an editorial remark that Calhoun and his friends will seek to produce a failure in the Presidential election here that he may succeed [as Vice-President]. Your informant is in error. . . . Every State where Mr. Calhoun has been supposed to have any strength will stand for General Jackson; and what more can the general's friends desire than that they should be true and firm to him? Do change your editorial remarks, and do build a contradiction, not on any communication received from Washington, but on your own calculation and the high confidence reposed in the integrity of Mr. Calhoun and those who are his friends."

So it was deemed necessary by one of these intriguers that Mr. Calhoun and his friends should be conciliated, and an expression put forth of "high confidence in his integrity and those who are his friends."

It was done as ordered. Mr. Crawford was denounced as "a Giant of Intrigue," and as having entered into a cabal, league, or intrigue with Clay, Cheves, and Webster, by Wm. B. Lewis, one of these intriguers. But subsequently it was feared they had gone too far in denouncing him: they began to perceive that he was not so formidable a candidate as they had supposed, and that he might be defeated. Mr. Lewis, therefore, wrote to Mr. Simpson thus: "Crawford's friends cannot believe he stands any chance of success. [This was after Mr. Crawford's health had become seriously impaired by paralysis.] I have no doubt they feel pretty sore. *Oil ought to be poured into their wounds by the friends of Jackson.* With the States that support *him* we may bid defiance to the 'Yankee nation,'—in other words, to Mr. Adams and his friends."

In a subsequent letter to Mr. Simpson, Mr. Lewis says, "The Crawford gentry feel quite sore under it [one of his denunciatory letters], and are just now amazingly restless."

On looking back and gathering together the different parts of the drama which was going on in 1823–4, we cannot fail to see these two active friends and confidants of General Jackson prominent in performing vedette, signal, and drill duty for him. Whatever move was made, or supposed to be made, by any candidate for the Presidency was immediately made known to Mr. Simpson, and the proper course for him to take in consequence thereof promptly indicated. Whoever was for the moment considered the most formidable rival of General Jackson was to be assailed; but if that candidate became weak, oil was directed to be poured into his wounds, and his friends conciliated, in the hope that they would finally come to the support of the general. After stigmatizing Mr. Crawford as a "giant of intrigue," and endeavoring to cast odium upon him, seeing that he is likely to be dropped out of the ring, they forthwith take steps to win his friends; "for," say they, "with the States that support *him* we may bid defiance to the *Yankee nation.*" Yet all this time the people were made to believe that General Jackson was indifferent to the result of the election, and only looked on as "a spectator of passing events," as he had said to the Dauphin County Committee he desired to be.

GENERAL JACKSON DENOUNCED BY THE LEADING DEMOCRATIC PAPERS.—IS IN FAVOR OF A PROTECTIVE TARIFF.—HIS COLEMAN LETTER.

I have already said that the leading organs of the Democratic party—the "Albany Argus," Noah's "New York Advocate," the "Richmond Inquirer," the "New Hampshire Patriot," and other papers, all friendly to Mr. Crawford and advocating his election —were open in their hostility to "Mr. Jackson," as Mr. Ritchie, of the "Richmond Inquirer," denominated him, and declared that "his election would be a CURSE to the country."

Pages of extracts from these papers, denouncing him in severe terms, could be quoted; but they have been so often reprinted that they could hardly be new, even to the generation born since they were promulgated. Yet in a brief space of time these organs of the party were as laudatory of "the hero of New Orleans" as they had been denunciatory of "*Mister Jackson.*"

William B. Lewis was a most astute, cool-headed politician, and a sagacious, prudent, far-seeing manager of the general's cause. He may almost be said to have made General Jackson President. He knew whatever was going on in any and every part of the Union calculated to affect the general's prospects, and promptly acted as circumstances demanded. He could hold within his own breast information both interesting and highly important to the general, for months, when he conceived it would do mischief to reveal it before the proper time arrived to use it with effect. By way of example: Mr. Crawford wrote a letter to Mr. Forsyth, undoubtedly intended for General Jackson's eye, revealing the secrets of Mr. Monroe's cabinet, stating that Mr. Calhoun proposed in cabinet meeting that General Jackson should be called to account—brought before a court of inquiry, or otherwise—for his invasion of Florida; in other words, exhibiting an unfriendly feeling to him.

This letter Mr. Lewis saw months before he let General Jackson know it was in existence. He well knew that, should the information it gave come to the knowledge of the general, an immediate quarrel between the two distinguished gentlemen would be inevitable; but a quarrel between them at that moment might, and probably would, seriously affect the interests of the Jackson cause; and so it was closely locked in Mr. Lewis's breast till it was prudent for General Jackson to quarrel with Mr. Calhoun and cast him off. Mr. Lewis had the wisdom and self-control to bide his time,—a most rare virtue in a politician. He seemed to have the entire confidence of the general, to which he was certainly entitled, and to act in the character of his privy councillor; and we have reason to believe that many of the published letters and other papers coming from the general were the inspiration of his mind and the production of his pen. He was a devoted, true, faithful, and judicious friend to the general so long as they both lived.

THE COLEMAN LETTER.

In order to present a continuous chain of events inseparably linked together, I have omitted, in its chronological order, to speak of another important letter written by General Jackson. The policy of giving protection to American manufactures and American labor, as opposed to what is termed *free trade* with foreign countries, was in 1824, as at this time, one upon which public opinion was divided. Pennsylvania, Ohio, Kentucky, a large portion of New York, and almost the entire population of the New England States, were ardently in favor of protection. General Jackson's views in regard to this matter, not being known, were drawn out and made public in a letter addressed by him to Dr. L. H. Coleman, of North Carolina, which became quite celebrated. It was certainly a very frank, unreserved, plain-spoken expression of opinions on this subject.

The letter was dated at Washington City, April 26, 1824, General Jackson being then in the United States Senate. It was long, but the following portion of it will speak for the whole:

"WASHINGTON CITY, April 26, 1824.

* * * * * * * *

"Providence has filled our mountains and our plains with minerals,—with lead, iron, and copper,—and given us a climate and soil for the growing of hemp and wool. These being the grand materials of our national defense, they ought to have extended to them adequate and fair protection, that our own manufactories and laborers may be placed on a fair competition with those of Europe, and that we may have within our country a supply of those leading and important articles so essential in war.

* * * * * * * *

"Where has the American farmer a market for his surplus product? Except for cotton, he has neither a foreign nor a home market. Does not this clearly prove, when there is no market either at home or abroad, that there is too much labor employed in agriculture, and that the channels for labor should be multiplied? Common sense points out at once the remedy. Draw from agriculture this abundant labor; employ it in mechanism and manufactures, thereby creating a home market for your breadstuffs, and distributing labor to the most profitable account, and benefits to the country will result. In short, sir, we have been too long subject to the policy of the British merchants. It is time we should become a little more *Americanized*, and, instead of feeding the paupers and laborers of England, feed our own, or else, in a short time, by continuing our present policy, we shall all be rendered paupers ourselves.

* * * * * * * *

"I am, sir, very respectfully, your most obedient servant,

"ANDREW JACKSON.

"DR. L. H. COLEMAN, Warrenton, N.C."

No one can doubt that in this letter General Jackson gave utterance to the strong convictions of his mind; and those convictions are expressed in language and with an emphasis and energy calculated to carry conviction to the minds of the great mass of the people. The letter, therefore, produced a marked effect upon the public mind; it was argument and demonstration combined, while it adroitly appealed to the pride and national feeling as well as patriotism of Americans.

His votes in the Senate clearly show that he expressed his honest sentiments in the Coleman letter, having voted in that body against removing the duty on cotton bagging, against reducing the duty on imported iron, and against reducing the duty on woolen goods; in each of these cases going with the friends and advocates of protection.

In regard to internal improvements by national means, his votes show that he went as far as the farthest in this direction, voting to authorize a subscription by the government to the Louisville and Portland Canal; a bill to extend the Cumberland Road; a bill to improve the navigation of the Mississippi, Ohio, and Missouri Rivers; a bill to subscribe to the stock of the Chesapeake and Delaware Canal; and other similar bills.

GENERAL JACKSON'S MONROE LETTERS.

Other letters written by General Jackson, many years previous, were made public about this time, and attracted much attention. They, moreover, did a good deal towards winning to his support that class of men who had once constituted the Federal party, and who had been exiled from positions at the disposal of the President and Senate since the advent of Jefferson to the office of chief magistrate.

These letters were denominated "the Monroe letters," being addressed to Mr. Monroe by General Jackson, with Mr. Monroe's replies. The correspondence was somewhat voluminous, the letters being pretty long. I shall make very brief extracts from them.

In his first letter, written mainly on business, and dated Nashville, 23d October, 1816, General Jackson takes occasion to say,—

. . . "Having learnt from General David Meriwether that Mr. Crawford is about to retire from the Department of War, I am inclined, as a friend to you and the government, to bring to your notice, as a fit character to fill that office, Colonel William H. Drayton, late of the army of the United States." . . .

His second letter, marked private, was dated

"NASHVILLE, November 12, 1816.

* * * * * * * *

"Everything depends on the selection of your ministry. In every selection, party and party feeling should be avoided. Now is the time to exterminate that *monster* called *party spirit*. By selecting characters most conspicuous for their probity, virtue, capacity, and firmness, without any regard to party, you will go far to, if not entirely, eradicate those feelings which, on former occasions, threw so many obstacles in the way of government; and perhaps have the *pleasure* and *honor* of uniting a people heretofore politically divided. The chief magistrate of a great and powerful nation should never indulge in party feelings. His conduct should be liberal and disinterested, always bearing in mind that he acts for the *whole* and not a *part* of the community. By this course you will *exalt the national character*, and acquire for *yourself* a name as imperishable as monumental marble. Consult *no party* in your choice; pursue the dictates of that unerring judgment which has so long and so often benefited our country, and rendered conspicuous its rulers. These are the sentiments of a friend; they are the feelings, if I know my own heart, of an undissembled patriot.

"Accept the assurances of my sincere friendship, and believe me to be respectfully your obedient servant,

"ANDREW JACKSON.

"The HON. JAMES MONROE."

To this letter Mr. Monroe replied, reflecting somewhat upon the Federalists, saying that "the contest between the parties [Federal and Republican] never ceased, from its commencement to the present time; nor do I think that it can be said now to have ceased." He, however, concurs in General Jackson's declaration that "the chief magistrate ought not to be the head of a party," etc., but intimates that in selecting his cabinet the wishes of his own friends should be consulted.

To this General Jackson rejoins in a third epistle, in which he fiercely denounces the Federalists, especially the Hartford Convention class, and declares that had he commanded the military department where the Hartford Convention met, if it had been the last act of his life, he would have punished the three principal leaders of the party. "I am certain," he says, "an independent court-martial would have condemned them, under the second section of the act establishing rules and regulations for the government of the army of the United States."

On reading these letters after a lapse of fifty odd years, one cannot but wonder at the great sensation they produced, and the influence they had upon the public mind. The declaration of General Jackson, however, that he would have punished,—hung or shot,—under the second section, the three principal leaders of the Hartford Convention, if it had been the last act of his life, was a bitter pill for his Federal friends. But it was swallowed with many wry faces, and excused as an ebullition of his impetuous temper.

THE PRESIDENTIAL CANVASS.—A CALM BEFORE A STORM.—THE STORM COMMENCES.—EXCITING TIMES.

The Presidential canvass and election went on, in 1824, in the various States, in a very quiet manner generally, there being no parties arrayed against each other. The contest was between individuals who had all belonged to the Republican or Democratic party. The number of candidates, by the withdrawal of Mr. Calhoun from the contest, was reduced to four. The immediate personal friends of each took a warm interest for their respective favorites; but this interest was confined to a comparatively few, no great principle or system of policy being at stake.

But upon the assembling of Congress in December, the interest in the conflict rapidly increased among the friends of those who were striving to win the high prize. The popular vote had been cast, and, as was expected, no one had a majority of the whole, except Mr. Calhoun, as the candidate for Vice-President.

The following were the votes cast for Mr. Adams: namely, Maine, 9; New Hampshire, 8; Vermont, 7; Massachusetts, 15; Connecticut, 8; Rhode Island, 4; New York, 26; Delaware, 1; Maryland, 3; Louisiana, 2; Illinois, 1. Total, 84.

For General Jackson, the following: New York, 1; New Jersey, 8; Pennsylvania, 28; Maryland, 7; North Carolina, 15; South Carolina, 11; Tennessee, 11; Louisiana, 3; Mississippi, 3; Alabama, 5; Indiana, 5; Illinois, 2. Total, 99.

For Mr. Crawford: Georgia, 9; Virginia, 24; New York, 5; Maryland, 1; Delaware, 2. Total, 41.

For Mr. Clay: Kentucky, 14; Ohio, 16; Missouri, 3; New York, 4. Total, 37.

The entire vote of North Carolina, 15, was cast for General Jackson, although Mr. Crawford had probably as many friends in the State as the general.

Had the bill in the Legislature of New York passed, giving the election of electors to the people, the entire electoral vote of that State would have been given to Mr. Adams,—36,—adding ten to his total, and making his vote 94, while it would have reduced General Jackson's to 98, and Mr. Crawford's to 36.

In Maryland, the Jackson and Crawford men united against Mr. Adams, and the same took place in Delaware. Neither candidate having a majority of the whole number of votes cast, by the Constitution, it devolved upon the House of Representatives to choose a President from the three who had the highest popular vote, or votes, of Presidential electors. These were General Jackson, Mr. Adams, and Mr. Crawford. Mr. Clay, having a lower number than the other three, was excluded from the list to be voted for; and instead of being voted for himself, it would become his duty to cast his vote for one of the three named. As his position was now most commanding, so it was one of great peril, politically, to himself.

It may be stated here that had not the election of electors of President and Vice-President been, by design, unfairly brought on in the Legislature of Louisiana in the absence of two or three of Mr. Clay's friends, he would have received the five electoral votes of that State, which would have sent him to the House as one of the three highest candidates, instead of Mr. Crawford; in which event the very strong probability, almost amounting to a certainty, was that Mr. Clay would have been elected President instead of Mr. Adams.

That his very elevated position at this time was a precipice from which he might be hurled with angry force so soon as he should have cast his vote, Mr. Clay was not unconscious, and he clearly foresaw that from being assiduously courted by certain sets of politicians, he was soon to become an object of the most rancorous calumny.

The well-remembered PLOT concocted against Mr. Clay, in January, 1825, which had for its object either to compel him to vote for General Jackson, or utterly to destroy his influence as a public man, was conceived in malignity and brought forth in baseness.

THE BEGINNING OF THE PLOT.—MR. CLAY CHARGED WITH BARGAIN AND INTRIGUE.

The first intimation the public had that bargain and intrigue were going on at Washington, with a view to elect either candidate who had been voted for by the people for President, was through the following letter, addressed, anonymously, to the "Columbian Observer," Philadelphia, the organ, as I have heretofore shown, of General Jackson and his friends:

"WASHINGTON, January 25, 1825.

"DEAR SIR,—I take up my pen to inform you of one of the most disgraceful transactions that ever covered with infamy the Republican ranks. Would you believe that men, professing democracy, could be found base enough to lay the axe at the very root of the tree of liberty? Yet, strange as it is, it is not less true. To give you a full history of this transaction would far exceed the limits of a letter. I shall therefore at once proceed to give you a brief account of such a BARGAIN as can only be equaled by the famous *Burr conspiracy* of 1801. For some time past the friends of Clay have hinted that they, like the Swiss, would fight for those who pay best. Overtures were said to have been made by the friends of Adams to the friends of Clay, offering him the appointment of Secretary of State for his aid to elect Adams; and the friends of Clay gave the information to the friends of Jackson, and hinted that if the friends of Jackson would offer the same price, they would close with them. But none of the friends of Jackson would descend to such mean barter and sale. It was not believed by any of the friends of Jackson that this contract would be ratified by the members from the States which had voted for Clay. I was of opinion, when I first heard of this transaction, that men professing any honorable principles could not, nor would not, be transferred, like the planter does his negroes, or the farmer does his team of horses. No alarm was excited. We believed the republic was safe. The nation having delivered Jackson into the hands of Congress, backed by a large majority of their votes, there was on my mind no doubt that Congress would respond to the will of the nation by electing the individual they had declared to be their choice. Contrary to this expectation, it is now ascertained to a certainty that Henry Clay has transferred his interest to John Quincy Adams. As a consideration for this abandonment of duty to his constituents, it is said and believed, should this unholy coalition prevail, Clay is to be appointed Secretary of State. I have no fear on my mind. I am clearly of opinion we shall defeat every combination. The force of public opinion must prevail, or there is an end of liberty."

Mr. Clay, in a public card, on the appearance of this calumnious accusation, indignantly pronounced it a falsehood, and its author, whoever he was, "a base and infamous calumniator, a dastard, and a liar."

Mr. GEORGE KREMER, a member of Congress from Pennsylvania, thereupon, in "ANOTHER CARD," referred Mr. Clay to the editor of the "Columbian Observer" for the name of the author, but declared that "in the mean time GEORGE KREMER holds himself ready to prove, to the satisfaction of unprejudiced minds, enough to satisfy them of the accuracy of the statements which are contained in that letter to the extent that they concern the course and conduct of 'H. Clay.' Being a representative of the people, he will not fear to 'cry aloud and spare not' when their rights and privileges are at stake."

Before going further in developing this infamous PLOT, I must do "honest George Kremer" the justice to say that he was more fool than knave; that he was the pliant tool with which to do the work of an arrant but cowardly set of knaves, instead of being himself the instigator of the PLOT. The composition of the letter addressed to the "Columbian Observer" was convincing proof, to all who knew the simple-minded, illiterate man, that he never wrote it; and the words, "that men professing any honorable principles could not, nor would not, be transferred, *like the planter does his negroes*," clearly prove that they were never written by a *Pennsylvanian*, but *were* written by a *Southerner.* Besides this internal evidence of the Southern paternity of the letter, Mr. Kremer told Mr. Crowningshield, a member of the House from Massachusetts, that he did not write the letter, and Mr. Brent, a member of the House from Louisiana, certified, in writing, that he "heard Mr. Kremer declare, at the fireplace in the lobby of the House of Representatives, in a manner and language which he believed sincere, that he never intended to charge Mr. Clay with corruption or dishonor in his intended vote for Mr. Adams as President; . . . that he was among the last men in the nation to make such a charge against Mr. Clay; and that his letter was never intended to convey the idea given to it."

Other members—Peter Little and Dudley Digges, of Maryland—heard and testified to the same statement of Mr. Kremer.

This shows that George Kremer did not write the letter he was induced to father; and if he sent it to the paper in which it appeared, he was evidently purposely deceived as to its purport.

It is hardly susceptible of doubt that Major JOHN H. EATON, the biographer and bosom friend of General Jackson, a Senator in Congress, and one of the PLOTTERS against Mr. Clay, was the writer of the letter. In a subsequent correspondence between Mr. Clay and Major Eaton,—commenced by the latter,—Mr. Clay said, "I did believe, from *your nocturnal* interview with Mr. Kremer, that you prepared or advised the publication of his card. I should be happy, by a disavowal on your part, . . . to know that I have been mistaken in supposing that you had any agency in the composition and publication of that card." To which Mr. Eaton replied, "You will excuse me from making an attempt to remove any belief which you entertain upon this subject. It is a matter which gives me no concern. . . . Suppose I did visit him; . . . that it was . . . 'a *nocturnal* visit;' was there anything existing that should have denied me this privilege?"

Major Eaton might feel very indignant at Mr. Clay's charge; but he could not deny its truth, nor escape its infamy.

Upon the appearance, in the "National Intelligencer," of Mr. Kremer's "*card,*" virtually assuming the authorship of the anonymous letter making the charge of "BARGAIN and IN-

TRIGUE," and declaring himself ready to prove the statements in that letter, Mr. Clay at once brought the matter to the notice of the House, over which he presided. "These charges," he said, "implicated his conduct in regard to the pending Presidential election. . . . If they were true, if he were capable and base enough to betray the solemn trust which the Constitution had confided to him, . . . the House would be scandalized by his continuing to occupy the chair with which he had been so long honored in presiding at its deliberations, and merited instantaneous expulsion. . . . He anxiously hoped that the House would be pleased to order an investigation to be made into the truth of the charges."

Mr. Forsyth, of Georgia, thereupon moved a resolution, which was, after some modification, passed, as follows:

"*Resolved,* That the communication made by the Speaker to the House, and entered on the journal of the House, be referred to a select committee."

One would naturally suppose that upon the earnest request of Mr. Clay, "that the House would be pleased to order an investigation into the truth of the charges" so boldly made, and the truth of which Mr. Kremer declared himself ready to prove, the resolution offered by Mr. Forsyth would have passed the House without a negative vote; but an investigation into the truth of this infamous charge was just what the "PLOTTERS" *did not want:* they knew it to be false; but to have it declared by a select committee of the House to be destitute of truth, and the author a calumniator, would spoil their PLOT. Accordingly, a very warm debate arose upon Mr. Forsyth's resolution, which occupied a day and a half. It was finally passed. The committee consisted of seven, not one of whom was the political friend of Mr. Clay.

In the course of this debate, Mr. Forsyth said,—

"If the charge is a true one, has not the bargain been made? And if it has, is it not corruption? And what then? It ought to be punished. Has not this House power not merely to reprimand, but to expel, any one of its members who shall have dared to be guilty of such conduct? If, on the contrary, it shall appear that any member of this House, governed by mere rumors, and under the influence of jealousy or mere surmises, shall have presumed to hold up as an infamous bargainer, as a contractor for votes and influence, a member or an officer of this House, will it be contended that we have no power to punish him? . . .

"If the charge is made, it ought to be investigated. If it is true, the member charged ought to be expelled from this House. If it is not true, the slanderer ought to be punished."

Mr. J. C. Wright, of Ohio, said, "We are told, sir, with this charge before us, that no offense is imputed; that all rests on rumors,—nothing affecting, in the slightest degree, the dignity of this House! that your presiding officer corruptly selling his own vote and those of his fellow-members is no offense to the dignity of the House! that no ulterior measures can grow out of such a charge, if true! and that it is beneath our dignity to notice such vague rumors! Sir, will you go to the election of a chief magistrate while corruption fills your halls and seeks to find its way into your ballot-boxes?" . . .

"Will any one," said Mr. Storrs, "undertake to convince this House that if its presiding officer should be convicted of theft (if I may suppose a case so offensive) we have not the power to dethrone him from the seat which he had thus dishonored? If he is charged with bribery, and the mean barter and sale of his vote as a member, is it an offense less involving the purity of the place? If the charge were proved, is there one among us who would not feel degraded in the occupation of these seats?" . . .

Unwilling, however, as the Jackson men were that an investigation should take place, lest the charge should prove to be, as they knew it was, a groundless calumny, they dared not set public opinion at defiance by refusing to appoint a committee charged with the duty of investigating the matter. The resolution was therefore passed and the committee appointed. And now, where is Mr. Kremer and his proofs? Does he come forward to sustain his charge? Quite otherwise. Having been notified to produce his proofs, he addressed a long communication to the committee, from which the following are brief extracts:

"GENTLEMEN,—I have received your note of yesterday, in which you inform me that you will meet at ten o'clock this morning, and will there be ready to receive any evidence or explanation I may have to offer touching the charges referred to in the communication of the Speaker of the 3d instant. . . . I can discover no authority by which the House can assume jurisdiction of the case. . . .

"Nor can I be ignorant of the fact that this body, thus unlimited in its rules and in the extent of its powers, is at all times, but more especially at a crisis like the present, subject, by its very constitution and the nature of its functions, to be acted upon by some of the most powerful passions that actuate the human breast, which unfit it to perform, in that cool and deliberate manner, the duties which properly belong to a court and jury. If it should be considered as proper that members be held responsible here for the communication of their opinions out of the House, on public men and public affairs, it would be much more safe that they should be placed at once under the operation of the *sedition law;* and so far as the members of this House are concerned, the repeal of that famous law might be considered as a calamity rather than a blessing. Thus regarding the constitutional power of the House, and the nature of that which is proposed to be exercised in my case, I have determined, under a deep sense of duty to myself and my constituents, not to submit to a procedure fraught with such dangerous consequences."

And so "honest George Kremer," who was so ready to prove the charge he had made, and with patriotic fervor to "cry aloud and spare not," when put to the test ignominiously backs out, and as a subterfuge denies the authority of the House to take cognizance of the matter, intimating that such a tribunal would exercise power in a very dangerous and arbitrary manner, "acted upon by some of the most powerful passions that actuate the human breast," under which it would be "unfit to perform, in that cool and deliberate manner, the duties *which properly belong to a court and jury*"!

The entire communication is worthy the PLOTTERS who concocted it for Mr. Kremer; for—poor soul, or poor dupe—everybody knew he had no hand in writing it. They had made a charge they dared not meet, and therefore must find a way of evading the call for proof. In doing this, they endeavored to put Mr. Kremer on the stilts of patriotism; he must protest against the jurisdiction of a "star-chamber court;" he must show the awful consequences that would result from submitting to such a tribunal, and bring in, for effect, the "*sedition law*," though it had no more to do with the case than the laws of Draco; he must assume a dramatic air of patriotism, defy the committee, and *stand upon his dignity!*

And the committee—what action did they take? Why, instead of reporting to the House that the charge had not been proved, that the accuser had failed to appear, and therefore the House must consider the charge a false accusation, and the Speaker's character unimpugned, they close their report by saying,—which is the gist of the whole of it,—"they have felt it to be their duty only to lay before the House the communication (Mr. Kremer's) which they have received." Most lame and impotent conclusion!

So ended, in a *fiasco*, the investigation by the House of this charge of "BARGAIN and INTRIGUE;" thus keeping it alive for future use. And great use, indeed, was made of it, so long as Mr. Clay was alive and likely to be a candidate before the people.

The subject will come up again when General Jackson shall have publicly made the charge against Mr. Clay of having attempted to make a bargain with him in regard to the Presidency, or of sending an emissary to him.

The very warm debate, which occupied a day and a half, on Mr. Forsyth's resolution tended to draw a line between those who had always before belonged to the same party,—to separate the friends of Adams from the friends of Jackson. It was the beginning of new parties, not yet fully developed, but to become as inveterately hostile to each other, in time, as the old Federal and Republican parties ever were.

ELECTION OF PRESIDENT BY THE HOUSE OF REPRESENTATIVES. —MR. ADAMS ELECTED.

The election of President by the House of Representatives took place in the Representative hall, on the 9th of February, 1825, in the presence of the Senate of the United States. It was a solemn occasion, and all felt it to be so. Every member of the House seemed to feel the responsibility of his position, —that the fate of the nation depended on his individual vote.

The members were called by States, and took their seats, each delegation sitting together, by itself. After being thus called and seated, the Senate came in and occupied seats prepared for them, the Vice-President presiding, and occupying the chair of the Speaker. Every voice was hushed; oppressive silence prevailed. The galleries were crowded with anxious spectators, the ladies being largely represented.

It was not generally expected that a choice would be made on the first ballot, though three or four members only had reason to believe this would be the case. It was necessary to an election that one of the three candidates to be voted for should obtain the votes of a majority of the States,—the votes being given by States, each State, large or small, casting but one vote.

It was not expected that New York would be able to cast her vote on the first ballot, as the members were divided, some intending to vote for Mr. Adams, some for Mr. Crawford, and a few, it was known, preferring General Jackson. It was not believed that either candidate could count on a majority of the members from that State on the first ballot. The vote of Louisiana was also uncertain. Mr. Brent, it was known, would vote for Mr. Adams; Mr. Livingston for General Jackson; while Mr. Gurley, the other member from that State, declared that he would cast his vote for Mr. Adams or for General Jackson, as the case might be, whenever by voting for the one or the other an election could be accomplished.

The balloting commenced, and proceeded in a very impressive manner. Maine, New Hampshire, Massachusetts, Vermont, Connecticut, were severally called, and the individual member appointed for the purpose by the delegation of the State handed to the tellers the vote of the State, which was declared aloud by the presiding officer, and held up, written in large characters, so that the whole House could see it.

At length it came to New York: her name being called, the vote was handed in, proclaimed by the Vice-President, and held aloft for all to see. New York cast her vote for JOHN QUINCY ADAMS. The surprise was as great as the relief from dubious anxiety. Everybody drew a long breath, as if relieved from oppressive doubt and apprehension. It was now known that the vote of Louisiana would be cast for Mr. Adams, because, by its being so cast, an election would take place. Of course all uncertainty was now removed: Mr. Adams, it was known, would be elected. The voting proceeded to the end with less restraint. The result is known.

But how did it happen that an election took place on the first ballot, so contrary to general expectation? This question I am enabled to answer by communications made to me by General Dudley Marvin, a member of the House at that time from the Canandaigua district, New York, and by Colonel John Taliaferro (pronounced Toliver), a member of the same body from Virginia.

General Marvin stated that of the New York delegation two, at least, were favorable to General Jackson, or desired to cast one vote for him; but, not expecting an election to take place on the first ballot, they both intended, and so stated to him, to vote for Mr. Adams on the second ballot, by which the vote of the State would be cast for him.

Meantime, General Marvin, as he informed me, discovered that Mr. Van Buren had got many Crawford men to agree to unite with the Crawford men of New York to vote for Mr. Adams on the second ballot, which would result in electing Mr. Adams by a large majority,—a result for which the Crawford men, and Mr. Van Buren as their file-leader, would claim the credit, and, of course, the reward from Mr. Adams, in appointments and influence.

Having ascertained that such an understanding had been entered into by the friends of Mr. Crawford,—an arrangement which, if successful, would make Mr. Van Buren the Warwick of the day, or "master of the situation,"—and knowing the political antagonism between Mr. Van Buren and these two members, namely, General Stephen Van Rensselaer, of Albany, and Parmenio Adams, of Batavia, he (General Marvin) lost no time in acquainting them with the arrangement he had discovered, and referred them to others, from whom they could obtain further information.

That such an arrangement had been entered into, these gentlemen both became satisfied; whereupon, to prevent Mr. Van Buren from claiming the credit of having made Mr. Adams President, they came to the resolution of voting for Mr. Adams on the first ballot, and thus electing him on that ballot. Thus it was accomplished, and thus was Mr. Van Buren balked.

Some twenty years after, General Marvin related to me the facts I have here stated. I became personally acquainted with Colonel Taliaferro, and availed myself of an opportunity to relate to him the facts communicated by General Marvin, and asked him if he knew whether any such arrangement had been entered into by the Crawford men. He said there was a general understanding among the friends of Crawford, of whom he was one, that they would give Mr. Crawford a complimentary vote on the first ballot, and then, on the second, cast their votes for Mr. Adams. "I know," said he, "of my own knowledge, that eighteen of the twenty-two votes from Virginia were to be given to Mr. Adams on the second ballot, had there been no election on the first, as it was supposed there would not be."

"All these eighteen were Jeffersonian Republicans," said Colonel Taliaferro; "and among them were P. P. Barbour, Andrew Stevenson, William C. Rives, and William S. Archer. New York," continued Colonel Taliaferro, "was very much under the lead of Mr. Van Buren, whom I often heard abuse General Jackson, as did his organ, the 'Albany Argus.' John Forsyth would not hold social intercourse with General Jackson or his prominent friends, and Benton held him in utter detestation."

Mr. Brent and Mr. Gurley, members from Louisiana, both addressed letters to their friends in that State on the day the election of Mr. Adams took place, announcing the fact, and stating that "General Jackson could not have been elected under any circumstances." "Had the friends of Mr. Crawford abandoned him," said Mr. Brent, "they would have gone to Mr. Adams, which would have swollen his vote to eighteen" States. This corroborates the statement of Colonel Taliaferro. As it was, Mr. Adams had the votes of thirteen States; General Jackson, seven; and Mr. Crawford, four.*

It may be interesting to inquire what would have been the history of Mr. Adams's administration, and of subsequent political parties, had not Mr. Van Buren's nice little arrangement been frustrated, and if *he* had had the credit of effecting that result. It would have committed the friends of Mr. Crawford, who constituted "the Democratic party" *par excellence*, to Mr. Adams, and secured their support of his administration. It would have prevented them from uniting with the friends of General Jackson, who at this time was no favorite with them and was vigorously assailed by all the leading presses of that party.†

* Since the above was written, I have found the following editorial in "Niles's Register," vol. xlii. p. 324, copied from the "New York Courier and Inquirer," the editor then being a decided Jackson man:

"The fact no longer should be concealed that if Mr. Clay had not on the first ballot decided the election of Mr. Adams, he would have been elected on the second ballot by the very men who now sustain the money-changers. We dare Mr. Cambreleng to deny it. We dare the 'Argus' to deny their avowal at the time, that they preferred Mr. Adams to General Jackson. We dare the 'Argus' to deny that he preferred having Mr. Rochester, an Adams man, for Governor than a friend of Andrew Jackson. We dare him to deny that he denounced the editor of the 'Inquirer' bitterly for preferring a friend to Jackson."

† Mr. Van Buren, it is well known, was a very cautious politician, seldom committing himself in writing; but he had in a letter to Colonel John Williams, United States Senator from Tennessee, spoken in disparaging terms of General Jackson as a candidate for President. Some years after, when he (Mr. Van Buren) was Secretary of State under General Jackson, in conversing with the Hon. Joseph L. Williams, son of his friend Colonel John, he took occasion to speak in very eulogistic terms of General Jackson; whereupon Mr. Williams reminded him of the fact that he (Mr. Van Buren) had changed his mind, as there was a time when he held a very different opinion of the general. On this remark being made, Mr. Williams —from whom I had the anecdote—said Mr. Van Buren looked surprised and inquisitive. Mr. Williams went on to say to Mr. Van Buren that, as the executor of his father, he had possession of all his correspondence, and among his letters he found some from him, Mr. Van Buren, in one of which he had spoken of Gen-

eral Jackson, of whom he evidently had then quite a different estimation from that which he now expressed. "For once," said Mr. Williams, "Mr. Van Buren was dumfounded; he made no reply, but appeared to be most uncomfortable." After enjoying his anxiety for a short time, Mr. Williams said he remarked that his letters, having been written in the confidence of private friendship, would be held sacred by him. Mr. Van Buren, he said, was prodigiously relieved by this assurance, and became very generous in offers of public positions at his disposal, no one of which he would accept, as he was not a friend of the administration.

No wonder Mr. Van Buren felt anxious, and even alarmed, well knowing that he could reach the great object of his ambition only by General Jackson's aid, and that he could no longer look for that should it come out that he had ever spoken disparagingly of him, as was shown in General Jackson's quarrel with Mr. Calhoun.

CHAPTER II.

Mr. Adams forms his Cabinet; Mr. Clay Secretary of State.—General Jackson; his Journey Home; charges Corruption against Mr. Adams and Mr. Clay.—Arrival of Lafayette, the "Nation's Guest."—His Tour through the United States.—Is fêted at Washington by the House of Representatives.—He is sent Home in the Frigate Brandywine.—The Beginning of a Storm in Georgia.—Completion of the Erie Canal.—Celebration of the Event.—De Witt Clinton.—A Political Calm. —General Jackson resigns his Seat in the Senate.—His Letter to the Legislature of Tennessee.—Governor Troup and the Legislature of Georgia terribly excited; they "stand by their Arms."—The Opposition Party formed.—Scene between Colonel R. M. Johnson and Colonel Seaton.—The "Telegraph" Paper established.—Violent and Calumnious Character of the Opposition.—The War opened upon the Administration upon the Panama Question.—Mr. McDuffie's Resolutions to amend the Constitution.—Fierce and Vindictive Debate thereon.—He endeavors to provoke a Challenge from General Vance.—Duel between Mr. Randolph and Mr. Clay.—John Randolph.—How Mr. Clay came to be elected Speaker on the First Day he entered the House as a Member.—Deaths of Adams and Jefferson.—The Cry of "Retrenchment and Reform" clamorously raised.—The famous East Room Letter.—"The gorgeously furnished East Room."—Georgia and the Creek Controversy.—Sharp Epistolary Skirmish between General Gaines and Governor Troup.—The Jackson Party gain the Ascendency in the House of Representatives.—Mr. McDuffie challenges Governor Metcalf, but will not fight with Rifles.—No Duel.—Abduction of William Morgan.—Formation of the Anti-Masonic Party.—General Jackson charges Mr. Adams and Mr. Clay with "Bargain and Corruption" at his Own Table.—Carter Beverly's Letter.—Mr. Clay's Denial.—Demands the Name of the Witness.—General Jackson replies, and gives the Name of James Buchanan as his Author.—Mr. Buchanan's Half-and-Half Letter in Response.—Mr. Adams's Solemn Denial of the Truth of the Charge.—Agitation of the Protective Policy.—Meetings and Conventions North and South.—Language of the South.—General Convention at Harrisburg.—Nullification first heard of.—Suggested by Colonel Hamilton, of South Carolina.—His Inflammatory Language.—Election of Governor and Lieutenant-Governor of New York.—Mr. Van Buren elected Governor by the aid of the Anti-Masons.—Presidential Election in 1828.—General Jackson elected.—A Winter in Washington, 1828–9.—Mrs. Eaton.—"Bellona."—Tempest in a Teapot.—Mrs. General Porter.—General Jackson arrives at Washington.—Declines to pay the Customary Visit of Respect to the President. —A Great Multitude of Office-Seekers rush to Washington.—Editors by the Score.—Calhoun Heir-Apparent.—A Spicy Debate in the House.—Proclamation; Braggadocio Smythe.—Mr. Adams's Last Levee.—General Anxiety of Heads of Bureaus and Clerks on account of Threats of Sweeping Removals.

MR. ADAMS PRESIDENT.—GENERAL JACKSON AGAIN NOMINATED FOR PRESIDENT.

THE great excitement which preceded the election of President immediately died away upon the consummation of that event, and a calm, apparent at least, succeeded for a time. True, the very ardent friends of General Jackson immediately nominated him for election four years subsequently, and talked of his being cheated out of his election; taking the singular ground that, as he had been returned to the House with the highest electoral vote of the three, the House ought to have elected him,—that he was entitled to it. If this proposition were true, the House had no discretion in the matter, and an election by that body of one of the three candidates having the highest number of electoral votes, but neither candidate a majority of the whole number, if their choice *must* fall upon the one having the highest number of the three, would be a farce. This argument found no favor with the country at this time. He was, personally, on the most friendly terms with all the rival candidates, though his relations with Mr. Clay were less cordial than with either of the others.

Mr. Adams had most ably and successfully defended General Jackson for entering Florida at the head of his army and taking St. Mark's and Pensacola,—a service no other man could so successfully have done when complaint was made of this by the Spanish government, and he justified his course in Mr. Monroe's cabinet, when the President and all the other members of the cabinet disapproved it. General Jackson was therefore under the deepest obligations to him. We have seen, moreover, that General Jackson was treated with distinguished consideration by Mr. and Mrs. Adams, who gave a large and well-remembered party in honor of him on the 8th of January, 1824.

Mr. Adams and Mr. Crawford, and their respective families, were on terms of the most friendly cordiality, the latter taking occasion to say, in 1824, that by Mr. Adams and his family he had been treated with the utmost kindness, especially during his long illness, for which he expressed himself most grateful.

At this time—February, 1825—Mr. Crawford's broken constitution not permitting him to remain longer in public life, even if he were disposed to do so, he was preparing to return to his home in Georgia and to private life, after a long period of faithful service in various high public stations, impaired in health and disappointed in his aspirations. But for the attack of paralysis which struck him down some eight or nine months previous to the Presidential election, it is probable he would have been elected instead of Mr. Adams. It is well known that Mr. Clay was, and had long been, much devoted to him, and there can be little doubt that most of the Western and New York members, who went with him for Mr. Adams, had Mr. Crawford's health not been impaired, would have voted for the latter. But, like many other eminent men who have aspired to that high position, he was destined never to be President of the United States.

WILLIAM H. CRAWFORD.

Mr. Crawford was a truly great man. His name stands among those of the most eminent of our statesmen, and long will his memory be cherished by those who know how to value great intellect, purity of character, and faithful public services. From his entrance into the Senate of the United States, he was the political Mentor of that galaxy of young men who then appeared in Congress and soon became eminent as statesmen and orators. Among these were Mr. Clay, Mr. Forsyth, Mr. Lowndes, Louis McLane, Thomas W. Cobb, George M. Troup, Philip Doddridge, James Barbour, Andrew Stevenson, and others, chiefly from the South and West. John Randolph and Nathaniel Macon, whose names were for many long years upon the rolls of Congress, were his contemporaries and life-long devoted friends.

He was a man of commanding presence; tall, large-framed, sedate, but with an agreeable expression; and the outer corresponded with the inner man,—both inviting confidence, but repelling familiarity.

For a short time he represented this country at the court of Napoleon, having for his colleague Chancellor Livingston, of New York. He could not speak French, and Mr. Livingston was very deaf—which drew from Napoleon the witty remark that the United States government had sent a deaf and dumb embassy to negotiate with him.

Soon after the Presidential election he returned to Georgia, and never again appeared in public life, except that as a means of support, he being poor, his friends in that State elected him to the office of Judge of Probate, or of some inferior court, which he held till his death, a few years later.

General Jackson was still in Washington, a member of the Senate, and apparently in a very amiable mood; at least uttering no complaint as to the result of the election. On the 10th of February, the day after the election, the general was invited to partake of a public dinner. He declined the invitation, and in his letter, alluding to the recent election, he said, "Any evidence of kindness and regard such as you propose might, by many, be viewed as conveying with it EXCEPTION, murmurings, and feelings of complaint, which I SINCERELY HOPE BELONG TO NONE OF MY FRIENDS."

Had he believed that the election of Mr. Adams had been accomplished, and his own prevented, by a corrupt "bargain," is it likely that he would, the next day, have declined a public manifestation of regard for himself, lest it might imply an exception on his part against the result of the election so brought about, and earnestly deprecate on the part of his friends any "murmurings" or feeling of dissatisfaction? Besides, immediately on Mr. Adams being inaugurated, the general stepped forward, tendered him his hand, and in the most cordial manner congratulated him on his election.* Was General Jackson then playing the hypocrite, by expressing feelings he did not entertain, or did he rather feel no chagrin, not believing he had any cause for other than friendly feelings towards Mr. Adams?

* Giving an account of Mr. Adams's inauguration, the editor of the "National Intelligencer" said, "The meeting between him [Mr. Adams] and his venerated predecessor had in it something peculiarly affecting. General *Jackson*, we were pleased to observe, was among the earliest of those who took the hand of the President, and their looks and deportment towards each other were a rebuke to that littleness of party spirit which can see no merit in a rival and feel no joy in the honor of a competitor."

Had he believed he had been defrauded out of an election, can any one suppose he would have been the first (after Mr. Monroe) to tender his hand and congratulations to Mr. Adams? By no means. It would seem that whatever stories about Mr. Adams's friends making "overtures" to Mr. Clay had been brought to him by Mr. Buchanan, he had put no faith in them, considering them the idle rumors of the day, of which the atmosphere was full.

There was a calm again in politics. The atmosphere at Washington, and, indeed, over the whole country, was serene as a summer's morning. Not a cloud was to be seen,—no mutterings heard. People congratulated themselves that "the era of good feeling"—which expression had been used to characterize Mr. Monroe's Presidential term—was to continue, and universal harmony prevail.

Mr. Adams soon formed his cabinet, which was thus constituted: Henry Clay, Secretary of State; Richard Rush, Secretary of the Treasury; James Barbour, Secretary of War; Samuel L. Southard (continued), Secretary of the Navy; William Wirt (continued), Attorney-General. John McLean, Postmaster-General under Mr. Monroe, appointed in 1822, continued to fill the same office—not then a cabinet office—during the whole of Mr. Adams's term.

These gentlemen had, each and all, belonged to the Republican or Democratic party, or that party represented by Mr. Jefferson, Mr. Madison, and Mr. Monroe, so that there was no change of parties by the election of Mr. Adams. He himself had held the highest stations, save that of President, both at home and abroad, under each of these Presidents, with whose administrations he was identified and in perfect accord.

He was at this time considered by the American people the ablest, best trained, and most experienced diplomatist and statesman in the nation. As a *diplomatist*, indeed, he had no superior in Europe. His knowledge of the laws of nations, and of the public affairs and policy of every great power in Europe, seemed to be inexhaustible, and his pen to be driven by the force of steam. Residing with his father when a boy at Versailles and other European courts, where he attended school, he acquired, so as to speak as familiarly as his mother-tongue, several modern languages, among which were the French and Russian.

A member of the United States Senate in 1806 (where he first met Mr. Clay), he resigned in 1808, in consequence of a disagreement with his party—the Federal—in regard to some of Mr. Jefferson's measures. Shortly after this he was appointed professor of rhetoric in Harvard University, and delivered a course of lectures upon that subject, which were published, and for many years used in colleges in preference to Blair's; but, like other things of that day, they have passed away and are forgotten.

But Mr. Adams was soon drawn from this sphere, which was clearly not his proper element, to one more congenial and befitting his education and peculiar cast of mind, by Mr. Jefferson, by whom he was appointed, in 1809, minister to Russia.

He was a scholar, and a ripe and good one, but was more especially a diplomatist and statesman; and it was as such that he was supported for the Presidency.

At the period of which I am speaking, and previously, the usages and customs of the people in electing Presidents, Governors, Senators, members of Congress, etc., were very different in the Eastern, Northern, and Middle States from what they are now and have been for thirty years past. Candidates for these high positions, and, indeed, for all other elective offices, were brought very little in contact with the voters. Such a thing as a public political meeting addressed by the candidates for office and their friends was unknown. It was considered discreditable, indeed, for any candidate to solicit support, or to appear to *seek* the office for which he was proposed. The theory was that the fittest man for the place would be sought by the people, and it did not become any one to thrust himself forward uncalled for.

But the practice at the South and West was always different. There the candidates appeared before the people, whom they respectively addressed, and whose favor they sought to win. Two results grew out of this usage. First, it accustomed and trained men to speak in public and to carry on a debate with their opponents, thus preparing them to become orators and debaters in legislative halls and in Congress. Second, it brought the candidates into personal contact and association with the electors; each soon knew the other, and their relations were of a more personal and friendly character than they otherwise would have been. Hence it was that almost every member of Congress from the South and West was an off-hand, ready speaker, while very few from the North, comparatively, could participate in a running debate or address the house for two or three hours in an extempore speech. This art has been more cultivated at the North since the memorable Presidential contest of 1840 than it formerly was; and the custom now prevails there, as it does in every other part of the Union, of candidates addressing the people at public meetings.

MR. CLAY SECRETARY OF STATE.

The charge of "bargain and corruption," calumnious as it was and utterly destitute of truth, embarrassed both Mr. Clay and Mr. Adams; but they acted, nevertheless, as men will act who are conscious of the rectitude of their actions and the purity of their motives, trusting to the intelligence and discernment of the American people for a verdict of "not guilty of the charge," and a denunciation of it as a base slander.

The "charge" was cunningly devised. It was a stratagem to head off or destroy Mr. Clay. Its first purpose was to deter him from voting for Mr. Adams; this failing, its next was to kill him off, politically. If he did not vote for Mr. Adams their first and great object would be gained,—General Jackson would be elected President. If he did vote for Mr. Adams, and elect him, it would be alleged that the truth of the "charge" had been proved. If he were appointed Secretary of State, and accepted the office, it would be "proof strong as holy writ" of the truth of the "charge." In a private letter to his friend Judge Brooke, of Richmond, Virginia, dated February 3, 1825, Mr. Clay, speaking of the acceptance of the office tendered to him by Mr. Adams, says, "It was urged [by his friends] that whether I accepted or declined the office I should not escape animadversion; that in the latter contingency it would be said that the patriotic Mr. Kremer, by an exposure of the corrupt arrangement, had prevented its consummation; that the very object of propagating the calumny would be accomplished; . . . that I ought not to give the weight of a feather to the Kremer affair. . . ." He states that those of his friends who were at first averse to his accepting the office changed their opinion and advised it. Mr. Adams's friends in New England were unanimous and urgent that he should accept. He further states that several of Mr. Crawford's friends—Mr. McLane, of Delaware, Mr. Forsyth, of Georgia, Mr. Mangum, of North Carolina, and also some of General Jackson's friends in Pennsylvania, expressed to him their strong convictions that he ought to accept.

Such were the reasons which induced Mr. Clay's acceptance of the office of Secretary of State, against his own convictions and inclinations. But in doing so he made the great political mistake of his life, and one which forever barred him from the Presidential seat.

GENERAL JACKSON ON HIS JOURNEY HOME.

We have seen nothing, as yet, indicating that General Jackson considered himself wronged by the election of Mr. Adams, or that he was in bad humor in regard to the result. He had shown no ill feeling, but, on the contrary, had been the first, after Mr. Monroe, to tender his hand to and congratulate Mr. Adams on his election. How could he do that, unless he were playing the hypocrite, if he believed Mr. Adams had been elected by corrupt and disreputable means? And if he had the proofs that Mr. Clay had bargained with Mr. Adams that in consideration that Mr. Clay should effect the election of Mr. Adams the latter would appoint him Secretary of State, why did he not present the charge to the Senate when Mr. Clay's nomination was before that body? True, he voted with John Randolph, Major Eaton, Colonel Hayne, and others, fifteen in all, against the confirmation; but no accusation was brought against Mr. Clay by any one.

Soon after the cabinet was formed and the Senate adjourned, General Jackson took his departure from Washington for his home, near Nashville, via Wheeling and Cincinnati; and now we find him scattering accusations all along his way, wherever he stopped, against Mr. Adams and Mr. Clay, but especially the latter, which indicated a most rancorous feeling. He had said nothing of the kind in Washington; but a letter dated February 14, 1825, which he wrote in haste from there to his confidential friend Mr. Lewis, and which was afterwards published, is evidence that the calm demeanor which he manifested while there was only assumed; that quite in contrast with this were the implacable passions then burning in his breast towards Mr. Clay. Wherever he happened to be, or whoever, and in whatever numbers, were present, he spoke with the utmost freedom, and charged that "there was cheating, and corruption, and bribery going on" in the election at Washington, and declared that "if *he* would have made the same promises and offers to Mr. Clay that Mr. Adams had done, he would have been in the Presidential chair. But he would make no promises to any one; if he went into the Presidential chair he would go with clean hands and uncontrolled by any one."

In conversation with the Rev. A. Wylie, a clergyman of much distinction, when asked if a proposition had been made to *him* in regard to the Presidency, he replied, "Yes; such a proposition *was* made. I said to the bearer, 'Go tell Mr. Clay, tell Mr. Adams, if I go into that chair I go with clean hands and a pure heart, and that I had rather see them, together with myself, engulfed to the earth's centre, than to compass it by such means.' The very next day, or shortly after, Mr. Clay and his friends declared for Mr. Adams."

He further declared that "the people, in the late election, had been cheated; that corruptions and intrigues at Washington had defeated the will of the people in the election of their President." He said that the tender of the office of Secretary of State to Mr. Clay and its acceptance by him "was a proof of the bargain, and a fulfillment of the prediction of honest George Kremer."

It is a matter of astonishment that none of these broad, calumnious charges, made at public hotels, at the way-side, and on board of steamboats, did not reach the ears of Mr. Clay or find their way into the public papers. It would be otherwise at this day. Of course they could not be contradicted, as they were unknown; and, remaining uncontradicted, they had their effect in poisoning the public mind against Mr. Clay and Mr. Adams. The most that I have quoted as coming from General Jackson was uttered on board the steamer "General Neville," on which he took passage from Wheeling to Cincinnati, and which was crowded with passengers.

Such false and calumnious charges against men in every respect as eminent, as worthy of public esteem, as incorruptible, and as patriotic as himself, were disreputable, and unworthy of his lofty position before the world. They were the outpourings of disappointed ambition, and the overflowings of a heart charged with gall and bitterness. He was making a boast of his own incorruptibility while accusing others of corruption,—an ignobleness which did not escape the comment and censure, at the time, of his listeners.

Meantime, as Mr. Adams considered it improper for him, as President of the United States, to denounce the charge of "bargain and corruption" as false, and as Mr. Clay could find no one to hold responsible for the charge, and could therefore only denounce it as false and calumnious generally, as he had done before his constituents, it was left to do its silent but effective work upon the public mind, until General Jackson unintentionally became responsible for it, as we shall see hereafter.

ARRIVAL OF LAFAYETTE, "THE NATION'S GUEST."

This eminent and beloved patriot and early friend of America had been invited by our government to re-visit this country, the scene of his early chivalric services in the cause of liberty and the rights of man, and had been tendered a frigate to bring him to the United States. He was also tendered a free passage by the owners of the different lines of packet-ships running from New York to Havre and to Liverpool, which were all splendid models of naval architecture, and floating palaces. Having declined the use of a public ship, the "Cadmus," Captain Allyn, a fine ship belonging to the Havre line of packets, was the fortunate vessel in which he took passage. He arrived at Staten Island on Sunday, 15th of August, 1824, accompanied by his son, George Washington Lafayette, and his son-in-law, M. Le Vasseur. Here he remained until Monday, and was then met and welcomed by a distinguished committee from New York, who escorted him to that city. Every preparation had been made for the occasion, as the arrival of the vessel bearing him to our shores had been for several days expected. A great number of steamers were chartered and formed in procession, every boat dressed with the flags of all nations, the whole presenting a most animating and gorgeous display. The whole bay of New York, indeed, was covered with steamers and other vessels decked with flags from deck to top-gallant mast and from stern-post to bowsprit.

The committee on landing proceeded to Lafayette's quarters, accompanied by a great but orderly crowd, eager to see one who had so endeared himself to a grateful people and who was enshrined in the nation's heart. The meeting was most cordial, warm, affecting. Every one who could, seized the hand of the beloved patriot, who, overcome by this manifestation of regard, shed grateful tears, the only reply he could make.

On the return to New York, two steamers, one on each side, took the "Cadmus," decked all over with flags, in tow, and all proceeded up the bay to "the Battery," where the landing was made, and carriages and a large body of troops were in waiting.

On approaching the city, every house near the water was covered with people, every window filled with ladies waving their white handkerchiefs, every vessel black with men and boys, wherever one could find "coigne of vantage" or cling to a mast. The whole scene was the most animating and sublime that could be imagined. I had the good fortune to be on board the "Cadmus," and could take in the whole panorama at once.

As the procession passed up Broadway to the City Hall, every door, balcony, and window was occupied, and every house-top covered with eager people. It seemed as if the whole population of the city had congregated in that street; and yet, on arriving at the City Hall, the grounds around were densely packed with men, women, and children. Lafayette took a position on the steps of the Hall, and reviewed the troops as they marched by him.

The arrival of Lafayette was an event which stirred the

whole country; everybody was anxious to see him, and every State and city in the Union extended an invitation to him to visit such State or city; and he did so, being everywhere received with the most enthusiastic manifestations of love and respect. Indeed, each city seemed to vie with every other in its demonstrations and in the fêtes given to him.

He spent a little over a year in the United States, traveling most of the time, and carrying with him, on his return to France, the heartfelt benedictions of a whole nation.

Lafayette in his travels through the United States occasionally met with some of his old Revolutionary companions, or the widow of an old friend and associate who had passed away. Some of these meetings were exceedingly interesting and affecting, both to the parties who met and to those who witnessed them. How could it be otherwise? As young men they had fought and bled in the same noble cause; had endured hardship and privation together; together had suffered defeat, and together had exulted in victory. For a long series of years they had been separated by the Atlantic Ocean; they now met again as old men, many of them just upon the verge of the grave. Their meeting must be brief, their words few but full of feeling, their separation final. Lafayette had the peculiar faculty of remembering faces and recognizing those whom he had once known, though time had plowed its deepest furrows upon their countenances and whitened their heads with the snows of forty additional winters.

The visit of the distinguished patriot, "THE NATION'S GUEST," as he was styled, was a historic event, and one that will be remembered, by those who were old enough to remember anything at the time, as long as their memory shall last.

Having visited every portion of the United States and received the affectionate homage of the people, General Lafayette returned to Washington, where he became in fact "the Nation's Guest" at the Presidential mansion.

Soon after the meeting of Congress, in December, 1824, a bill was reported by a joint committee of the two Houses granting to him a township of land and the sum of two hundred thousand dollars, which became a law.

In order further to honor the old patriot and friend of liberty, a banquet was given him by Congress, on the 1st of January, 1825. Mr. Clay, Speaker of the House of Representatives, presided. The following eminent gentlemen, among others, were present: Colonel James Monroe, President; General Samuel Smith, General Jackson, Rufus King, General Chandler, and Mr. D'Wolf, of the Senate; J. Q. Adams, Mr. Calhoun, Smith Thompson, one of the Judges of the Supreme Court; Generals Dearborne, Scott, Macomb, Bernard, and Jessup; Commodores Bainbridge, Tingey, Stewart, and Morris.

Mr. Clay spoke briefly, but with great feeling and eloquence. Colonel Monroe, who was present less in his official character of President than as an officer of the Revolution, responded to a toast; but Mr. Charles Fenton Mercer enchained the attention of the company, not only by his very eloquent remarks, but also by relating many circumstances of the Revolutionary struggle, which he must have obtained from General Washington and "Light-Horse Harry Lee," who had both been his neighbors. Among other things, he spoke of the sad, forlorn, and dispirited condition of the army at Valley Forge,—barefoot, destitute of proper food, clothing, blankets, tents, and everything necessary to comfort, almost support. Washington, he said, then almost despaired, and was meditating the disbanding of the army from sheer necessity. Something occurred, however, to give a more cheerful tone to his despairing mind, and, forming his ragged, destitute, half-starved, barefooted men in line, he said, in a kindly, fatherly tone, "Boys, march slowly on to Chester."

Sadly they marched as best they could, leaving tracks of blood, to Chester, where the people received them with open arms, open hearts, open hands, and tearful eyes; furnishing them food, clothing, shoes, and shelter to the extent of their power, for which no men could have been more grateful. It was a crisis,—the turning-point of the Revolution,—but the crisis was now past. Hope, and confidence, and resolution once more animated the heart of the beloved general, and the hearts also of his compatriots and the forlorn little army. The rest is known.

Among the guests present was Caspar Everhart, a Methodist

preacher, and chaplain in the Revolutionary army, who had been sent for and brought here for the occasion from his residence at Frederick, Maryland. Being called upon, he made some remarks and told many amusing Revolutionary anecdotes. "How was it, Mr. Everhart," some one inquired, "that you, unarmed, took three British soldiers prisoners?" "But I *was* armed," he replied. "True, I had no gun, nor pistol, nor sword, but I had a powerful weapon, and one that, if used too often, is very deadly, and I used it on this occasion. It was a bottle of rum. I met these soldiers and entered into a little conversation with them, and, finally, invited them to go to a spring near by and take refreshing drinks. They required no persuasion, but went at once, stacked their arms, sat down, and soon became *hors du combat*, as our French allies used to say. Wishing to extend my hospitalities still further, I took their muskets, and then invited them to accompany me to our camp. Duly appreciating my kindness in taking care of them when not in a fit condition to take care of themselves, they did not refuse my pressing invitation."

We may well imagine what roars of laughter Mr. Everhart brought out by the quaint manner in which he related this heroic feat. This, however, was but one of many amusing circumstances of the times related by this beloved chaplain.

It was an occasion and a banquet long to be remembered, and is still vividly remembered by several gentlemen now living in Washington,—some of the "oldest inhabitants," of course, as it took place forty-nine years ago.

But what an assemblage of heroes, statesmen, patriots, generals, and commodores was here to do honor to the beloved "guest of the nation"! Not one among them but of whom Fame had proclaimed "her loudest O yes!" not one whose name was not already familiar to the lips of every American and inscribed high upon his country's scroll of honor; not one who had not rendered eminent service to his country, in her cabinet councils, in her halls of legislation, on the field of battle, or on the briny ocean,—where had been won the laurels of victory, now so gracefully worn.

The frigate Brandywine had been prepared to convey General

Lafayette from our shores to those of France. The ship had been named the "Brandywine" in commemoration of the gallantry of Lafayette and his being wounded in the battle of that name.

The day at length arrived when he was to bid a final adieu to America, and when the nation, through its chief magistrate, was to bid him farewell. The occasion was made a public and imposing one. An eye-witness of it says, "The 7th instant (September, 1825) was the day appointed for his departure. The civil and military authorities, and the whole people of Washington, had prepared to honor it. The banks were closed, and all business suspended.

"At about twelve o'clock the authorities of Washington, Georgetown, and Alexandria, the principal officers of the general government,—civil, military, and naval,—some members of Congress, and other respected strangers, were assembled in the President's house to take leave of Lafayette."

Everything being prepared, the President addressed him in language exceedingly eloquent and touching.

" . . . In the lapse of forty years," Mr. Adams said, "the generation of men with whom you co-operated in the conflict of arms has nearly passed away. Of the general officers of the American army in that war, you alone survive. . . . A succeeding and even a third generation have arisen; . . . and their children's children, while rising up to call them blessed, have been taught by them . . . to include in every benison upon their fathers the name of him who came from afar, with them and in their cause to conquer or fall.

"You have traversed the twenty-four States of this great confederacy. You have been received with rapture by the survivors of your earliest companions-in-arms. You have been hailed as a long-absent parent by their children, the men and women of the present age. . . . You have heard the mingled voices of the past, the present, and the future age joining in one universal chorus of delight at your approach, and the shouts of unbidden thousands which greeted you on your landing have followed every step of your way, and still resound, like the rushing of many waters, from every corner of our land.

"You are about to return to the country of your birth. . . .

The first service of a frigate recently launched at this metropolis [will be that] of conveying you home. The name of the ship has added one more memorial to distant regions and future ages of a stream already memorable at once in the story of your sufferings and of our independence."

To this eloquent and pathetic valedictory Lafayette replied in language equally eloquent and touching; and there were few tearless eyes among the distinguished persons, men and women, there present.

Immediately after this scene, Lafayette left the Presidential mansion and the city, and proceeded down the Potomac to its mouth, where the Brandywine awaited his coming, and on board of which he left our shores, never to return. He was accompanied to the frigate by the Secretary of the Navy (Mr. Southard); the Mayors of Washington, Georgetown, and Alexandria; the Commander-in-chief of the Army, General Brown; Commodore Bainbridge, Mr. Custis of Arlington, and many other distinguished personages.

Among the distinguished characters present at the Lafayette banquet I have mentioned General Dearborne, of Boston. At that day gentlemen, especially lawyers, were much in the habit of taking snuff, and in this habit the general had so long indulged, and to such excess, that he had almost entirely lost his voice. Mr. Clay was also fond of snuff,—so fond that he would never carry a box, lest he should indulge the habit to such excess as to injure his voice,—his splendid, silver-toned, melodious voice. There was, however, a tobacco-store on "the Avenue," where he usually stopped on passing to get a pinch of fine maccaboy. Passing the place the morning after the great dinner in company with General Dearborne, he stopped, as usual, inviting his friend in to test the quality of Mr. Tobacconist's snuff. As they were snuffing away, General Dearborne remarked that snuff injured some men's voices, "but," said he, with what little vocal power snuff had left him, "it has never affected mine in the least."

Mr. Clay used to relate this anecdote with great humor, imitating, in doing so, General Dearborne's piping tones, to the infinite amusement of his company.

THE BEGINNING OF A STORM.

Hark! Is that distant and faint rumbling thunder? The skies are clear, but something gives warning of a coming storm; and it may be a tempest that shall carry desolation over the land. It comes from the South,—from Georgia. Listen: Governor Troup, in an official communication to the Legislature of that State, warns them of danger and entreats them to *stand by their arms!* The storm is coming; this is the first faint indication of it; but in thirty-five or forty years it will sweep like a tornado from the Potomac—ay, from the Susquehanna—to the Rio Grande, and the South, having sown the wind, shall reap the whirlwind.

On the 23d of May, 1825, Governor G. M. Troup sent a message to the Legislature of Georgia, which he had called together, in which occur these passages:

"Since your last meeting, our feelings have been again outraged by officious and impertinent intermeddlings with our domestic concerns. Besides the resolution presented for the consideration of the Senate by Mr. King, of New York, it is understood that the Attorney-General of the United States, who may be presumed to represent his government faithfully and to speak as its mouth-piece, has recently maintained, before the Supreme Court, doctrines on this subject which, if sanctioned by that tribunal, will make it quite easy for the Congress, by a short decree, to divest this entire interest [slavery] without cost to themselves of one dollar or of one acre of land. . . . I entreat you, therefore, most earnestly, now that it is not too late, to step forth, and, having exhausted the argument, to stand by your arms."

Surely Mr. Rufus King and Mr. Attorney-General Wirt must have committed some grave offense! What was it? Mr. King introduced a resolution into the Senate of the United States, resolving that "so soon as the portion of the funded debt, for the payment of which the public lands were pledged, should be paid off, then the whole public lands of the United States, with the net proceeds of all future sales, should constitute a fund to be applied to the emancipation of such slaves, and the removal of such free persons of color in any of the States, as by the laws of the said States may be allowed to be emancipated or removed without the limits of the United States." The resolution was never called up or acted on; yet Governor Troup, in his nervous alarm, saw in it something very dangerous, and forthwith invoked the Legislature of his State to *stand by their arms.*

Governor Troup's message was taken up for consideration in the Georgia House of Representatives, when Mr. Lumpkin submitted the following resolution:

That they concur in the sentiments of the Governor, and, "having exhausted the argument," we will "stand by our arms."

COMPLETION OF THE ERIE CANAL, AND THE CELEBRATION OF THE EVENT.

The completion of this great channel of commerce from the Atlantic to Lake Erie was a most important event,—one of the most important in its consequences which had ever occurred in the great Empire State. It was of national importance. It was the opening of the door and a channel of commerce between the East and the great, rich Northwest, then but very partially settled,—much of it primeval forest or prairie,—but which, immediately after this event, began to be settled with amazing rapidity, and is now filled with its teeming millions of industrious inhabitants, its large and elegant cities, its wonderful network of railroads, its churches, colleges, and common schools, rivaling those of the oldest States.

It was very properly determined that the completion of this great work should be celebrated with a grand procession of boats, to commence at Buffalo and end at Sandy Hook, where the waters of the lake should be mingled with those of the ocean. The completion of the canal, and the letting in of the waters of the lake, took place on the 27th of October, 1825.

Cannon had been placed at suitable distances from Buffalo to Sandy Hook, and upon the letting in of the waters the gun at Buffalo was fired, and the next, as soon as the report of the first was heard, and so on to Sandy Hook, thus announcing the important event. The first gun was fired at ten o'clock A.M., and the gladsome sound reached New York at twenty minutes past eleven. The cannon, when their boom had reached Sandy Hook, were fired in reversed order, one extremity thus replying to the other.

Simultaneously with the letting in of the waters at Buffalo, boats gayly decorated and drawn by four and six horses started for New York. They were joined by others, similarly decorated and drawn, at Rochester, Syracuse, Utica, and other principal towns on the canal, and these formed quite a fleet by the time they reached Albany. Here they entered the North or Hudson River, and were towed down by a fleet of steamers, the whole presenting a most gay and animating scene. There was the "Seneca Chief," from Buffalo; the "Niagara," from Black Rock; and the "Young Lion of the West," from Rochester. With the fleet from Albany came Governor De Witt Clinton, to whom the canal owed its existence. This fleet was met above New York and escorted to the city by another fleet of steamers, gayly decorated with flags and streamers, arriving about nine o'clock A.M. on the 4th of November. At a given signal, all the vessels and forts in the harbor were ornamented with flags, and a grand salute was fired. The fleet, consisting of twenty-one steamers with several large vessels in tow besides the boats that had come through the canal, proceeded down the bay to Sandy Hook amidst the roar of cannon. On arriving at "the Hook," Governor Clinton performed the ceremony of uniting the waters, by pouring a keg of the waters of Lake Erie into the Atlantic, upon which occasion he made an appropriate speech. After other ceremonies, the drinking of toasts, etc., the fleet returned to the city. Thus was completed the great work which had for more than ten years employed the mind and energies of DE WITT CLINTON, whose name the canal ought to bear, and to whose memory it is a noble monument, more enduring than brass or marble. It was a triumphant day to him; it was a proud day for the State of New York; it was a great day for the nation. It was the beginning of that system of internal navigation by canals, which, before railroads were thought of as channels of internal commerce, furnished an outlet to the rich fields of the West, for its stores of produce, almost valueless before, but immensely valuable so soon as the means were thus provided for its being transported to the sea-board cities.

The Erie Canal originally cost about seven millions of dollars, but added more than a thousand millions to the value of the property owned by the people of New York, and, prospectively, untold millions to the wealth of the nation. And yet it did not come into existence without the most virulent opposition. It was scouted and ridiculed as a chimerical idea, a work too gigantic to be accomplished in a generation, if at all. It was hooted at as "Clinton's Big Ditch;" and at its commencement (when I was a student of law in Troy) I frequently heard "Bucktails," or "Tammany men," or "Anti-Clintonians," declare that they should be glad to be assured of living till "the ditch" was completed, but that event no one then living would behold! Perhaps the wish, inspired by political hostility to Clinton, was father to the idea that the canal never could be finished. It never *would* have been, had the hostility to Clinton been as powerful as it was intense.

The completion of the Champlain, Oswego, and other smaller canals soon followed that of the Erie, as also the canal from Lake Erie, at Cleveland, to the Ohio River, and the great Pennsylvania canals, each and all the legitimate offspring of the Erie or CLINTON Canal.

DE WITT CLINTON,

to whose genius and perseverance New York is indebted for her magnificent works of internal improvement, which have added thousands of millions to her wealth, was fortunate in living to witness the completion of the great work which had for so many years occupied his thoughts and called forth his energies. He lived to enjoy his own triumph, almost his own apotheosis,—to see those who had sneered and scoffed at him and cast ridicule upon him, who had thrown every obstacle in his way they possibly could, now put to shame, and made to feel how unjust, how unpatriotic, how base, how mean had been their persecution of and opposition to him and the great work in which they now could not, as citizens of New York, but indulge a lofty pride. New York owes him a debt she can never pay.

Mr. Clinton died very suddenly, a little more than a year after the completion of the Erie Canal, at Albany, being then Governor of the State.

In manly beauty of form and features De Witt Clinton had no superior. His deportment was dignified, but wanting in warmth and geniality. It was as impossible for him to fawn and flatter as it would have been, with his large and portly frame, to play the part of an acrobat. Dignity and reserve distinguished him everywhere and at all times. He had warm friends who admired, but bitter enemies who hated him. He lacked the winning manners of a CLAY or a JACKSON, as well as the tact and judgment to assuage the rancor of his opponents.

A CALM.—GENERAL JACKSON RESIGNS HIS SEAT IN THE SENATE. —HIS LETTER OF RESIGNATION.

During the spring, summer, and autumn of 1825 the country was as free from political strife as it had been during Mr. Monroe's administration. Not a murmur was heard against the election of Mr. Adams, save now and then from the South and from some very ardent friend of General Jackson. But there was rancor in the breasts of those whose hopes had been disappointed. They at once proclaimed General Jackson a candidate to succeed Mr. Adams, and were as persevering as they were unscrupulous in their efforts to elect him, till they accomplished their purpose.

On the meeting of the Legislature of Tennessee, in October, that body formally nominated him, at the same time passing eulogistic resolutions commending him to the people of the United States as a fit man to fill the office of President.

General Jackson, on the 13th of October, 1825, addressed a letter to that body resigning his seat in the United States Senate. Subsequent events gave great importance to this letter, which is now a historical document. As a reason for resigning, he says, "Having been advised of a resolution of your honorable body, presenting *again* my name to the American people for the office of chief magistrate of this Union, I could no longer hesitate on the course I should pursue; doubt yielded to certainty, and I determined forthwith to ask your indulgence to be excused from any further service in the councils of the nation.

"Thus situated,—my name presented to the freemen of the United States for the first office known to the Constitution,—I could not, with anything of approbation on my part, consent either to urge or encourage an altercation [what altercation?] which might wear the appearance of being induced by selfish consideration, by a desire to advance my own views. I feel a thorough and safe conviction that imputation would be ill founded, and that nothing could prompt me to any active course on the subject [what subject?] which my judgment did not approve; yet, as from late events [the election by the House of Representatives] it might be inferred that the prospects of your recommendation could be rendered probable only by the people having the choice given to them direct, abundant room would be afforded to ascribe any exertions of mine to causes appertaining exclusively to myself. Imputations thus made would be extremely irksome to any person of virtuous and independent feeling; they would certainly prove so to me; and hence the determination to retire from a situation where strong suspicions might at least attach, and with great seeming propriety. I hasten, therefore, to tender this my resignation.

*　　*　　*　　*　　*　　*　　*　　*

"With a view to sustain more effectually in practice the axiom which divides the three great classes of powers into independent constitutional checks, I would impose a provision rendering any member of Congress ineligible to office, under the general government, during the term for which he was elected, and for two years thereafter, except in cases of judicial office. . . .

"The effect of such a constitutional provision is obvious. By it Congress, in a considerable degree, would be free from that connection with the executive department which at present gives strong ground of apprehension and jealousy on the part of the people. Members, instead of being liable to be withdrawn from legislating on the great interests of the nation through prospects of executive patronage, would be more liberally confided in by their constituents; while their vigilance would be less interrupted by party feelings and party excitements. Calculations from intrigue or management would fail; nor would their deliberations or their investigation of subjects consume so much time. The morals of the country would be improved, and virtue, uniting with the labors of the representatives and with the official ministers of the law, would tend to perpetuate the honor and glory of the government.

"But if this change in the Constitution should not be obtained, and important appointments continue to devolve on the representatives in Congress, it requires no depth of thought to be convinced that *corruption will become the order of the day*, and that, under the garb of conscientious sacrifices to establish precedents for the public good, evils of serious importance to the freedom and prosperity of the republic may arise. It is through this channel that the people may expect to be attacked in their constitutional sovereignty, and where tyranny may well be apprehended to spring up in some favorable emergency.

* * * * * * * *

"My name having been before the nation for the office of chief magistrate during the time I served as your Senator, placed me in a situation truly delicate; but, delicate as it was, my friends do not and my enemies cannot charge me with descending from the independent ground then occupied, with degrading the trust reposed on me by intriguing for the Presidential chair. As by a resolution of your body you have thought proper again to present my name to the American people, I must entreat to be excused from any further service in the Senate, and to suggest, in conclusion, that it is due to myself to practice upon the maxims recommended to others, and hence feel constrained to retire from a situation where temptations may exist and suspicions arise of the exercise of an influence tending to my own aggrandizement."

This letter was generally published, and attracted much attention. Prone as the mass of the people generally are to credit charges of corruption against those in power, the "imputation" that members of Congress were liable to be corrupted by being appointed to office by the President found ready credence, and the proposed mode of preventing this great evil was hailed with approbation. General Jackson rose still higher in public estimation, as a wise patriot and a very honest, "virtuous," and incorruptible man. I may truly say that he was looked upon, by a large majority of the people of the United States, as far above and scorning all intrigue; wholly indifferent to the Presidency, and a very paragon of honesty, purity, and elevation of character. "Imputations" and warnings, therefore, coming from him, fell upon the public mind with great force; no sinister motive could be imputed to or actuate *him*.

At this time—1825—those contrivances to catch votes, those mean-nothing, party manifestoes called "platforms," had not been invented. The public services of each candidate for the Presidency, and his well-known principles, constituted his "platform," and this, if the candidate had been long before the public as a member of the Senate or the House of Representatives, or had filled high civil stations, was a far more reliable guarantee to the people than any "platform" gotten up for the occasion and filled with professions and political platitudes which are forgotten as soon as written.

This letter of General Jackson's was his "Platform," his "Pronunciamiento" to the people of the United States. It was the key-note to his friends and advocates, and so they understood and used it.

Following up, or rather in accordance with, General Jackson's tocsin of alarm that the appointing of members of Congress to Federal offices would result in corruption becoming "the order of the day," Mr. Benton, in February, 1826, introduced into the United States Senate a resolution to amend the Constitution of the United States as follows, to wit, that

"No Senator or Representative shall be appointed to any civil office, place, or emolument, under the authority of the United States, until the expiration of the Presidential term in which such person shall have served as a Senator or Representative."

The passage of this resolution was never pressed,—probably

never desired. We shall see, hereafter, how, in respect to appointing members of Congress to Federal offices, General Jackson practiced upon the maxims he recommended to others.

GOVERNOR TROUP AND GEORGIA TERRIBLY EXCITED.—THEY "STAND BY THEIR ARMS."

The stillness that had so long prevailed in the political atmosphere proved to be but the calm which precedes the storm. Mutterings had been occasionally heard from the South and Southwest, and there were certain other indications which were unmistakable signs of a violent change. But no organized opposition as yet existed to the administration.

Governor Troup, of Georgia, seemed to be in a very excitable condition, and highly irritated against the President and certain officers sent to Georgia by the general government to look after the Indians and certain lands lately ceded to the government by treaty. A very caustic correspondence took place between him and General Gaines, who had been ordered to that State; and the Governor addressed some extraordinary letters to the President, complaining of the "arrogance," "self-sufficiency," "haughty and contemptuous carriage, and most insulting interference with our local politics" by the government officials sent there, and demanding to know "if these things have been done in virtue of your instructions . . . or authority; . . . and if not, whether you [the President] will sanction and adopt them as your own, and thus hold yourself *responsible to the government of Georgia?*"

"Most unquestionably," says Mr. Niles (see "Niles's Register," September 10, 1825), "the Governor of Georgia had determined either to *bully* the government of the United States into submission to his schemes, or *fight* his way to success in them, if the Georgians would '*stand by their arms*' and support him."

This was one of the means adopted to raise up hostility to the administration, by arousing Southern prejudice. "State rights! State rights! the sovereignty of the State is invaded! the federal government is assuming unlimited power!" were the cries by which the people were to be aroused and alarmed.

FIRST SESSION NINETEENTH CONGRESS.—PANAMA MISSION RECOMMENDED.

The Nineteenth Congress commenced its session on the 5th day of December, 1825, and the first message of President Adams was sent in the next day. In speaking of the South American Republics, he said,—

"Among the measures which have been suggested to them by the new relations with one another, resulting from the recent changes of their condition [from that of subject colonies to independent republics], is that of assembling at the Isthmus of Panama a congress, at which each of them should be represented, to deliberate upon subjects important to the welfare of all. The republics of Colombia and Mexico and of Central America have already deputed plenipotentiaries to such a meeting, and they have invited the United States to be also represented there by their ministers. The invitation has been accepted, and ministers on the part of the United States will be commissioned to attend at those deliberations, and to take part in them so far as may be compatible with that neutrality from which it is neither our intention, nor the desire of the other American States, that we should depart."

The message was universally commended at the North as a most able state paper; at the South, however, a few of the leading journals raised an outcry against it, declaring that "a fearful crisis was at hand;" that "the message formed an era in the government;" that "a higher-toned message had not been seen since the days of John Adams, or one so directly looking to the establishment of a magnificent, overshadowing government."

The Legislatures of Pennsylvania and Maryland both adopted resolutions expressing confidence in the administration, and approving of its course in regard to the proposed congress at Panama. Upon this question a most protracted and heated debate took place in both branches of Congress during the session of 1825–6, occupying a large portion of the entire time of that session.

THE OPPOSITION PARTY FORMED.

A party opposed to the administration was formed, mainly by the efforts of Mr. Calhoun and his friends, though Mr. Randolph and Colonel Benton were among its master-spirits. Among these also were Colonel Hayne, Mr. McDuffie, and Colonel Hamilton, of South Carolina, Mr. Forsyth and Mr. Berrien, of Georgia, Mr. Livingston, of Louisiana, Richard M. Johnson, of Kentucky, Colonel King, of Alabama, Mr. Van Buren and Mr. Cambreleng, of New York, Messrs. Buchanan and Ingham, of Pennsylvania, Mr. Woodberry and Isaac Hill, of New Hampshire, and others eminent for talent, including all who had supported General Jackson at the preceding election.

Two motives induced the old prominent, ambitious Federalists of the country generally to join the "Combination," or Jackson, party: *first*, their resentment against J. Q. Adams, who had, in former years, deserted them and supported the measures of President Jefferson; *second*, the advice of General Jackson to Mr. Monroe to destroy the "monster, party," and make up his cabinet irrespective of parties, at the same time recommending Colonel Drayton, a Federalist, as Secretary of War. They had been long excluded from the enjoyment of official honors, and longed to return to the pleasant seats they had once occupied.

Of the most prominent men of this "Combination," Mr. Randolph had always been opposed to internal improvements by government means, against all surveys by the government of roads and canals, and against making them, including the great Cumberland Road, leading through Maryland, Pennsylvania, Ohio, Indiana, etc., which was *the* great work in its day, and most useful and important to the West. He was also the sworn enemy of "the protective system."

Mr. Calhoun, on the contrary, had been the strong advocate of *protection* to domestic manufactures, and made a celebrated speech in favor of that policy, as a *national policy*, in 1816, when South Carolina wished to drive out of our market India cotton goods and replace them by cloths made of South Carolina cotton. He was also the earnest advocate of internal improvements.

Mr. Benton had been the advocate of protection to domestic

manufactures, as the whole West was at one time, and the political friend of Henry Clay, the author of "the American system." He had also been in favor of internal improvements by government means, if we can judge by his votes in favor of appropriations for continuing the Cumberland Road. Similar remarks could be made of other prominent members of this new party. Many had had personal differences of long standing. The feeling of the Georgians towards General Jackson had been very hostile for many years—ever since his famous letter to Governor Rabun, of that State.

In forming a new national party, it became necessary to settle the policy or principles which were to constitute its creed and become a common bond of union for all its members. How could this be done where the leaders had held and long advocated principles so diverse and irreconcilable? There could be but one way: somebody, more than one, must give up cherished opinions, favorite measures, approved systems of policy, the championship of which had gained them whatever favor they had with the country, and adopt and advocate creeds, measures, and doctrines the reverse of all they had before professed and supported.

But "the Combination" was formed; and what was the inducement to all this surrender of cherished opinions, this laying upon the altar of party principles long professed and earnestly advocated? Had the administration committed any great crime? Had it violated any republican principle? Were its measures condemned by the people? Had it assumed any unwarranted powers? This could hardly be alleged; and certainly, up to that time, not a voice was raised, north of the Potomac, against it, nor was any opposition to it in that portion of the country anticipated, it being as free from party feeling and strife as it had been for eight years past.

In an interview between Mr. Calhoun and Joseph McIlvaine, of Philadelphia, which took place in December, 1825, or January, 1826, as related to me by Mr. McIlvaine, he being, at the time he related it to me, Recorder of Philadelphia, Mr. Calhoun urged him to join the new party, in opposition to the administration. Mr. McIlvaine objected, on the ground that it had done nothing objectionable, and should be judged by its measures. Certainly he could not oppose it so long as its measures met his approbation, as they had thus far.

Mr. Calhoun replied that such was the manner in which it came into power that *it must be defeated at all hazards, regardless of its measures.*

Mr. McIlvaine rejoined that this was very different from the principles he had learned from him (Mr. Calhoun), and it was too late for him to unlearn them and learn others. He perceived that their respective political roads now diverged, and he would therefore respectfully bid him adieu.

This interview was at the instance of Mr. Calhoun, and held in the Vice-President's chamber, in the Capitol.

The interview between these two gentlemen, and the language used by Mr. Calhoun, are strikingly similar to a colloquy between Colonel William W. Seaton and Colonel Richard M. Johnson, an account of which, from the pen of Colonel Seaton, was published in the Washington "Telegraph" of April 18, 1827. In this conversation Colonel Johnson declared that "as for this administration [Mr. Adams's], we will turn them out as sure as there is a God in heaven."

To this Mr. Seaton replied, "But how can you say so, colonel, before you see what course the administration will adopt? Suppose they consult the public interest and pursue a course that you think right?"

Colonel Johnson: "I don't care [speaking with warmth]; for, by the Eternal, if they act as pure as the angels that stand at the right hand of the throne of God, we'll put them down."

Colonel Johnson was one of those whom Mr. Clay consulted as to the propriety of his accepting the office of Secretary of State, and who strenuously urged him to accept it, saying that on account of the interests of the West he should not decline.

But what could be Mr. Calhoun's motive for so actively and zealously opposing Mr. Adams, whose election he at one time favored, and of whom, in a letter to General Peter B. Porter, he spoke as "that great and good man"? It was quite apparent: he had linked his fortunes with those of General Jackson: the general had declared himself in favor of an alteration of the Constitution, limiting the service of President to a single term.

He was considered, therefore, bound to limit his own service to a single term. But that term he must have before Mr. Calhoun could step to the front. Here, then, was Mr. Calhoun's short road to the Presidency. Of course he was deeply interested in electing General Jackson, and thus removing the only apparent obstacle in his way, at the same time entitling himself to his and his friends' support as his successor, of which he could not entertain a doubt. Alas! what did subsequent events prove? Would he have been so earnest and unwearied in his efforts to form this new party had he foreseen what those events were to be,—that for all the wheat he was sowing he was to have naught but chaff, and that with insulting derision?

It was reported, and, I have reason to believe, correctly, as I had it from those who were in accord with the new party, that various meetings of the leaders of the opposition took place early in the session of 1825–6, when Mr. Calhoun invariably urged upon them the necessity of having a press at their command. This, it was said in reply, would cost a good deal of money. "Very true," said Mr. Calhoun; "but if the play is worth the candle, buy the candle: if not, let us give up the play." The argument had the desired effect: a considerable sum of money (fifty thousand dollars) was raised, and the "United States Telegraph" was established.

General Duff Green, of Missouri, became the editor and proprietor of the "Telegraph;" and a more fit and capable man for the services required could not have been found. General Green had an extensive knowledge of the public men of the day, great intelligence, embracing a great variety of subjects, strong powers of mind, unwearied industry, and wielded a vigorous pen. The purpose for which he had been sought was to write *down* one set of men and to write *up* another. If this could be done by simple, plain, unvarnished statements of facts, why, well; if not, so much the worse for the facts.

The two parties were now in the field, with their respective organs,—the administration party, and the "combination," afterwards the "Jackson party;" the former to become eventually the "National Republican," the "Whig," and, finally, the "Republican party" of the present day.

There was one purpose in forming the new party, common to each member: namely, the putting down of the Adams administration. In this there was unity; beyond this, division and hostility.

General Green opened his batteries with a vigor and clamor heretofore unprecedented in this country, to rouse public opinion and set it against the administration, and especially against Mr. Adams and Mr. Clay. Charges of the grossest corruption and extravagance were made in so bold, positive, and confident a manner, and in such thundering tones, and these charges were so oft repeated, that the people of the United States, not then accustomed to hearing such allegations against the highest officers of the government, and not knowing that all this was done for political effect,—that there was not a grain of truth to a pound of falsehood in them,—were astounded, and some even convinced.

It was the *rôle* of the opposition party to *attack*, and keep the administration on the defensive; and in this they had a decided advantage. They were a scattered army in the field besieging a citadel; every shot of theirs "told," while those in the citadel must fire at random, and at least only hit individuals; and individuals, as all know, are of no account in an army. The administration was denominated the "coalition," the "monarchical party." It was charged that "the great contest was between power and liberty, patronage and the ballot-box." The people were assured that the aim of the administration was "a great radical change of our system, by which it would ultimately receive a direction that would end in monarchy," and much more of the same kind.

After Mr. King's return from England, Mr. Gallatin was appointed Minister to Great Britain. He was an old-time Republican or Democrat; had been a Senator from Pennsylvania, Secretary of the Treasury under Presidents Jefferson, Madison, and Monroe,—twelve years in all,—Minister Plenipotentiary with Adams, Bayard, Clay, and Russell at Ghent, and Minister to France. But upon his appointment it was insinuated that he had been tampered with by, or was willing to sell himself to, the administration. "He had frequently visited Washington," it was said, and it was asked "if that had anything to do with his appointment." The question implied that there was corruption in the appointment; but indeed every act of the administration was distorted in the vilest manner and attributed to base motives.

The malevolence of the assaults upon and misrepresentations of the administration at this time has no precedent, except in the war waged upon General Washington's administration during the last four years of his service, or his second term. The "Telegraph" daily teemed with falsehoods, uttered with the most positive asseveration, as if they were gospel truths. Thus sent forth, they were caught up and republished, with comments calculated and intended to excite the minds of the people, by all "the affiliated presses" in every part of the country. To contradict them was useless, as the contradiction could never overtake the falsehood, and this no one knew better than the editor himself.

In recommending the erection of observatories for astronomical purposes, such as we now have, Mr. Adams spoke of them as "light-houses of the skies;" for which expression he was ridiculed by the whole opposition press, which also jeered and scoffed at observatories as if they were utterly worthless.

Mr. Adams was strongly in favor of the system of internal improvements by the general government, which had been begun by Mr. Calhoun and so strenuously advocated by him. Speaking of this subject in his Inaugural Address, he said, "The magnificence and splendor of their public works are among the imperishable glories of the ancient republics. The roads and aqueducts of Rome have been the admiration of after-ages, and have survived thousands of years after all her conquests have been swallowed up in despotism or become the spoil of barbarians. Some diversity of opinion has prevailed with regard to the powers of Congress for legislation upon objects of this nature. The most respectful deference is due to doubts originating in pure patriotism and sustained by venerable authority. But nearly twenty years have passed since the construction of the first national road was commenced. The authority for its construction was then unquestioned. To how many thousands of our countrymen has it proved a benefit! To what single individual has it ever proved an injury?"

In his first annual message he again brought the subject of internal improvements before the Congress and the nation, saying, "The spirit of improvement is abroad upon the earth. It stimulates the heart and sharpens the faculties, not of our fellow-citizens alone, but of the nations of Europe and their rulers.

* * * * * * * *

"While foreign nations, less blessed with that freedom, which is power, than ourselves, are advancing with gigantic strides in the career of public improvements, were we to slumber in indolence or fold up our arms and proclaim to the world that we are palsied by the will of our constituents, would it not be to cast away the bounties of Providence and doom ourselves to perpetual inferiority?" . . .

"*Palsied by the will of our constituents.*" This was another expression which the opposition rang the charges upon, and used with great effect.

But, however virulent the war made upon him and his administration, Mr. Adams would take no steps to counteract it. It was well known that men holding high federal offices were in opposition to him and exerting great influence in favor of General Jackson, and he was strongly urged to remove them and appoint his own friends; but this he persistently refused to do, saying that they had a right to support whom they deemed most fit for President, and he would not punish them for preferring another to himself. It was safe, therefore, for any one to join the opposition, but not so to adhere to the administration.

About this time, or a little later, Mr. Hezekiah Niles, of Baltimore, editor of "Niles's Register," and an old Republican, visited Washington, and, on returning home, gave expression to his thoughts and feelings. Speaking of the violence that characterized the contest of parties, he says, "It is not our purpose to inquire whence the necessity of such a state of things; why the excitement that already prevails among *politicians*, though the *people* are calm; why the heat manifested against, and the abuse heaped upon, distinguished gentlemen hitherto regarded as among those who did honor to their country and marked the character of the age, and whose claims to the most exalted standing, for private probity and public worth, were never questioned until PARTY had conjured up its chimeras to confound the understandings of men and lead them into captivity blindfolded by passion. . . . We look on and wonder at the *transformations* of the character of persons and of the fitness of things.

"Individuals who were supposed to be the wisest and best, the most discreet or patriotic of our citizens, a little while ago, are now spoken of as corrupt and base; and others that were among the least approved for character, discretion, or moral worth, are exalted into beings of a very superior order, though neither, perhaps, have changed their opinions or principles, or in any respect prescribed new rules of conduct for themselves. Such, however, is the *necromancy of party*, that makes men as devils or as gods, at will, imputing all that is base and claiming all that is excellent."

This is a dispassionate statement of the political condition of things at Washington at that time. Mr. Adams and Mr. Clay were among those "individuals who were supposed the wisest and best, the most discreet and patriotic of our citizens, a little while before;" men whom the country delighted to honor, of whose public character it was proud, and for whose eminent services it was grateful; and yet, if the representations of the opposition press and orators were true, they were the most infamous of men, unworthy to associate even with honorable thieves! Such a sudden transformation of public men from eminence to infamy, from lofty patriots to the meanest panders of vice and pollution, was never before witnessed, and could have been effected only by "the *necromancy of party*."

But of abuse and vilification the opposition did not enjoy an entire monopoly. These ignoble and disreputable weapons were common to both parties. General Jackson was assailed by whatever it was supposed would operate against him, true or false; and probably truth itself was so distorted as to become falsehood. Among other things, both he and Mrs. Jackson were held up to scorn on account of his having taken her from her husband, Mr. Roberts, aided her to obtain a divorce, protected her while doing so, and married her immediately upon its being obtained.

The "Coffin Handbill," put forth by Mr. Binns, of Philadelphia, which made such a sensation at the time, is still remembered by some now living, and has been heard of by hundreds born since that day.

General Jackson had caused six militia-men to be executed, whose offense was starting for their homes in Tennessee at the expiration of their terms of enlistment. True, their terms, and those of a large portion of his force, had expired; but he was not in a condition to dispense with their services, and must retain them until reinforced. Six, however, left, were followed, arrested, tried, condemned, and executed as a terror to others.

A pictorial handbill represented these six men hanging on the gallows, with six pretty large and very black coffins beneath them. The lamentable story of their execution for wishing to return to their families was told in print, emphasized by the illustrations. It was supposed that these handbills, which were scattered over the country, would produce a great sensation and effect. They did so,—but were like the gun represented by Hudibras, which, shot at plover, kicked its owner over. The sensation and effect were all against the authors of these handbills, which became extensively known as "the Coffin Handbills."

The executions of Arbuthnot and Ambrister in Florida, by General Jackson, were also attempted to be used against him; nor were his killing of Dickinson in a duel, his desperate fight with the two brothers Benton, Colonel and Jesse, his quarrel with Judge Fromentin at Pensacola, and many other of his acts, forgotten. But while the assaults upon Mr. Adams and his administration told with damaging effect, those upon General Jackson only increased the popular enthusiasm which pervaded the country and was bearing him on to the Presidential seat.

OPENING OF THE WAR ON THE ADMINISTRATION UPON THE PANAMA QUESTION.

The opposition opened its batteries upon the administration early in the first session of the Nineteenth Congress, upon the proposition to send ministers to the congress to be held at Panama. The debate upon this, both in the Senate and in the House of Representatives, was one of the warmest and the most protracted that had occurred in either body for many years. In the Senate it lasted over two months, and called into requisition all the ability and resources of the ablest members on both sides. It was strictly *partisan*, and the language of the speakers was piquant, though not personal, for personalities were not at that day used to give force to argument instead of reason and illustration. It must be presumed the debate took a wide range from the fact that a number of Senators occupied two or three days in delivering their respective speeches against the measure; though those in reply were much more brief. In the Senate the attacking party were Messrs. Randolph, Van Buren, Hugh L. White, Hayne, Benton, Macon of North Carolina, Berrien and Cobb of Georgia, Woodbury, and Dickerson. On the other side were Messrs. Lloyd of Massachusetts, Edwards of Connecticut, Robbins of Rhode Island, Harrison of Ohio, Barton of Missouri, Bouligny and Johnson of Louisiana, and Thomas of Illinois. In the House the principal speakers against it were Messrs. McDuffie, Forsyth, Cambreling, Buchanan, Ingham, Stevenson, and others. Opposed: Messrs. Webster, Everett, John Davis, Crowningshield, Dwight, Peleg Sprague, Tristam Burgess, Henry R. Storrs, Charles Fenton Mercer, Joseph Vance, Samuel F. Vinton, John C. Wright, Robert P. Letcher, Thomas Metcalf, Wm. L. Brent, Daniel P. Cook, and others.

But what was the proposition of the administration which called forth such determined opposition? What was the purpose of this Panama convention? In a message sent to the Senate on the 25th of December, 1825, nominating Richard C. Anderson, of Kentucky, and John Sergeant, of Pennsylvania, as envoys and ministers, and Wm. B. Rochester, of New York, as secretary to the ministers, Mr. Adams defines the objects of this mission to be—1. The adoption of principles of maritime neutrality, and favorable to navigation and commerce in time of war; 2. The doctrine that free ships make free goods; 3. An agreement between all the parties represented that each will guard, by its own means, against the establishment of *any future European colony within its borders*,—in other words, agree to enforce "the Monroe doctrine," promulged two years before; 4. The advancement of religious liberty.

As a reason for the last object, the President states that "some of the southern nations are, even yet, so far under the dominion of prejudice that they have incorporated with their political constitutions an exclusive church, without toleration of any other than the dominant sect." At the same time it was distinctly understood that no entangling alliances were to be entered into, and that there was to be no departure from that strict neutrality which has ever been our fixed policy.

The opposition saw, or professed to see, in this mission, or its objects, something extremely dangerous to liberty and republican government,—a tendency to monarchy; an assumption of power hitherto unprecedented. But, while this very animated, and even heated, debate was going on at the Capitol, the country was never more calm and unconcerned. The "Telegraph," the organ of the opposition at the seat of government, and the "Richmond Inquirer" might proclaim, daily, in well-feigned tones of alarm, that "a great contest was going on between Power and Liberty, Patronage and the Ballot-box;" that "a great change was taking place in our system, which will end in monarchy;" that "Mr. Adams's policy was ambitious, daring, and dangerous," and that he was supported by every "Hartford Convention" press. The people could not be aroused, or made to believe they were sleeping over a political abyss into which they were every moment liable to be plunged. It was, indeed, puzzling to them to know what it all meant; in truth, they cared not a fig whether a deputation was sent to Panama or not.

Considering what has since been said of the "Monroe doctrine," and the great importance that has been, and is, often attached to it, it appears passing strange that the proposition to make Mr. Monroe's declaration—or "doctrine"—the subject of consideration at the Panama convention, with a view "to make effectual the assertion of that principle, as well as the means of resisting interference from abroad with the domestic concerns of the American governments," should have been one of the grounds of opposition to the convention. It was urged that this would be imitating the "Holy Alliance," and challenging them to do what Mr. Monroe had declared we could not, with unconcern, see any European nation do.

It is proper to say that Southern gentlemen saw, or professed to see, danger to their "peculiar institution" in this movement, as they apprehended that one object of this convention would be to adopt means to bring about a revolution and the abolition of slavery in Cuba and other West India islands, slavery having been abolished in all the South American states that had shaken off the yoke of Spain. This, of course, was enough to bring out all the fiery eloquence of the Southern Hotspurs to "prepare the hearts of the people" of that portion of the Union "for war" upon the administration.

The friends of the administration in the Senate finally triumphed by confirming the nominations of ministers by a few votes. Mr. Seaton, in his letter to Colonel Johnson, dated April 18, 1827, of which I have before spoken, says that a Senator,—understood to be Mr. Van Buren,—"on being rallied on the triumph of the administration party on the Panama mission, replied, '*Yes; they have beaten us by a few votes, after a hard battle;* BUT IF THEY HAD ONLY TAKEN THE OTHER SIDE, AND REFUSED THE MISSION, WE SHOULD HAVE HAD THEM!'"

MR. M'DUFFIE'S RESOLUTION TO AMEND THE CONSTITUTION.—FIÈRCE DEBATE THEREON.—HE ATTEMPTS TO PROVOKE A DUEL.

While the debate upon the Panama mission was going on in the Senate, an equally important and far more spirited and acrimonious one was carried on in the House of Representatives. Mr. McDuffie, one of the leaders of the opposition in that body, and decidedly the most violent and aggressive speaker arrayed against the administration, introduced a resolution to amend the Constitution so as to elect the President and Vice-President by districts, by the direct vote of the people, and that no person should hold the office of President more than one term. It was not disguised that this was a direct attack upon the administration: it was distinctly charged that the late election of President by the House of Representatives was a fraud upon the people; that it was accomplished by "bargain and corruption," and a "coalition" between Adams and Clay; and it was urged that the Constitution should be so altered that the people themselves should elect the President by a direct vote. The speakers in this debate took a wide range, indulged in great freedom and asperity of remark, and manifested a heat and acerbity indicative of personal disappointment and revenge. It became, therefore, a sort of Homeric conflict, or a hand-to-hand fight. Mr. McDuffie put forth his whole strength, and called out all the powers of his impassioned eloquence. He was the leader, and ably did he justify his title to that distinction.

He was replied to, first by Henry R. Storrs, of Utica, N.Y., a most accomplished speaker, quick and ready in debate, of fine, commanding presence, splendid voice, and polished manners. No personal asperities ever gave piquancy to his sentences; no language escaped him that did not become a high-toned gentleman and the representative of an enlightened constituency. His scimitar was keen, but it was polished, and could not but be admired even by those who saw its flashes and felt its sharpness. And be it remembered that, as members of Congress *debated* in those days, their weapons must be ready at a moment's notice. True, they took time to prepare for a long speech, either of attack or of reply; but they would have been laughed out of the House had they come into the hall with, and attempted to *read*, a written speech. *Tout cela est changé.* A member now is not compelled to draw on his brains for thoughts, arguments, wit, and illustrations, but may draw on a *friend* and procure them ready written out for *reading*, or draw a speech, or a dull essay, from his pocket, and, without reading, have it published in the "Globe" as his *speech.*

Mr. Everett, of Massachusetts, also replied to Mr. McDuffie

in an elaborate, argumentative, classical speech, which fully sustained his high reputation as an orator, scholar, and statesman.

Mr. McDuffie rejoined to Mr. Everett, and in doing so indulged in the most intemperate and virulent accusations against Mr. Adams and Mr. Clay, personally, ever listened to in that hall. It is impossible to conceive of a more vituperative outpouring of gall and wormwood than was witnessed on that occasion.

This abuse of Mr. Clay, and, by implication, of Mr. Clay's friends who voted with him for Mr. Adams as President, elicited a reply from General Vance, of Ohio.

General Vance was a man of noble aspect: tall, portly, and athletic,—a true son of the West; born and reared on the verge of civilization, and accustomed from boyhood to toil, privation, rough life, the rifle, and the Indian. He knew the *people* well, for he was one of them, and they knew and loved him. No man was more esteemed and beloved in the House by his fellow-members.

Although naturally quiet and sedate, by no means vehement in his language or boisterous in his delivery, he could be severe without being personal or malevolent. Not content to stand altogether on the defensive, he carried the war into Africa, gathering up the shafts of his adversary and hurling them back with a force and precision that made him wince. After indignantly repelling the charge of intrigue, bargain, and corruption, reiterated by Mr. McDuffie against Mr. Clay and his friends, himself among the number, in relation to the Presidential election, and showing that after Mr. Crawford had become incapacitated by paralysis they had no other course than to support Mr. Adams or General Jackson, whom they could not support; after showing who many of the men now so malignantly assailed were, and the heroic part they had borne in the War of 1812,—their sufferings, privations, labor, fortitude, and courage,—he went into a review of some things of the past, which were by no means pleasant to the ears of Mr. Calhoun's friends. There was no bitterness of language, no noisy denunciation of any one, no pounding of his desk,—*à la* McDuffie,—but quiet allusions were made retaliatory of Mr. McDuffie's charges, which showed the latter that while he was hurling missiles at Mr. Clay and his friends, his own and his friends' armor was not impenetrable. The severity of General Vance's remarks and allusions provoked a quasi challenge from Mr. McDuffie, to which General Vance replied that he had no life to throw away; that he harbored no malice and sought no revenge.

Thus baffled, and unable to provoke General Vance to anger, Mr. McDuffie became still more inflamed and personal. "Now, sir, once for all," he exclaimed, in a passion, "I give the Secretary of State [Mr. Clay] to understand that when he wishes to avoid the responsibility of repelling imputations upon his character, and chooses to send his minions and tools and understrappers to utter insolence and scurrility on this floor, I shall not feel bound to notice them, *in a certain way*, until he commissions men who have, at least, the semblance of gentlemen!"

This ebullition of splenetic vulgarity, bad temper, and bluster was intended to overwhelm General Vance, whose calm self-possession it did not in the least disturb, and whose courage was too well tested and established during the War of 1812, by feats of bravery and gallantry, to render it necessary that he should accept the challenge of a blustering Gascon to avoid the stigma of cowardice.

"But," continued Mr. McDuffie, "I should be willing, in order to avoid any possible imputation on my personal honor, to admit that they are gentlemen, *pro forma*, and for that occasion merely, though in point of fact they have no pretension to that character."

It will be seen hereafter that Mr. McDuffie was soon afforded an opportunity to display his vaunted fighting propensities, when he deemed "discretion the better part of valor," and showed a wise repugnance to face a Kentucky rifle in the hands of an old Kentucky hunter.

Mr. McDuffie may have supposed that in offering and supporting a resolution to amend the Constitution so as to prevent any person from holding the office of President more than one term, he was acting in accordance with the President's views, since this principle had been proclaimed by General Jackson, and became well understood by his supporters during his candidacy. Especially was it so understood and insisted by Mr. Calhoun's friends, as they expected Mr. Calhoun to succeed General Jackson in 1832.

Moreover, in accordance with this understanding, the President, in his first annual message, December 8, 1829, said, "I would, therefore, recommend such an amendment of the Constitution as may remove all intermediate agency in the election of President and Vice-President. The mode may be so regulated as to preserve to each State its present relative weight in the election; and a failure in the first attempt may be provided for by confining the second to a choice between the two highest candidates. In connection with such an amendment, it would seem advisable to limit the services of the chief magistrate *to a single term of either four or six years.*"

In his second annual message, December 7, 1830, General Jackson refers to his recommendation in his preceding message, and adds, "I cannot too earnestly invite your attention to the propriety of promoting such amendment of the Constitution as will render him [the President] ineligible after one term of service."

In his third annual message he said, "I have heretofore recommended amendments of the federal Constitution, giving the election of President and Vice-President to the people, and limiting the service of the former to a single term. So important do I consider these changes in our fundamental law, that I cannot, in accordance with my sense of duty, omit to press them upon the consideration of a new Congress."

No report was made upon Mr. McDuffie's resolutions at this time. A committee was constituted the next year, to whom they were referred, and on the 22d of December, 1830, Mr. McDuffie, chairman, reported the following joint resolution:

"*Resolved,* That the following amendment of the Constitution of the United States be proposed to the several States, to be valid to all intents and purposes as part of the said Constitution when ratified by the Legislatures of three-fourths of the said States, viz.:

"'No person shall hereafter be eligible to the office of President of the United States who shall have been previously elected to the said office, and who shall have accepted the same or exercised the powers thereof.'"

Mr. McDuffie's resolutions, coming to a vote on the 5th of March, 1831, failed to pass by a two-thirds majority of the House,—failed, because other schemes had entered the heads of the Jackson men: namely, to run "the old Roman" for another term. Mr. Lewis, General Jackson's most trusted friend, had already laid a plan to have the general renominated by the Legislature of Pennsylvania, which was easily accomplished, and which was a flank movement against those who would hold the general to his avowed principle of limiting the service of any one man in the Presidency to a single term. Mr. Lewis's movement will be seen hereafter.*

But though Mr. McDuffie's amendment failed to obtain the requisite two-thirds of the House, his purpose was, in part, obtained. He had made a fierce assault upon the administration, and sent abroad his charges over the whole country, giving the cue to the opposition presses, raising a general clamor, and putting the administration on the defensive. Whether his accusations were true or false, whether the administration were guilty or not guilty, he knew there are always those ready to condemn upon accusations boldly made and oft repeated though wholly destitute of truth. Indeed, there are never wanting in any community those who are prone to believe evil reports of others, and would rather not be convinced that such reports are false and malicious, especially if made against men in power.

Little dreamed this fiery Southron that all his impassioned eloquence and frenzied denunciations were to inure, not to the benefit of his friend Mr. Calhoun, but to the benefit of those who would thrust Mr. Calhoun aside and wrest from him the coveted prize, the Presidency, now almost within his grasp; that even then, perhaps, the unsuspected intriguer was meditating the means of accomplishing a *coup de main* upon him with whom he was now lovingly laboring to overthrow the administration.

* Thus, while the President was urging the adoption of the *one-term* principle, his most trusted friend was preparing the way for his re-election! Was he ignorant of this movement, and did he discountenance it? *Credat Judæus.*

But such is political life. Such it was then, such it is now, such it ever will be. Politicians are grateful for services *expected*. The value of a political *friend*—it is a desecration of the word so to use it—consists in what he *can* and *will* do, not in what he *has* done.

DUEL BETWEEN MR. RANDOLPH AND MR. CLAY.

Exciting events crowd themselves into the period of which I am speaking. While the very animated debate was going on in the Senate upon the Panama mission, and in the House upon Mr. McDuffie's resolutions to amend the Constitution, a personal affair arose between Mr. Randolph and Mr. Clay. Mr. Randolph, it is well known, indulged in great liberties of speech, and hurled his barbed shafts right and left, regardless, apparently, whom they hit, or intending probably to hit every opponent of importance enough to become his mark.

In his speech in opposition to the mission to Panama, in one of his heated outbursts he designated the union of Mr. Adams and Mr. Clay as "the coalition of Blifil and Black George,—the combination, unheard of till then, of the Puritan and the blackleg." This language, which charged Mr. Clay with being a blackleg, was very insulting; but Mr. Randolph also virtually charged Mr. Clay with forging a certain dispatch which purported to have been written and addressed to him by a foreign minister; and Mr. Randolph refusing to make any retraction of these charges or give any explanation of his language, Mr. Clay had no other alternative than to call him to the field. General Jessup bore the challenge as Mr. Clay's friend, and Mr. Tatnall, of Georgia, acted as the friend of Mr. Randolph. The injury complained of by Mr. Clay, as stated by General Jessup in his note to Mr. Tatnall, was "in this: that Mr. Randolph has charged him with having forged or manufactured a paper connected with the Panama mission; also, that he has applied to him in debate the epithet of blackleg. The explanation which I consider necessary is, that Mr. Randolph declare that he had no intention of charging Mr. Clay, either in his public or private capacity, with forging or falsifying any paper, or misrepresenting any fact; and, also, that the term blackleg was not intended to apply to him."

To this Mr. Tatnall replied, "Mr. Randolph informs me that the words used by him in debate were as follows: 'That I thought it would be in my power to show evidence sufficiently presumptive to satisfy a Charlotte (county) jury that this invitation was manufactured here,—that Mr. Salazar's letter struck me as bearing a strong likeness in point of style to the other papers.* I did not undertake to prove this, but expressed my suspicion that it was so. I applied to the administration the epithet puritanic,—diplomatic,—blacklegged administration.' Mr. Randolph, in giving these words as those uttered in debate, is unwilling to afford any explanation as to their meaning or application."

The meeting took place on the 8th of April, 1826. There was an exchange of shots; Mr. Clay's ball cutting Mr. Randolph's coat near the hip, and Mr. Randolph's striking a stump in the rear of and nearly in a line with Mr. Clay. Another was required by Mr. Clay. Mr. Randolph received the fire of his antagonist, raised his pistol and fired in the air, saying, "I do not fire at you, Mr. Clay," and immediately advanced and offered his hand. "He was met," says Colonel Benton, who was present, "in the same spirit. They met half-way and shook hands, Mr. Randolph saying, jocosely, 'You owe me a coat, Mr. Clay' (the bullet had passed through the skirt of the coat near the hip), to which Mr. Clay promptly and happily replied, 'I am glad the debt is no greater.'"

"The joy of all," says Colonel Benton, "was extreme at this happy termination of a most critical affair, and we immediately left, with lighter hearts than we brought."

Colonel Benton concludes this account as follows:

"On Monday the parties exchanged cards, and social relations were formally and courteously restored. It was about the last high-toned duel that I have witnessed, and among the highest-toned I have ever witnessed, and so happily conducted to a fortunate issue,—a result due to the noble character of

* The implication was that Mr. Clay manufactured a letter purporting to be addressed to him by Mr. Salazar, Minister from Colombia.

the seconds, as well as to the generous and heroic spirit of the principals. Certainly dueling is bad, and has been put down, but not quite so bad as its substitute,—revolvers, bowie-knives, blackguarding, and street-assassinations under the pretext of self-defense."

JOHN RANDOLPH.

Who has not heard of "John Randolph of Roanoke"? A man of extraordinary powers of mind; possessed of a wonderful fund of information of every kind, which he dealt out in an extraordinary manner; of extraordinary habits and eccentricities, and of extraordinary personal appearance. A professed republican, yet an enthusiastic admirer of the British government, British aristocracy, English horses, and English books,—everything, indeed, English. He would not have in his possession an American book, not even an American Bible. Professedly a Republican, he opposed the measures and administration of every Republican President,—Jefferson, Madison, and Monroe,—and bitterly the administration and measures of both the elder and the younger Adams. It seemed impossible for him to agree with any one. If the House, or Senate, were engaged in debating a bill or measure of any kind, and he got the floor, ten to one he would not allude to the subject of debate in a three or four hours' speech, but would discuss "everything and all things besides." He had stores of learning, was quick at repartee, sarcastic, bitter, misanthropic; indulged in personalities, and rambled everywhere, "through field and flood, brier, brake, and wood," throwing his shafts right and left, hitting promiscuously those around him as well as those absent; nothing was too grave or sacred, nothing too trivial, to be brought into his speeches. In his rambles over the fields of history, sacred and profane, ancient and modern, biography, poetry, and politics, he gathered and scattered fruit, flowers, precious stones, and worthless pebbles. To listen to one of his interminable harangues was at once a rich repast and a tedious task. To report him was impossible. His transitions from one subject to another, the two having no relation to each other, were so sudden and frequent that no reporter could have followed him, especially as he spoke rapidly, and his parenthetical sentences, thrown between the noun and the verb, were so long and frequent that the two parts of speech appeared to have no relation the one to the other. Indeed, it not unfrequently occurred that he would commence a sentence, but, some other idea crossing his mind, would leave it unfinished,—a noun without a verb,—and rush on in an opposite direction from that he first took, and before he sat down would have boxed the compass many times. To attempt to follow the thread of his discourse would be to attempt to follow the thread of the spider in its already-formed web. It was not one thread, but a thousand. Woe to any member who called him to order! if he did not receive a shaft at the moment, it was sure to come, and that when it was least looked for; very likely it would be thrown as the Australian throws his boomerang: aimed, apparently, at an object in front, the boomerang flies in that direction for a space, when it suddenly turns, comes back, and hits the real object in the rear of the thrower. Down would come the Randolphian boomerang upon the head of some luckless member who least expected it, and who was perhaps watching its flight in another direction, as he supposed, towards some other object.

There was a member in Congress from Maine who became so famous for calling the "previous question" as to acquire the sobriquet of "Previous Question Cushman." He had greatly annoyed Mr. Randolph, who, in one of his long harangues, spoke of the great mechanical ingenuity of the Germans, and gave an account of some of the clocks made by them, in which were automatic birds that would come out and sing, or figures of men which would perform various and curious antics, make a bow, and retire. There was one that especially attracted his attention: it was a clock out of which the figure of a man—looking at the doomed member—would frequently pop up, cry out, "Previous question!" "previous question!" and then pop down again out of sight. The boomerang hit the mark; the House burst into a roar of laughter; but poor Mr. "Previous Question" was never seen or heard afterwards, and the place in the House that had known him for several years, knew him no more forever after that session.

But Mr. Randolph was not always so fortunate in killing the game he attacked, and sometimes came off "second best." Among those he came in conflict with was Mr. Tristam Burgess, of Rhode Island, an "ugly customer," as many a lawyer in his own State could testify,—one not to be intimidated by or to shun an encounter with even "John Randolph of Roanoke." He was just the man for a slander suit, a case of crim. con. or divorce, and similar cases, especially for the defense. He could bully and browbeat, perplex, entangle, and bother a witness till he could hardly tell what he had sworn to or what he really knew, and could black-ball his client's opponent until he made him almost hideous to himself. He had unbounded audacity; nothing could abash him,—not even a reprimand from the court. Was it likely that such a man would quail before that "spook" of a man, whose face put you in doubt whether he were a white man or an Indian, and whose squeaking voice might be taken for that of a woman or a boy, or "who might be mistaken for an ape walking on stilts"? Both soon understood that their natures were as incompatible as their politics were adverse, and that they would necessarily "lock horns." In every assemblage of animals, whether of the genus *homo*, "those that cleave the hoof," or those that do not, if they are any length of time together, contests for mastery will take place, until it is settled who, or which, shall be master. Turn any number of horses, mules, or cattle into a yard where there are others, and a conflict will soon ensue to settle which shall drive all the rest. And so it was when Mr. Burgess entered the body where John Randolph had found no one but Mr. Clay who could cope with him, though the hands of all were against him, as his were against all.

Those who were in Congress at that time, or were spectators in the galleries, have a vivid recollection of the encounters between these eminent gladiators, and the sharp words uttered by them. Mr. Randolph's weapon was the fine-tempered rapier of sarcasm: it flashed and penetrated like an electric bolt, and left a sting behind, if it did not kill. Mr. Burgess, on the other hand, dealt his blows with a tomahawk, a battle-axe, or a broad-sword, either of which was more effective from its force than from its keenness. In one of these encounters, it is well remembered, Mr. Burgess, after characterizing Mr. Randolph and likening him to some hideous monster, exclaimed, "But, thank God, Mr. Speaker, monsters cannot perpetuate their species!" alluding to the generally-received opinion that Mr. Randolph could never be a father.

When Mr. Randolph came to reply, he said, "Mr. Speaker, the gentleman makes a boast of his virility: he boasts of that in which the goat is his equal, and the jackass his superior."

"There were giants in those days." Their weapons were drawn impromptu from the armory of a well-supplied brain,—not wrapped up in paper and carried in the pocket. Mr. Randolph was tall and very slender; his body short in proportion to his legs, so that when he was sitting or riding he appeared to be below medium height. He rode much on horseback, always followed, forty paces in the rear, by his faithful servant Juba, who, like his master, rode a fine blooded horse. Each had his own, and neither ever rode the other's. He frequently rode to the House and entered the hall with whip and spur, and sometimes, but rarely, with his dogs.

Mr. Randolph undoubtedly had the most exalted notions of honor and propriety, and, with all his eccentricities and personal sarcasms, he had a manly, generous disposition, and could make the *amende honorable*, where he felt it to be due, in a princely manner.

In his duel with Mr. Clay he had previously told Colonel Benton that he did not intend to fire at Mr. Clay. Why? Because he felt that he had done him an injury, and, according to the notions which governed all Southern men at that time, Mr. Clay could not do otherwise than call him out. In doing this Mr. Clay retained Mr. Randolph's respect; had he not done it, he would have lost it. After Mr. Clay had fired the second time, Mr. Randolph, saying, "Mr. Clay, I do not fire at you," stepped forward and tendered his hand with the jocose remark I have already given. This was true chivalry, and it put an end to the quarrel. Mr. Randolph did not say that he regretted making the insulting remark concerning Mr. Clay, but his actions spoke louder than words, and were well understood by Mr. Clay.

Mr. Randolph prided himself on the fact that he had royal blood in his veins, being in some way a descendant of Princess Pocahontas, to whom Captain John Smith owed his life. His complexion and features bore testimony to the fact that he was part Indian; and his brilliant intellect, his morbid sensibilities, and his incomprehensible idiosyncrasy may have come more from his Indian than from his Anglo-Saxon ancestors.

Arriving at Washington, on his way to Philadelphia for medical aid, and hearing that Mr. Clay was addressing the Senate on some important subject, he had himself taken to the Senate-chamber and laid down on a sofa in the rear of and near the Senator, whose voice, he said, he wished to hear once more. As Mr. Clay closed, seeing Mr. Randolph, he immediately accosted him in the most friendly manner, and inquired after his health. "Dying, sir, dying," Mr. Randolph replied; "and I came here expressly to have this interview with you." They grasped hands, and remained silent for some time, each shedding tears.

Mr. Clay was moved at this manifestation of regard from his old antagonist, now his friend, and the more so as it was evident that Mr. Randolph had made a great effort to see and hear him once more, and that this would be his last visit to the Capitol and his last interview with Mr. Clay, as it proved to be. Can we wonder that two such men at such a moment, all the past rushing to their memories, all the future to them but a span, should turn from each other with tearful eyes? Both had generous, noble hearts, and where there is a *heart* there will sometimes be a *tear*.

The two great orators and statesmen, who had for twenty-five years met in the arena of the hall of the House of Representatives in many a keen encounter and upon the field in deadly conflict, parted forever as cordial friends.

WHY MR. CLAY WAS ELECTED SPEAKER OF THE HOUSE OF REPRESENTATIVES ON THE FIRST DAY HE ENTERED IT AS A MEMBER.

It is, or used to be, well known that an apparent rivalry or hostility existed between these two distinguished men from the moment they came together in the House of Representatives. From the first appearance of Mr. Clay in the House, Mr. Randolph seemed to perceive, as if by instinct, that a member had appeared over whom he could not ride rough-shod, at least without a severe contest; and, as he had had it all his own way in that body for many years, it is quite in accordance with the workings of the human heart that he should feel a degree of hostility towards the new-comer, which was ere long manifested.

It is unwritten history, except as it is recorded in the journals of Congress, that Mr. Clay was elected Speaker of the House of Representatives on the first day he entered that body as a member. Why so unusual an incident as this should have taken place I will relate as it was related to me by Jonathan Roberts, of Pennsylvania.

Mr. Roberts said, "Near the close of the Fourteenth Congress, a number of members being together, the conversation turned upon the condition of the House, its irregularities, want of order and decorum, etc., which were lamented by all, and it was insisted that a reform must be effected. 'But how is this to be done?' asked one. 'By electing a Speaker who will enforce order,' replied another. 'Then it must be some man who can bridle John Randolph,' said a third, 'for he disregards all rules.' This was assented to by all. 'Then,' said one, 'he must be a man who can meet John Randolph on the floor or on the field, for he may have to do both.' This being assented to, 'But where is the man who can do this?' it was asked. 'I'll tell you,' said Mr. Roberts: 'young Harry Clay will be a member of the next House, and is the very man to do it.' All assented, and it was agreed that he should be elected Speaker of the next House, as he was, and brought about the reform which was expected of him. A collision between him and Mr. Randolph was inevitable, and occurred on several occasions."

DEATH OF ADAMS AND JEFFERSON.

On the 4th of July of this year, 1826, the fiftieth anniversary of our national independence, passed from earthly existence two of the most venerable and venerated characters in the nation; than whom no other two had performed a more important part in bringing about the entire separation of the colonies from England, and in framing the Declaration of Independence. The death of Adams and Jefferson on the same day, just fifty years from the day upon which they put their hands to that immortal paper and it was proclaimed to all the world that these United States were a free and independent nation, amid the ringing of bells, the firing of cannon, and the exulting shouts of the people, was a circumstance so extraordinary that it produced the most profound impression throughout the entire limits of the land, and even in foreign countries.

Adams and Jefferson, two of the three survivors, on the morning of the fiftieth anniversary of Independence, of that patriotic and immortal band who put their names to that instrument, had long been looked up to and venerated as the Fathers of the Republic. Their names had been inseparably connected in the minds and upon the lips of the people, as their labors were united in bringing about the events of the Revolution and its final triumph. Mr. Jefferson was the writer, Mr. Adams the orator, of the Congress of '76. The one penned the Declaration of Independence, the other was pronounced "the pillar of its support, and its ablest advocate and defender." Mr. Jefferson called Mr. Adams "the colossus of the Congress;" the most earnest, laborious member of the body, and its animating spirit.

For the loss of these men, though they fell as a ripe shock of corn falleth,—both having arrived at an advanced age, Mr. Adams over ninety,—the whole nation clothed itself in mourning, and its ablest orators were called upon to pronounce their eulogies: Mr. Webster in Boston, Mr. Everett in Charlestown, Chancellor Kent in New York, General Smith in Baltimore: in all the large cities, indeed, the ablest pens paid tribute to the memory of the illustrious departed. One signer of the Decla ration of Independence was yet left, and only one: Charles Carroll, of Carrollton, the last survivor of that band of patriots who in placing their names to it put their lives and their fortunes to the hazard of a die or the chances of war.

"RETRENCHMENT AND REFORM."

In the first session of Congress after Mr. Adams's election—1825–26—Mr. Macon moved in the Senate that the select committee appointed upon Mr. Benton's resolutions in regard to the amendment of the Constitution should also be charged with an inquiry into the expediency of reducing the patronage of the Federal government, where it could be done without impairing its efficiency. The committee consisted of nine Senators; all, save one, and he rather doubtful, were the friends of General Jackson, and opponents of Mr. Adams.

The purpose undoubtedly was to operate on the public mind to the prejudice of the administration, and in favor of the Jackson party, as the party in favor of reducing the Executive patronage, the number of officers of the government, and the public expenses; conveying the idea, of course, that *they* were the true friends of the people and opposed to all extravagance.

Mr. Benton, from the committee, made an elaborate report, which was accompanied by six bills, namely:

1. To regulate the publication of the laws of the United States, and of the public advertisements.
2. To secure in office the faithful collectors and disbursers of the revenue, and to displace defaulters.
3. To regulate the appointment of postmasters.
4. To regulate the appointment of cadets.
5. To regulate the appointment of midshipmen.
6. To prevent military and naval officers from being dismissed the service at the pleasure of the President.

Each of these bills presupposes that there was an evil which was necessary to be corrected; an abuse of power on the part of the Executive which an additional law was needed to arrest.

In regard to bill No. 1,—to regulate the publication of the laws, etc.,—the ostensible reason for that was, that Mr. Clay, as Secretary of State, had, like all his predecessors, designated the papers which should publish, "by authority," the laws of the United States, and in making this selection did not designate certain papers, which were violently opposed to, and denunciatory of, the administration, but which had previously published the laws by authority.

Mr. Clay was fiercely assailed in the House on this account, Mr. Saunders, of North Carolina, offering a resolution calling upon him for the *reasons* for his action in the premises. This caused a warm debate, which lasted for several days. The resolution failed, sensible men, even though opposed to the administration, perceiving the absurdity of demanding *reasons* from him who was necessarily required to exercise his own discretion in the matter.

In regard to the second bill,—to secure in office faithful collectors, etc.,—no collector had been removed by Mr. Adams, and there had been no instance of defalcation to require the removal of a defaulter.

Mr. Thompson, collector of customs of the port of New York, was known to be opposed to Mr. Adams and in favor of General Jackson; and Mr. Adams's friends strenuously urged his removal; but he peremptorily refused to comply with their request, though they assured him that if he acted on the policy of retaining his active opponents in office in that State he would surely lose it,—as he did. Mr. Thompson got his reward by being removed by General Jackson. Mr. Adams took the high ground in this case, as he did in that of Mr. McLean, Postmaster-General, that every man had a right to exercise and act upon his own opinion; and if officers of the government believed General Jackson a more fit man for President than himself, they were right in supporting him, and so long as they discharged the duties of their office faithfully he would not remove them. This would now be considered rather Quixotic purity.

In regard to the other three bills, there was as little occasion for them in anything that had occurred under Mr. Adams's administration as there was for the others.

Speaking of this report, which he says he wrote twenty-five

years ago, Colonel Benton says, in his "Thirty Years' View," "The crowds which congregate at Washington at every change of an administration, suppliants for office, are humiliating to behold, and threaten to change the contests of parties from a contest for principle into a struggle for plunder."

Very true; but when did this begin? Who inaugurated this "spoils system"? General Jackson himself, whom Colonel Benton supported with all his ability, energy, and industry.

The second bill reported by the committee required "that in all nominations to fill vacancies occasioned by removals, the fact of the removal shall be stated, and the reasons for such removal given." This was intended to recognize the principle that, as appointments are made by the advice and consent of the Senate, that body should also be consulted in regard to removals, which Colonel Benton claims was the intention of the framers of the Constitution. These bills, however, were never acted on. Perhaps it would be uncharitable to suppose that it was never expected or intended they should be.

Resolutions were subsequently introduced in the House by Mr. Chilton, of Kentucky, for the appointment of a special committee on "Retrenchment and Reform;" this being intended as a sort of Congressional indorsement and confirmation of the allegation of the Jackson press that monstrous "extravagance and corruption" prevailed at Washington, which called for the retrenching and reforming hand of Congress.

Upon these resolutions—a part of the system of attacks to be made upon the administration—a protracted, heated, and ill-tempered debate ensued, during which all possible missiles were hurled at it, and absurd and unfounded charges brought against it, calculated and intended to alarm and prejudice the people.

It may surprise some at the present day to learn that the "*enormous expenditures*" of Mr. Adams's administration, about which such a clamor was raised, were twelve million five hundred thousand dollars per annum!

"THE GORGEOUSLY FURNISHED EAST ROOM."

During the Presidential canvass a letter appeared in and addressed to the "Richmond Inquirer," purporting to be written by "a distinguished member of Congress," who had just visited the White House, January 1, 1827, and seen "the gorgeously furnished East Room," representing and giving the public to understand that Mr. Adams was living in a more princely manner than any President had ever lived in before, and that extravagant sums of the public money had been expended in "gorgeously" furnishing the Presidential mansion.* The letter made quite a sensation for a time, and served the unmanly purpose intended. It was an utter *mis*representation. The "gorgeous" furniture existed nowhere but in the imagination of the writer. The East Room was at that time most meagerly furnished; nay, not furnished at all. There were three marble-top centre-tables in the room, which remained there till a very few years ago; but besides these and some mirrors there was not fifty dollars' worth of furniture in the room. There were no chandeliers, and the only mode of lighting the room was by sperm candles held in long tin candlesticks hung to nails driven into the walls. From these candles dripped the sperm upon the clothes of those who came under them, as I well know from experience, having several times got my coat besmeared with the drippings, as many other gentlemen did. Such was the "*gorgeously furnished* East Room" in the winter of 1828–9.

The auther of this famous "East Room Letter" was reputed to be a United States Senator. It was in consonance with other means used to excite the prejudice of the people against Mr. Adams.

GEORGIA AND THE CREEK CONTROVERSY.

I have alluded to the difficulty that arose between Georgia and the Creek Indians, and the sharp correspondence between Governor Troup and General Gaines, who was sent by the general government to protect the Indians.

* See Niles's Register, vol. xxxvii. p. 116.

The governor assumed a very arrogant and imperious tone, not only towards General Gaines but towards the President and the general government, demanding that a treaty purporting to have been made at Indian Springs by the chiefs and head-men of the Creeks should be executed, and threatening to enter upon the Indian lands purporting to have been ceded by this treaty to Georgia, have them surveyed, and drive the Indians off. The treaty was undoubtedly a fraud; its validity was denied by the real chiefs and head-men, and not recognized by the general government. General Gaines, being sent to protect the Indians and prevent a collision, necessarily had much correspondence with Governor Troup, which became excessively sharp and personal on both sides. In a letter to the President, complaining of General Gaines and other officers sent to Georgia, Governor Troup says, "Now, sir, suffer me in conclusion to ask if these things have been done in virtue of your instructions, expressed or implied, or by authority of any warrant from you whatever; and if not so done, whether you will sanction and adopt them as your own, and thus *hold yourself responsible to the government of Georgia?*"

The attitude of the governor during the whole of this controversy had been exceedingly imperious and insulting, as may be judged from the above language. His letters to General Gaines were of this character; but the general in his replies showed that his pen was not less sharp than his sword, and that he could use the one with as much skill and effect as he could wield the other.

The unjustifiable course pursued by Georgia to drive the Indians off and get possession of their lands had given the general government much trouble. It was bound to protect the Indians against unjust claims and aggressions, and in the peaceable possession of their lands until relinquished by treaty, and such a treaty was greatly desired; but the impatience of Georgia, the fraudulent treaty effected by her at Indian Springs, and the constant threats of the governor that he would take forcible possession in spite of the general government, very much embarrassed the action of the latter.

At length, however, the real chiefs and head-men of the

nation were induced to come to Washington, where a treaty was made with them by which they gave up all their lands in Georgia and Alabama and took lands west of the Mississippi, where they still remain.

THE JACKSON PARTY GAIN THE ASCENDENCY.

So much prejudice had been excited against the administration by the continued cries of "bargain and corruption," "extravagance," the cheating of General Jackson out of his election, and other clap-trap means of operating on the public mind, that the elections which took place in the fall of 1826 for members of Congress resulted in a sweeping Jackson majority in the House of Representatives, as there had been for two years in the Senate.

General Jackson was represented as an Irishman; or, if not himself, his father was. Of course the Irish were for him to a man. Nevertheless, very much the largest portion of the intelligent, sober, moral, exemplary citizens of the Northern, Eastern, Middle, and Western States—full four-fifths—were friends of the administration.

The general was largely possessed of the elements of popularity: knew the people, and how, now and then, at proper times, to address them without seeming to do so. He knew the importance of keeping himself in their minds,—of being talked about, and even abused. Added to this was the fact that he had rendered services to the country which the most unlettered of the people could appreciate. He was a *hero*,—had won a great battle: there was, therefore, something in and about him to excite the imagination and stir up enthusiasm.

On the other hand, there was nothing *heroic* or attractive in Mr. Adams. His name excited no enthusiasm; he had no elements of popularity; even those who knew him personally were never inspired by any ardent feelings towards him, inasmuch as he was cold, stiff, and reserved in his manner, which rather repelled than attracted. Ezekiel Webster spoke the truth when he wrote to his brother Daniel, in February, 1829, that "the people always supported Mr. Adams's course from a cold sense of duty, and not from any liking of the man. We soon satisfy ourselves that we have discharged our duty to the cause of any man, when we do not entertain for him one personal kind feeling."

A CHALLENGE, BUT NO DUEL.

Party feeling ran high in Congress during the first session of the Twentieth Congress: the speeches, especially in the House of Representatives, were of a very heated and virulent character. The Presidential election was to take place in the coming fall, and consequently the two parties were in the very heat of the great battle which was to decide which should have possession of the government. So far as Congress could take part in this great battle, it was the last charge, the bayonet contest, the hand-to-hand encounter; and as one of the results of this state of things, a challenge to single combat was sent by Mr. McDuffie to Governor Metcalf, of Kentucky, the especial friend of Mr. Clay. The language of Mr. McDuffie, in his reply to General Vance, which I have quoted, will be remembered. That language seemed maliciously designed to insult Mr. Clay, and probably had no little influence in shaping Governor Metcalf's to Mr. McDuffie. The latter seemed to be impatient for a personal conflict with Mr. Clay or some one of his friends, and it is evident that Governor Metcalf was disposed to accommodate him, but upon his (Governor Metcalf's) own terms. I may state it still more strongly: the correspondence between them, I think, shows a decided determination on the part of Governor Metcalf to compel Mr. McDuffie to challenge him. Of course the challenge came, and Governor Metcalf selected rifles as the weapons. But General Hamilton, Mr. McDuffie's friend, flatly refused to recognize the rifle as a proper dueling-weapon, and no duel ensued.

Mr. McDuffie had the reputation of being "a dead shot" with the pistol, and hence, it is presumed, the determination of Governor Metcalf to draw the challenge from him,—the challenged party having the right to name the weapons. No one can blame Mr. McDuffie for not wishing to face a rifle in the hands of a Kentuckian, or Governor Metcalf for refusing to become a mark for a pistol in the hand of one who could use it with fatal skill. Probably the object which Governor Metcalf wished to accomplish was attained,—of silencing audacious personal abuse and putting a stop to gasconading. There were no more challenges after this.

ABDUCTION OF WILLIAM MORGAN.—FORMATION OF THE ANTI-MASONIC PARTY.

An extraordinary event took place in the western part of New York, in 1826, which created a most intense excitement among the people of the western counties,—Erie, Chautauqua, Niagara, Genesee, Monroe, Livingston, Orleans, and Ontario, —and finally in other parts of the State. William Morgan, a Mason, living at Batavia, had announced that he should publish a book which would reveal the secrets of Masonry. Instead of laughing at this pretended exposure as a joke or a humbug, —a mere catch-penny,—the Masons treated the matter very seriously, showing anger whenever the subject was mentioned, and making threats of injury to Morgan should he publish the book. It was published in spite of their threats and various forcible attempts to prevent it.

Morgan was immediately arrested on some pretended criminal charge brought against him by a party of men from Canandaigua, where he was taken. On examination he was of course acquitted and discharged, but he was immediately again arrested for debt, and thrust into jail. This was done merely to keep possession of him until arrangements could be made to dispose of him otherwise. These being completed, he was discharged from jail, but was taken at once, after nine o'clock P.M., thrust into a close carriage, gagged and bound, and driven rapidly, by relays of horses, and finally lodged in the magazine of Fort Niagara, on the river of that name, at the head of Lake Ontario.

His seizure and disappearance roused the people of Batavia and other places. Public meetings were held and committees appointed to ascertain and make known all the facts of this mysterious outrage upon a citizen against whom no crime was or could be alleged. These committees ascertained that he had been taken, as I have mentioned, from Canandaigua towards Rochester, but could not trace him, at that time, any farther.

His disappearance, and the mystery attending it, his unknown fate, and the suspicions that were created by the Masons justifying these outrageous proceedings, impressed upon the public mind the belief that he had been murdered, and created an excitement which became almost a frenzy.

Meanwhile, the perseverance of those who sought to unravel the mystery was crowned with at least partial success. They became satisfied that Morgan had been confined in Fort Niagara for a time, and had finally been taken out in a boat upon the river and dropped in, with a cannon-ball attached to his feet. That he was thus disposed of was afterwards proved before a special court held at Lockport, by Judge Marcy, appointed for that special purpose, under an act of the Legislature of New York, authorizing a special court to be held for the trial of those implicated in this nefarious transaction. Some convictions were made and punishments inflicted; but, best of all, the whole transaction from beginning to end was judicially laid open, and the intense desire of the public to know the facts gratified.

In consequence of this feeling which had arisen towards Masonry and Masons, there were, for many years, no Masonic celebrations. The appearance of a Masonic procession in full regalia in almost any part of the Northern States would probably have raised a mob: it certainly would in any one of the western counties of New York.

Soon after the death of Morgan, and when the excitement was at fever-heat, a few gentlemen met at a room, or office, in "the Kremlin," a building so called, in Buffalo, and then and there initiated the "Anti-Masonic party," which soon became a powerful organization in New York, Pennsylvania, Vermont, and some other States. To this party Mr. Seward, of New York, and Mr. Ritner, of Pennsylvania, owed their elections as governors of their respective States.

GENERAL JACKSON CHARGES MR. ADAMS AND MR. CLAY WITH BARGAIN AND CORRUPTION.—CARTER BEVERLY'S LETTER.—MR. CLAY'S DENIAL.—DEMANDS THE NAME OF THE WITNESS.—GENERAL JACKSON REPLIES, AND GIVES THE NAME OF JAMES BUCHANAN AS HIS AUTHOR.

I have given a very brief account of the charge of "bargain and corruption" gotten up against Mr. Adams and Mr. Clay at the time of, and subsequent to, the election of the former as President by the House of Representatives, in February, 1825, and the part played by Mr. Buchanan at that time. Up to the 5th of June, 1827, no one was responsible for this charge: it was made in such a way that neither Mr. Clay nor Mr. Adams could fix the authorship upon any one. But now General Jackson made the charge at his own house, before all his company, and thus assumed its authorship. The contest between the Adams party and the Jackson party was carried on at this time with great virulence: consequently General Jackson's charge produced a profound sensation. It came out in this manner. In a letter addressed to and published in the "Fayetteville (N. C.) Observer," by Carter Beverly, dated March 8, 1827, he says,—

"I have just returned from General Jackson's. I found a crowd of company with him. . . . He told me this morning, *before all his company*, in reply to a question I put to him concerning the election of J. Q. Adams to the Presidency, that Mr. Clay's friends made a proposition to his friends that if they would promise for *him not* to put Mr. Adams into the seat of Secretary of State, Clay and his friends would, in *one hour*, make *him*, Jackson, the President." . . .

Mr. Clay, seeing this publication, positively denied that there was any truth in General Jackson's statement, as put forth by Mr. Beverly, and expressed his unwillingness to believe Jackson had made such a statement, upon which Mr. Beverly addressed a letter to General Jackson, who replied, reiterating his former declaration, and stating that a gentleman, without naming him, called on him, previous to the election by the House, and informed him that he had a communication to make, etc., and then detailed the conversation which took place, and which he considered a proposition from Mr. Clay to him.

This letter was dated June 5, 1827. Mr. Clay, having obtained a copy of General Jackson's letter to Mr. Beverly before its publication, came out immediately with a positive, indignant denial of the whole and every part of General Jackson's allegations, and called upon him to produce his evidence. In response to this demand, General Jackson put forth a somewhat lengthy publication, argumentative and accusatory of Mr. Clay, and giving the name of James Buchanan as the gentleman who came to him with corrupt propositions, as he believed, from Mr. Clay. This drew from Mr. Buchanan the following letter, addressed to the editor of the "Lancaster (Pa.) Journal," dated 8th of August, 1827:

* * * * * * * *

"On the 30th of December, 1824, I called upon General Jackson. After the company had left, . . . I told him I wished to ask him a question in relation to the Presidential election; that I knew he was unwilling to converse upon the subject; that, therefore, if he deemed the question improper, he might refuse to give it an answer; that my only motive in asking it was friendship for him, and I trusted he would excuse me for thus intruding a subject about which I knew he wished to be silent.

"His reply was complimentary to myself, and accompanied with a request that I should proceed. I then stated to him that there was a report in circulation that he had determined he would appoint Mr. Adams Secretary of State in case he were elected President, and that I wished to ascertain from him whether he had ever intimated such an intention; that he must at once perceive how injurious to his election such a report must be.

* * * * * * * *

"After I had finished, the general declared he had not the least objection to answer my question. That he thought well of Mr. Adams, but had never said or intimated that he would or that he would not appoint him Secretary of State. That these were secrets he would keep to himself,—he would conceal them from the very hairs of his head.

* * * * * * * *

"I called upon General Jackson, on the occasion which I have mentioned, solely as his friend, upon my individual responsibility, and not as the agent of Mr. Clay or any other person. I never have been the political friend of Mr. Clay.

* * * * * * * *

"The conception never once entered my head that he (General Jackson) believed me to have been the agent of Mr. Clay or of his friends, or that I had intended to propose terms to him of any kind for them."

* * * * * * * *

Mr. Buchanan further states that, in answer to a letter from the editor of the "United States Telegraph," dated 12th of October, "I promptly informed him, on the 16th, by return mail, that I had no authority from Mr. Clay, or his friends, to propose any terms to General Jackson in relation to their votes, nor did I ever make any such proposition."

To an ordinary mind this reply of Mr. Buchanan seems to be a full and positive denial that he went to General Jackson as the agent of Mr. Clay or his friends, or made any propositions by Mr. Clay's authority or suggestion. "He called on General Jackson," he states, "*solely as his friend*, and not as the agent of Mr. Clay, and it never once entered his head that General Jackson believed him to have come to him as Mr. Clay's agent."

Mr. Clay thought Mr. Buchanan's statement strong and explicit. Mr. Webster wrote to Mr. Clay, saying, "Many persons think Mr. Buchanan's letter candid. I deem it otherwise. It seems to me he labored very hard to protect the general, as far as he could without injury to himself. The general's friends this way, however, affect to consider Buchanan's letter as supporting the charge." This was the cue given, immediately on the publication of the letter, to the press, which then persistently insisted that Buchanan's letter proved General Jackson's charge, and the hue and cry of "corruption, bargain, and sale" was raised afresh. Had Mr. Buchanan been a truly honest witness, he would have denied at once, as his meaning, the interpretation which the Jackson press put upon his letter; but he was a moral coward, and afraid of offending General Jackson: he therefore kept silent, and allowed the friends of the general all the benefit they could derive from proclaiming that the charge had been proved by his, Mr. Buchanan's, testimony. In this affair, however, he lost the confidence of the general.

Mr. Clay did not allow the subject to drop, but issued a circular to his constituents, and addressed the citizens of Louisville in a most indignant and animated speech, vindicating himself from the calumnies his enemies had originated against him and were now attempting to overwhelm and ruin him with.

In due time he obtained the testimony of every member of Congress who acted with him in the Presidential election, Western members generally, besides many others, thirty-four in all, including Lafayette, going to prove General Jackson's charge utterly false, and that he had, even before leaving Kentucky to attend Congress, declared to some of his friends that, in case he should be so situated as to be required to vote for a candidate for President, instead of being voted for, he should support Mr. Adams. This he early avowed to Lafayette, who made the inquiry of him, and who certified to the fact.

Upon obtaining this testimony, he issued, December, 1827, a stirring address to the people of the United States, which was accompanied by a mass of overwhelming testimony.

In a letter to Mr. Clay, dated January 1, 1828, Mr. Webster, after stating that he had read Mr. Clay's address, says, "The statement is clear, and the evidence irresistible. I am satisfied, upon my conscience, that the whole business originated with General Jackson himself: whether through mistake or from intention I cannot say."

In 1829, after Mr. Adams had retired from the Presidency, in reply to a letter from a committee of gentlemen in New Jersey, he spoke of Mr. Clay as follows, and thus denounced the charge of "bargain and corruption:" "Upon him the foulest slanders have been showered. . . . Prejudice and passion have charged him with obtaining that office by bargain and corruption. Before you, my fellow-citizens, in the presence of our country and Heaven, I pronounce that charge totally unfounded. This tribute of justice is due from me to him, and I seize with pleasure the opportunity afforded me by your letter of discharging the obligation. As to my motives for tendering to him the Department of State when I did, let that man who questions them come forward; let him look around among statesmen and legislators of this nation and of that day; let him then select and name the man whom, by his pre-eminent talents, by his splendid services, by his ardent patriotism, by his all-embracing public spirit, by his fervid eloquence in behalf of the rights and liberties of mankind, and by his long experience in the affairs of the Union, foreign and domestic, a President of the United States, intent only upon the honor and welfare of his country, ought to have preferred to HENRY CLAY. Let him name the man, and then judge you, my fellow-citizens, of my motives."

In 1843, Mr. Adams, taking a tour to the West for the purpose of delivering an address at Cincinnati on the establishing there of an astronomical observatory, stopping, on his return, at Maysville, Ky., was addressed by the mayor on behalf of the citizens. In reply he said, "I thank you, sir, for the opportunity you have given me of speaking of the great statesman who was associated with me in the administration of the general government at my earnest solicitation; who belongs not to Kentucky alone, but to the whole Union, and who is not only an honor to this State and this nation, but to mankind. The charges to which you refer, after my term of service had expired and it was proper for me to speak, I denied before the whole country, and I here reiterate and reaffirm that denial; and as I expect shortly to appear before my God, to answer for the conduct of my whole life, should those charges have found their way to the throne of eternal justice, I WILL, in the presence of OMNIPOTENCE, pronounce them FALSE."

In replying to an address of the mayor of Covington, Ky., or the chairman of a committee, Mr. Adams used similar language.

On the 27th of January, 1844, the Legislature of Tennessee passed a resolution declaring that "so much of a resolution passed by the Legislature of this State, in 1827, as sustained the allegation, either expressed or implied, of an improper and corrupt combination, or, as it has been more generally denominated, *corruption*, *bargain*, and *intrigue*, between John Q. Adams and Henry Clay, is, in the opinion of this General Assembly, unsupported by proof and not believed."

Yet, in the face of all this, General Jackson never ceased to reiterate the charge, and was followed by thousands of politicians, who found it to be too effective among the ignorant of their party to be given up, and the clamor was therefore kept up almost to the day of Mr. Clay's death. It was kept up in Pennsylvania with more virulence than in any other State. Mr. Buchanan had the power at any time to nail it to the counter as a calumny. Why did he not do it? Because he had not sufficient manliness and candor.

AGITATION OF THE PROTECTIVE POLICY.—MEETINGS AND CONVENTIONS NORTH AND SOUTH.—LANGUAGE OF THE SOUTH.—GENERAL CONVENTION AT HARRISBURG.—"NULLIFICATION" FIRST HEARD OF.—SUGGESTED BY COLONEL HAMILTON, OF SOUTH CAROLINA.—HIS INFLAMMATORY LANGUAGE.

Another subject in which both the North and the South took a very deep interest, but upon which their views were antagonistic, had been for some time before Congress and ably debated. The interest and feeling manifested in regard to it were not confined to the halls of Congress, but pervaded the whole country. Meetings of the people were held, resolutions were passed, and the subject was discussed with warmth and ability at those meetings and in the public papers.

A meeting was held in Baltimore, which declared that "it is the business and duty of the general government to encourage and support the national industry in all its lawful pursuits, whether in relation to agriculture, manufactures, or commerce; and the people of Maryland, generally, have been greatly benefited by the degree of encouragement that has already been extended to certain branches of manufactures, which have furnished a large and valuable home market for the products of our farmers."

Similar meetings were held in various parts of New York, and one, especially, at Albany, which was addressed by Chief-Justice Ambrose Spencer, General Van Rensselaer, Martin Van Buren, and other eminent men. Mr. Van Buren, who was acting with and courting Southern men, professing to be "a Northern man with Southern principles," found it necessary to participate in the proceedings of the meeting. He did so, and made a speech; but it would puzzle a Philadelphia lawyer to discover whether he was for or against the measure.

The "Woolens bill" passed the House, but was lost in the Senate by the casting vote of the Vice-President, Mr. Calhoun, Mr. Van Buren dodging the vote, when, if he had voted for it, it would have passed.

Meantime, the South was not indifferent or inactive. Meetings were held in South Carolina, and at Charleston especially, at which strong denunciatory language was used and intemperate speeches were delivered. In a memorial from the citizens of South Carolina to the State Legislature, the memorialists declared that the Northern and Middle States were to be enriched by *the plunder of the South*, which was to be made tributary to them.

At the North a general convention was held at Harrisburg, Pa., on the 30th of July and several subsequent days, in which all the States of the Union were represented except Indiana.

The convention was composed of "agriculturists and manufacturers, and others friendly to the encouragement and support of the domestic industry of the United States," and was called for the purpose of taking into consideration the important subject of giving protection and encouragement to domestic manufactures and home industry.

It was, probably, as able a body of men, in point of talent, business capacity and experience, character and influence, as could be got together for any purpose whatever. The venerable Hezekiah Niles, the life-long, able advocate of "protection," was chairman of a committee to prepare an address to the people of the United States, and Thomas Ewing, of Ohio, afterwards United States Senator, Secretary of the Treasury, and first Secretary of the Interior, was a member.

Of the ninety-six members who composed the Harrisburg Convention I know of but two now (1871) living; namely, Thomas Ewing, of Ohio,* and Gideon Welles, of Connecticut:

* Mr. Ewing died a month or two after this was written.

all the rest have passed away; but the question they met to discuss—the great controversy between the advocates of "Protection" and those of "Free Trade"—still survives and occupies the public mind. Not only is it not settled, but it never will be. Sometimes one side has been in the ascendant in Congress, sometimes the other, producing such a vacillation as seriously to injure the interests of manufacturers, and with theirs the farmers'.

The contest between the friends and advocates of "protection" and those who denounced it as unconstitutional and oppressive, became more and more ardent. The friends of the "Woolens bill," which had been defeated in the Senate, at the last session of Congress, by the casting vote of the Vice-President, Mr. Calhoun, thrown upon him by Mr. Van Buren's dodging, brought the measure forward again at the session of 1827–28. Meantime, the public mind at the South, particularly in South Carolina and Georgia, continued to be inflamed against it by the leading politicians, who harangued the people everywhere and kept up a continued blast of denunciation through the papers. A dinner having been given to Colonel Hamilton, representative in Congress, at Walterboro', in the fall of 1827, he made a long, inflammatory speech, denouncing the protective policy as unconstitutional and oppressive, and proposing "NULLIFICATION" AS THE "RIGHTFUL REMEDY." This is the first we hear of "NULLIFICATION;" though probably that measure had been discussed and agreed upon among and by the leaders. It is not easy to conceive the heat, fury, and passion of these leaders as manifested by their language.

A new tariff bill was passed by both houses of Congress, after a severe struggle in the House and Senate, and became a law on the 19th of May, 1828.

It was not such a bill as the advocates of protection desired; indeed, many of them were strongly opposed to it, for it was purposely made as obnoxious as possible by the South, with a view, it was alleged, to its defeat; but, rather than have no alteration in the tariff, the friends of protection accepted it with all its obnoxious features. It was derisively denominated the "Bill of Abominations."

The political ferment which pervaded the country during the summer and autumn of 1827 was greatly increased by the appearance of the Carter Beverly letter to the "Fayetteville Observer;" General Jackson's letter to Carter Beverly, charging Mr. Clay with "bargain and corruption;" Mr. Clay's prompt and indignant denial; General Jackson's announcing the name of James Buchanan as the person who made proposals to him; Mr. Buchanan's letter, and Mr. Clay's appeal to the public.

With all these exciting subjects before the country, a Presidential contest of no ordinary character on hand, and the MORGAN, or *Anti-Masonic*, fever raging in New York, it may be supposed the people did not need wholesale murders by railroads, steamboats, coal-mines, collisions at sea, and daily and nightly assassinations, to produce "sensations."

In the mean time, the "Adams men" took the name of "NATIONAL REPUBLICANS," while their opponents were designated, and called themselves, "Jackson men," and their party the "Jackson party," showing that parties were then divided by preferences for *men*, and not by difference of views in regard to *policy* or *principles.* The only great questions of this kind which divided the public mind, and upon which public men differed, were those of internal improvements by the general government, and the protection of domestic manufactures. In favor of both these, Pennsylvania was foremost; and yet, strange to say, a very large majority of her voters were in favor of Jackson for President and Calhoun for Vice-President, both Southern men, both now opposed to her policy, and both ardently supported by those who were threatening to "nullify" the tariff act which her influence and agency had done more to obtain the passage of than any other State! True, the "wool" was pulled over her eyes by persuading her people that General Jackson was "a good tariff man," and referring to his famous "Coleman letter" in proof of it, and thus the honest but ignorant German population were deceived by their dishonest leaders. Adams and Rush, the other candidates for President and Vice-President, were both Northern men. Mr. Rush, a Pennsylvanian, had put forth very elaborate and able arguments, in his reports as Secretary of the Treasury, in favor of protecting domestic manufactures. Yet neither the fact that he was a native of Pennsylvania, nor his masterly advocacy of Pennsylvania's favorite policy, had the least weight with her population. The only answer to appeals to her sound judgment, self-interest, and consistency to support men who advocated her principles was, "Hurrah for Jackson!" and this was all-sufficient.

ELECTION OF GOVERNOR IN NEW YORK.—THE PARTIES AND THE NOMINEES.

The Anti-Masonic party had become somewhat important in the State of New York in 1828, the year of the Presidential election, inasmuch as it held the balance of power between the other two. It was evident that whichever candidate for President obtained the vote of that State would be elected: the struggle for it, therefore, was a vigorous one.

The election for governor, lieutenant-governor, members of Congress, etc., took place before that for Presidential electors, and, as the result of these elections would have a very potent influence upon the next, each party nominated a powerful ticket. The National Republicans nominated for governor Smith Thompson, formerly chief justice of the State, then Secretary of the Navy, and, finally, one of the justices of the Supreme Court of the United States; for lieutenant-governor, Francis Granger. The Jackson party nominated Martin Van Buren for governor, and Enos T. Throop for lieutenant-governor. The Anti-Masonic party placed in nomination Francis Granger for governor, and John Crary for lieutenant-governor.

Mr. Granger was a National Republican as well as an Anti-Mason; and knowing that if the latter party put a ticket into the field and voted for their candidates it would be the means of defeating the National Republicans and electing Van Buren and Throop,—a result he had no desire to bring about,—he withheld his reply to the committee appointed to inform him of his nomination (which he declined) as long as he could, with a view to prevent any other person being nominated in his place.

But it was of vital importance to Mr. Van Buren and the Jackson party that the Anti-Masons should vote their own ticket; and he was equal to the occasion. By his management Solomon Southwick was put in nomination, or rather nominated himself, as the Anti-Masonic candidate, and issued a spirited address to the Anti-Masons, well calculated to rouse their passions and induce them to "stand by their flag, and lock their shields like a Macedonian phalanx." It had the desired effect: the result of the election was, for Van Buren and Throop, 136,785; for Thompson and Granger, 106,415; and for Southwick and Cramer, 33,335. Van Buren and Throop's plurality over Thompson and Granger, 30,370,—2966 less than a majority of the whole vote of the State.

While the gubernatorial campaign was in progress, there appeared a letter from Mr. Adams, addressed to a Mr. Hartwell, of Canandaigua, known as "the Hartwell Letter," in answer to one from Mr. Hartwell to Mr. Adams, inquiring whether he was a Mason; to which Mr. Adams replied that he never had been and never should be a Mason. This exceedingly provoked the Masons, many of whom who up to that time had been National Republicans went over in great anger to the Jackson party, and zealously supported Van Buren, Throop, and Jackson.

Had Mr. Adams been as sagacious and cautious a politician as Mr. Van Buren, he would simply have replied, if he replied at all, that he was not a Mason. The answer he gave was construed to imply either contempt for, or hostility to, the Masonic order.

GENERAL JACKSON'S ELECTION.—WHAT IT TRIUMPHED OVER.—COLONEL BENTON CONTROVERTED.

The election for President resulted in favor of General Jackson. Colonel Benton says, "It was a triumph over the high protective policy and the federal internal improvement policy." Did Pennsylvania give her immense majority for Jackson as a rebuke to her own high protective policy?*

* The venerable Andrew Stewart, of Pennsylvania, who entered Congress in 1823, and continued a member till 1833, and was also a member of the Thirtieth Congress, 1847 to 1849, writing to me on the 11th September, 1871, says, "I think you ought to notice in your work the sudden change of Buchanan and Ingham on

A WINTER IN WASHINGTON, 1828–29.

I spent the winter of 1828–29 in Washington. I arrived near the last of December, and at that time heard much talk about the marriage of Major Eaton, Senator from Tennessee, to Mrs. Timberlake, which had taken place a few days previous. The happy couple had then gone on a bridal tour to Philadelphia. They returned in a few days, and Mrs. Eaton soon left cards with such officials, and their wives, as etiquette required a Senator to make the first call upon. Among these were Mr. and Mrs. Calhoun, Vice-President; Mr. and Mrs. Rush, Secretary of the Treasury; General and Mrs. Porter, Secretary of War; Mr. and Mrs. Southard, Secretary of the Navy.

Good society was in commotion. Who Mrs. Eaton was and had been, the old residents of Washington knew, and they were now anxious to know what was to be her social position. Peggy O'Neil, subsequently Mrs. Timberlake, the wife of a purser in the navy, and then the wife of Senator Eaton, was born and had always resided in Washington. Unfortunately for her, the tongue of scandal had, justifiably or unjustifiably, made free with her name for some year or two previous to her marriage with Major Eaton. If her calls (by card) were returned by Mrs. Calhoun, Mrs. Rush, Mrs. Porter, and Mrs. Southard, the question would be settled; if not, other ladies of an official rank below hers would be at liberty to consult their own inclinations and sense of propriety in regard to calling on her.

It was soon privately whispered about that no one of the

the tariff policy. They warmly supported the tariff bill of 1824, and the general policy of *protecting* American manufactures, but opposed the woolens bill in 1827, which was quite as important to the farmers and manufacturers as that bill was. This was done in pursuance of a *contract* between the Democracy of the North and the Democracy of the South, by which the former were to have the offices and the latter to dictate the *policy* of the country, the North to have the *men* and the South the *measures;* and they adhered to the contract most faithfully. The Democrats of the North all went for the tariff of 1824; but in 1827 they had changed sides. After this infamous contract was made, I quit the Democratic party, and adhered to our old friend Henry Clay's 'American System,' the tariff, and internal improvements." *

* Mr. Stewart died a few months after this letter was written.

ladies who had been "carded" by Mrs. Eaton would leave cards with her in return. But whispers in social circles are trumpet-sounds to curious and anxious ears. To call, or not to call, was now the important question among the ladies constituting "good society" in Washington, and kept it in a ferment the whole winter. General Jackson arrived in February, in the midst of this *émeute*, and was soon appealed to by Mrs. Eaton. He took a deep interest in her troubles,—let off, on the occasion, some strong expletives, and swore, "by the Eternal," that he would place Major Eaton in such an official position as would compel the ladies of Washington to call on his wife. But some of these, more spunky or independent than others, replied, with a spirit equal to his own, that neither General Jackson nor any other man should compel them to call on any woman they did not choose to call upon. Even his own niece, the lady of the White House, refused to visit Mrs. Eaton, and was banished, for a time, to Tennessee, but was finally brought back and reinstated.

Society was divided: a portion visited and received Mrs. Eaton, while another portion refused to do so; but, sustained by the President, she bore herself proudly wherever she appeared. She was at this time a splendid-looking woman, and must have been beautiful when young.

Arriving in Washington the latter part of March, when this commotion was at fever-heat, and when General Jackson was earnestly engaged in endeavoring to effect the admission of Mrs. Eaton into society, Mr. Van Buren soon saw and comprehended the situation. Nothing could have been more fortunate for him, as it enabled him to bring into action his tact and adroitness in effecting conciliation. With Mr. Vaughan and Baron Krudener, the British and Russian ministers, he was on the most friendly terms, and soon induced them—both of them being bachelors—to aid him in his friendly purposes towards Mrs. Eaton; and they both gave a ball and party for her special benefit, and made every possible demonstration of honor to her. But at the ball given by the Russian minister a circumstance happened which was most significant, and exceedingly mortifying to "Bellona" (Mrs. Eaton). Mrs.

Huygens, the wife of the minister from Holland, on being escorted to the supper-table, perceived Mrs. Eaton already seated at the head of the table, and an empty chair by her side which was intended for Mrs. H. Having declined, although requested by Mr. Van Buren, in her own Dutch tongue, to be introduced to Mrs. Eaton, she now refused to occupy the seat to which she had been escorted and thus be compelled to *appear* to be on social terms with her; and, taking her husband's arm, with stately dignity, she walked out of the room, and immediately took her carriage home.

This display of dignity, spirit, and self-respect by Mrs. Huygens greatly incensed General Jackson, who threatened to send the Dutch minister home. But Mr. Van Buren had won his heart, and from this time to the death of the general never lost it.

The winter was a gay one, though not comparable to the gay seasons of late years. Parties were frequent, not large, but the more cheerful and agreeable. The receptions at the Executive mansion were not then those multitudinous and promiscuous gatherings which now occur there. No one then thought of attending them who had not the *entrée* to the best circles of Washington society: they were made up, therefore, of the most distinguished and refined people in the city, either permanently or temporarily resident here. Party politics had its influence, to be sure, so far as to prevent some from attending parties given by those who were specially obnoxious to their opponents of either side.

Mrs. General Porter's parties were the delight of all,—Adams men and Jackson men alike,—and her rooms were always crowded. General Porter was Secretary of War, had distinguished himself by his gallant conduct in the War of 1812, on the northern frontier, had received the thanks of Congress, and been presented with a gold medal, voted by Congress. Upon the appointment of Mr. Barbour as minister to England, in June, 1828, General Porter succeeded him as a member of Mr. Adams's cabinet. He had been a member of Congress when the War of 1812 was declared, and had raised a large volunteer force in Western New York, of which he had the command.

He was a man of great mental and physical vigor, and agreeably surprised the prominent men at Washington, who had known little of him, by the ability he exhibited as Secretary of War.

Mrs. Porter was a model woman, wife, mother, and mistress of her household. She was the daughter of Mr. Breckinridge, of Kentucky, at one time Attorney-General of the United States, and sister of the eminent divines the Revs. Robert and John Breckinridge. Like the Roman matrons and the royal ladies of England in ancient times, the members of Mr. Breckinridge's household, as of all others, seventy-five years ago, were accustomed to perform domestic duties, and deemed it no degradation: the knowledge and ability to do so were then necessary accomplishments for a lady and wife. No one possessed these accomplishments in a higher degree than the daughter of Attorney-General Breckinridge and wife of Major-General Porter. But no one shone with more brilliancy in the drawing-room than the accomplished, domestic housewife. Easy, graceful, self-possessed, quick in repartee, piquant in her remarks when she chose to be, a keen observer of character, with great tact, few were her equals in conversation, few could keep a circle gathered around her, of gentlemen or ladies, in better humor or more entertained with her playful badinage and sprightly wit. Yet, with all her playful wit and brilliant conversation, she had a large, generous heart, full of sympathy, as every poor or unfortunate or suffering person who came within the sphere of her observation, appealed to her benevolence, or sought her counsel, had reason to know. Her piety was as genuine as it was unostentatious. She was a proud woman; yet to the ordinary observer, and to the humble, she was as free from pride as the most humble. She was proud of her lineage,—of father, mother, and brothers; proud of her husband and children, as she had reason to be.* Her pride was the consciousness that she was the peer of the highest and best in the land; but she felt, at the same time, that the poor and heart-stricken, if virtuous, were her own peers. She seemed

* The late gallant Colonel Peter Augustus Porter, who was killed at the battle of Cold Harbor at the head of his regiment, was her son, and a son worthy his parents. No more valuable life was lost during the rebellion.

to feel above no one, but that no one was above her: pride and humility beautifully blended formed her character. She was equally admired and beloved by high and low, rich and poor, bond and free; for who could resist her winning manner? She was the life, soul, and spirit of the administration circles while in Washington, from June, 1828, to the 4th of March, 1829.

The following anecdote of her is characteristic, and may not be uninteresting.

Her ordinary apparel was very plain. Being in the vicinity of Batavia, whither she went with her carriage on business, she stopped at the hotel to feed her horses and dine. Going in to dinner, she left her bonnet, which was a very plain one, upon the table of the sitting-room. Meantime, a wedding-party arrived, full of fun and glee, and on her return to the sitting-room one of the gentlemen of the party had her bonnet on the end of his cane, carrying it about and offering it for sale at auction. Mrs. Porter waited a few moments, and then said to the auctioneer that if he could not get a satisfactory bid for it she would take it; whereupon he tossed it to her as if she had been some one as inferior as the bonnet, by which he judged the owner. Mrs. Porter then entered her carriage and left for home.

Next day two or three gentlemen called upon General Porter, at Black Rock, to whom they had letters of introduction, and were invited to dine with him the day after. Coming down from Buffalo, where they had stopped, they and the ladies with them were ushered into the parlor, and in a few minutes General and Mrs. Porter entered. In Mrs. Porter the party immediately recognized the *woman* whose bonnet they had made so much sport of. She received them with all the grace and dignity natural to her, perhaps with a little more than was her wont, as she immediately recognized them. Their feelings during the dinner may be guessed, but nothing was said; nothing could be said without making matters worse. Mrs. Porter was amply revenged as she saw their mortification and embarrassment.

The auctioneer said, afterwards, that he hunted for a knot-hole out of which to escape, and he was sure he must have behaved very awkwardly at dinner.

Tried by the usual standard, she would hardly be ranked among "the first ladies of the land," certainly not as a *fashionable* one, as she never spent her summers and her thousands at Newport, Long Branch, or Saratoga, or her winters in Paris. She was so unfashionable and destitute of taste as to prefer her own beautiful, happy home, immediately on the banks of the Niagara, to all the fashionable watering-places in the world, with their crowds of pleasure-seekers, who find no rational enjoyment at home, nor contentment anywhere.

GENERAL JACKSON DECLINES TO PAY THE CUSTOMARY VISIT OF RESPECT TO THE PRESIDENT.

On arriving at Washington, General Jackson declined to pay the customary visit of respect to the President, on the ground, as alleged, that he could not shake the hand of one who had attained the office by bargain and corruption. This incident caused much comment among all parties, and was warmly condemned by the most discreet of his own friends. They had not forgotten that he was on the occasion of Mr. Adams's inauguration one of the first to step forward and tender him his hand and congratulations, and they knew that he had no more evidence now that unfair and dishonorable means had been used to elect Mr. Adams, than he had then; and if he could take Mr. Adams by the hand *then*, why not *now?*

Simultaneously with the arrival of the President elect came, for the first time in the history of our government on such an occasion, crowds of office-seekers; those who had joined and swelled the hue and cry of denunciation of "extravagance," "corruption," "bargain and intrigue" against the administration, and had hurrahed for Jackson. The city was full to overflowing of these cormorant patriots. That they were to be "rewarded" was thus announced to them by the "Telegraph," the organ of the party, on the 2d of November, 1828:

"We know not what line of policy General Jackson will adopt. We take it for granted, however, that HE WILL REWARD HIS FRIENDS AND PUNISH HIS ENEMIES."

That this "line of policy" was to be adopted seemed to be a well-understood fact among the leading seekers, a large number of whom were editors of the principal Jackson papers. But there was a multitude gathered here belonging to a class far below them, the like of whom had never before been seen at the capital as expectants of office, and whose presence was mortifying to many of the high-minded friends of the general, especially from the South, whence none of this class came, and, indeed, very few of any class.

Mr. Calhoun was looked upon at this time as "lord of the ascendant," "heir-apparent," and sure of succeeding to the Presidency at the end of four years, as the Jackson creed and cry had been "one term," which had taken with the people and aided his election. How he "missed his mark" will appear hereafter.

A SPICY DEBATE.

Mr. Smyth, of Virginia, supposing General Jackson was sincere in recommending an alteration of the Constitution so as to prevent any one man from holding the office of President for more than one term, had introduced into the House, at a previous session, a resolution to alter the Constitution in accordance with General Jackson's idea; but, being informed that his proposition was a very good one for the *outs*, but very bad for the *ins*, he rose one morning in the House and withdrew his resolution. As quick as thought John C. Wright, of Ohio, rose, was recognized by the Speaker,—Stevenson,—and removed Mr. Smyth's resolution.

Mr. Wright had been endeavoring during the whole session —this was, I think, in February—to obtain the floor, but in vain: the Speaker would never see him. He had got it now, in the morning hour, and could hold it, day by day, indefinitely. He determined to avail himself of it to say what he had to say. He was a speaker of no mean ability, fluent, sharp, caustic, and sarcastic.

A short time previous to Mr. Smyth's withdrawal of his resolution, anonymous notes had been laid upon the desks of some members, calling upon them to vote for it; and as an inducement to do so, the writer endeavored to show how much better would be their chances of obtaining the Presidency if the

Constitution should be so altered as to limit its possession by any one man to a single term. There was not a doubt that these notes emanated from the mover of the resolution.

Mr. Wright, in commencing his remarks, alluded to these notes, and exhibited one of them, which drew a crowd of members around him. He said they reminded him of a certain proclamation issued by a general on the Niagara frontier during the war.

Mr. Smyth here sprang to his feet and called the member from Ohio to order. Mr. Wright sat down. The Speaker said, "The gentleman from Virginia will state his point of order."

Mr. Smyth said "his point of order was, that the member from Ohio had alluded to and spoken of a proclamation which was not before the House."

The Speaker, with a peculiar mischievous twinkle of his eye, said, "The *cheer* cannot decide whether the gentleman from Ohio is in order or not until the *cheer* hears the proclamation read."

This produced great merriment in all parts of the House, and, as General Smyth had no particular desire to have the proclamation read, he sat down, and Mr. Wright proceeded.

Every one understood then what the proclamation was; there are few living now who know anything about it. An explanation is therefore necessary.

General Smyth was at one time in command on the Niagara frontier, during the War o 1812, and issued a grandiloquent proclamation to the people of Western New York, calling upon them to volunteer and join his army: "come in regiments; come in companies; come in squads; come in pairs; come singly, and march with me into Canada." He made a great bluster about invading Canada, but finally did nothing, and was removed. Everybody was disgusted with his bluster and brag, and he became the laughing-stock of the nation, obtaining the sobriquets of "Proclamation" and "Braggadocio Smyth." Hence the Speaker's sly humor in saying, "the *cheer* cannot decide without hearing the proclamation read,"—the very last thing General Smyth desired.

Mr. Wright now resumed the floor, and went on till the close of the morning hour, in running a parallel between the *notes* and the proclamation: "Come, all you patriots who want to be President, and vote for my resolution. Come in regiments; come in companies; come in squads; come in pairs; come singly."

Mr. Wright occupied the morning hour, or that portion of it not taken up by other business, for three or four days, hitting right and left, and paying off old scores; this being the only opportunity he would have of doing it.

CHAPTER III.

General Jackson inaugurated.—His Inaugural Address.—The Multitude enter the White House with Him.—A Terrible Jam.—A Disorderly Rabble fill the House and scramble for the Refreshments designed for the Drawing-Room.—They damage the Chairs and Sofas with their Hob-Nailed Shoes and Mud from the Canal.—General Jackson's First Cabinet.—"Retrenchment and Reform."—"Rewarding Friends and Punishing Enemies."—Reign of Terror.—Why and how Judge McLean became a Justice of the Supreme Court.—Excitement at the South on the Subject of the Tariff, and at the North on account of Morgan's Abduction.—The Case of Tobias Watkins.—The Twenty-first Congress meets December 7, 1829.—General Jackson sounds the First Blast of War against the United States Bank in his Message.—The Great Debate between Mr. Webster and Colonel Hayne.—Colonel Hayne.—Coolness between General Jackson and Mr. Calhoun.—General Jackson fires a Shot into Nullification.—His Celebrated Toast, "Our Federal Union: it must be preserved."—Georgia and the Cherokees.—Rupture between General Jackson and Mr. Calhoun.—The Breaking-up of General Jackson's First Cabinet.—Mr. Van Buren appointed Minister to England.—A New Cabinet appointed.—Mr. Livingston.—Mr. McLane.—The Kitchen Cabinet.—Anti-Masonic Nomination for President, October, 1831.—Mr. Wirt nominated.—National Republican Convention nominates Mr. Clay for President.—First Session of the Twenty-second Congress.—Mr. Clay in the Senate.—Brings in a Bill to reduce Revenue Duties.—Makes an Able Speech.—Colonel Hayne replies.—A Brutal Assault upon a Member of the House.—Hot Discussion in the House on the Occasion.—The President charged with inciting his Myrmidons to attack Members to silence Opposition.—General Houston, the Assailant, reprimanded by the Speaker, by Order of the House.—Attempt of Heard to assassinate Mr. Arnold, a Member of the House.—Young Men's National Convention at Washington.—Incidents.—Rejection of the Nomination of Mr. Van Buren as Minister to England.—In the Debate, Senator Marcy proclaims the Dogma that "to the Victors belong the Spoils of Office."—How the Nomination of General Jackson for a Second Term was procured.—William B. Lewis's Letters.—Baltimore Jackson Convention.—Nomination of Mr. Van Buren as Vice-President.—Mr. William C. Braddley, of Vermont, nails the Charge of Bargain and Corruption to the Counter in this Convention.—Distribution of the Proceeds of the Public Lands.—Tariff Bill of 1832.—The Case of the Cherokees.—General Jackson assumes the Right to support the Constitution as he understands it, independent of the Supreme Court.—Application of the Bank of the United States for a Re-Charter.—Mr. Adams's Report.—The New Hampshire Intrigue to obtain Control of the Bank.—The Veto of the Bank Bill.—Passage of the "Force" or "Bloody Bill."—Verplanck's Tariff Bill.—Mr. Clay's Compromise Bill.—Mr. Webster opposed to it.—It is passed.—Anecdote of Mr. Calhoun and Mr. Simmons.—Mr. Clay's Land or Distribution Bill.—An Episode.—Mr. Webster and Mr. Poindexter.—Presidential Election, 1832.—General Jackson re-elected by an Overwhelming Majority.

GENERAL JACKSON'S INAUGURAL ADDRESS.—THE MULTITUDE ENTER THE WHITE HOUSE WITH HIM.—TERRIBLE JAM.—HIS CABINET.

GENERAL JACKSON was sworn into office as President of the United States on the 4th of March, 1829. His inaugural address was artfully drawn to mean anything or nothing, except where it was intended to give a back-handed blow to the outgoing administration. For instance, with the exciting questions of protection to domestic manufactures and internal improvements he deals in Delphic generalities.

The following paragraph, however, *had* meaning, and both indirectly or impliedly cast censure upon Mr. Adams's administration, and foreshadowed the use to be made of offices, as well as the proscription for opinion's sake, which immediately followed:

"The recent demonstration of public sentiment inscribes on the list of executive duties, in characters too legible to be overlooked, the task of *reform;* which will require, particularly, the correction of those abuses that have brought the Federal government into conflict with the freedom of elections, and the counteraction of those causes which have disturbed the rightful course of appointment, and have placed or continued power in unfaithful or incompetent hands."

There are very serious implied charges in this sentence. *First,* that the Federal government, under Mr. Adams, had in some way interfered with elections; a charge never before made, never attempted to be sustained, and utterly destitute of truth.

Second. What is meant by "disturbed the rightful course of appointment" no one could ever explain.

Third. The charge of having "placed or continued power in unfaithful or incompetent hands" is equally untrue.

Mr. Adams was both careful and fortunate in selecting not only *competent* men, but men of superior abilities, for all the offices he filled. One only of all his appointees proved unfaithful, and the amount the government lost by him was very trifling.

Whatever might be said or believed then, we now know that his administration was one of the purest, ablest, and most economical we have ever had. Even Washington's was not more so. It was calumniated out of existence, and damning obloquy cast upon it, so long as the people could be made to believe the falsehoods uttered against it.

From the Capitol, at the east front of which General Jackson was sworn in by Chief-Justice Marshall and delivered his inaugural, he proceeded to the White House with such an accompaniment as was never before beheld in Washington.

A Washington lady of high culture and social position thus described the scene:

"The President was literally pursued by a motley concourse of people, riding, running, helter-skelter, striving who should first gain admittance into the Executive mansion, where it was understood that refreshments were to be distributed. The halls were filled with a disorderly rabble scrambling for the refreshments designed for the drawing-rooms! the people forcing their way into the saloons, mingling with the foreign ministers and citizens surrounding the President. . . . China and glass to the amount of several thousands of dollars were broken in the struggle to get at the ices and cakes, though punch and other drinkables had been carried out in tubs and buckets to the people."

Another writer who witnessed the scene says, "A profusion of refreshments had been provided. Orange-punch by barrels full was made; but, as the waiters opened the door to bring it out, a rush would be made, the glasses broken, the pails of liquor upset, and the most painful confusion prevailed. To such a degree was this carried, that wine and ice-creams could not be brought out to the ladies, and tubs of punch were taken from the lower story into the garden to lead off the crowd from the rooms. . . . It was mortifying to see men, with boots heavy with mud, standing on the damask-satin-covered chairs and sofas."

Judge Story wrote, "The President was visited at the palace by immense crowds of all sorts of people, from the highest and most polished down to the most vulgar and gross in the nation.

I never saw such a mixture. The reign of King Mob seemed triumphant."

I was then in the city, and the reports of those present confirmed the above accounts.

GENERAL JACKSON'S FIRST CABINET.

General Jackson's first cabinet was constituted as follows: Martin Van Buren, New York, Secretary of State; Samuel D. Ingham, Pennsylvania, Secretary of the Treasury; John H. Eaton, Tennessee, Secretary of War; John Branch, North Carolina, Secretary of the Navy; John M. Berrien, Georgia, Attorney-General; William T. Barry, Kentucky, Postmaster-General.

Of these gentlemen, Messrs. Eaton, Branch, and Berrien were members of the United States Senate, and Mr. Ingham of the House of Representatives. Mr. Van Buren had been a member of the United States Senate up to the first of January, only two months before.

Of members of Congress, besides those named as cabinet officers, the following were immediately appointed, namely:

Louis McLane, of Delaware, Senator, Minister to England; John Chandler, of Maine, Senator, Collector of Customs; Geo. W. Owen, of Alabama, member of the House of Representatives, Collector of Customs; Francis Baylies, Massachusetts, member of the House of Representatives, Collector of Customs; John G. Stower, New York, member of the House of Representatives, District Attorney, Florida; T. P. Moore, Kentucky, member of the House of Representatives, Minister to Colombia.

But these were not all: during the first six months of General Jackson's administration more "Federal appointments devolved upon members of Congress" than had before fallen to their lot from the commencement of the government, in 1789, down to the 4th of March, 1829,—forty years. Thus did the President "practice upon the maxims he recommended to others."

The Washington lady whom I have already quoted, speaking of the condition of things at the capital at this period, says,—

"With the advent of Jacksonism was inaugurated proscription for opinion's sake, and a state of party hostility ensued which not only strictly separated political opponents, but pervaded social relations and severed friendly ties. It was indeed a dark era in the capital, which had been characterized by elegance of manners and the charm of high breeding."

It is hardly possible for a person not familiar with the circumstances to conceive the anxiety and distress which this new order of things, this "reign of terror," produced in Washington.

It must be remembered that up to that time no person had been removed from an office in one of the departments for any other cause than incompetency or unfaithfulness; and these cases were exceedingly rare. Heads of bureaus, and clerks, upon accepting office and entering upon their duties, did so with no expectation of its being a mere temporary arrangement. They gave up all other business and devoted themselves to the duties of their office; and it was *then* thought that the longer the service the more capable and useful became the officer.

But now came a change, "a great political revolution," as the new Secretary of the Treasury designated it: a sweep was to be made of all, in the departments and elsewhere, who did not "belong to the household of the faith." The axe fell upon scores who had held their positions many years,—had families, some of them large, and no other means of support than their salaries. They were unfitted for entering into other business; some of them, indeed, were too old to do so. What was the prospect before them? Hunger and want. What was the humane, the *refined* and *feeling* reply to statements of this kind? "*Root, hog, or die.*" So said the "Telegraph."

WHY AND HOW JUDGE MCLEAN BECAME A JUSTICE OF THE SUPREME COURT.

What I am about to relate in regard to Judge McLean's appointment was stated by General Cass, at General Porter's, in my presence, on the evening after the conversation between General Jackson and Judge McLean, which I here give, occurred, and which, he said, he had just had repeated to him by the latter gentleman, with whom we knew he was on very intimate terms.

Mr. McLean had been Postmaster-General about six years, under Mr. Monroe and Mr. Adams, and was understood, as he was "a Jackson man," to be an aspirant for the position of Secretary of War. But, as General Jackson had determined to put Major Eaton at the head of that department, Mr. McLean's wishes could not be gratified. But the general proposed that if he would remain where he was the salary of the office should be raised, and it should be made a cabinet office. With this Mr. McLean was content, and the new arrangement was soon publicly understood.

It was soon known, however, that General Jackson would adopt the policy indicated by the "Telegraph" in the preceding November: viz., that of "*rewarding his friends and punishing his enemies.*" As Mr. McLean had always refused to make appointments and removals upon the ground of party affinities, and had strongly condemned such a practice, the inquiry was naturally made, "If General Jackson adopts this policy, what will Mr. McLean do? Will he carry it out, or refuse?"

This question was so often put, and so emphatically answered by his nearest friends in the negative, that the general deemed it proper to come to an understanding with, and sent for, Mr. McLean, to whom he stated that he should adopt the policy of removing from office such persons as had, during the canvass for President, taken an active part in politics, and asked whether he had any objection to this line of action.

To this Mr. McLean replied in the negative; "but," said he, "if this rule should be adopted, it will operate as well against *your* friends as those of Mr. Adams, as it must be impartially executed." To this General Jackson made no reply; but, after walking up and down the room several times, as if cogitating with himself, he said, "Mr. McLean, will you accept a seat upon the bench of the Supreme Court?" This was answered in the affirmative; and he was in due time nominated, as we, who had had the story related to us, expected.

EXCITEMENT AT THE SOUTH AND AT THE NORTH.

The effervescence and agitation at the South on the subject of the tariff continued with unabated heat during the vacation of Congress, and was culminating into a serious if not alarming crisis.

At the North, in the western part of New York and in Pennsylvania, the public feeling was scarcely less demonstrative on another subject, that of the abduction of William Morgan, before spoken of.

In May, at a sitting of the Court of General Sessions, at Canandaigua, Judge Howell presiding, Eli Bruce, sheriff of Niagara County, and John Whitney were convicted of kidnapping Morgan, and sentenced, the one to close confinement for two years and four months, the other for one year and three months.

On the trial it was proved that Morgan had been taken in a close carriage, his eyes bandaged, from Batavia to Lockport, where he was put into a cell and confined during the night, and from thence next day to Fort Niagara, at the mouth of the Niagara River, where he was confined in the powder-magazine. I shall speak of his fate hereafter.

CASE OF TOBIAS WATKINS.

During the summer it was discovered that Dr. Tobias Watkins, late Fourth Auditor, was a defaulter to the amount of about two thousand dollars. For this he was indicted, tried, convicted, and imprisoned. The affair caused a great stir in Washington, and was availed of to prove the corruptions and defalcations charged upon the outgoing government. Defalcations being then of rare occurrence, hardly known, indeed, the affair caused a great sensation, and was looked upon in a more criminal light than such transactions now are, since, unfortunately, they have become so frequent and of vastly larger proportions.

Dr. Watkins was a man of prominence, highly esteemed in social life, and one of the last who would have been suspected of doing a wrong act or attempting to defraud the government. That he had no such intent, but merely used the money as a temporary relief from pecuniary embarrassment, his personal friends claimed and believed. The matter assumed a political significance, and was the cause of as much exultation on the one side as of mortification and regret on the other. He was imprisoned in a cell, over which was painted, in large letters, "*Criminal Apartment*,"—a pleasant sight to his affectionate and faithful wife, who visited him as often as she was permitted to do so. He lived many years after undergoing this imprisonment, a broken-down and ruined man. He had been prosecuted with a display of exultation and vindictiveness altogether disproportioned to the offense he had committed, and which must have been prompted by the very unfriendly feelings entertained towards Mr. Clay, his friend, by Amos Kendall. There is no other way of accounting for the malice shown towards him, and the insatiable desire to punish and disgrace him.

But how this case sinks into insignificance when compared with the stealings and defalcations of a host of Federal officers in 1834, '35, '36, and '37, under General Jackson, and exposed in 1837,—to say nothing of the stupendous stealings of the Tammany ring in New York! Did the administration which so patriotically prosecuted Dr. Watkins utter a word against Swartwout, who pocketed over one million two hundred thousand dollars, or Price, who took seventy-five thousand dollars? Not a word. And the host of land-office defaulters might have never been heard of but for Mr. Wise's committee of investigation, which brought those defalcations to light and exposed them to the world.

The Twenty-first Congress assembled on the first Monday, 7th, of December, 1829. With the exception of two or three paragraphs, the message contained nothing worthy of note. In this document was sounded the first blast of war upon the United States Bank from the Executive. Thus spoke the President:

"The charter of the Bank of the United States expires in 1836, and its stockholders will most probably apply for a renewal of their privileges. In order to avoid the evils resulting from precipitancy in a measure involving such important principles and such deep pecuniary interests, I feel that I cannot, in justice to the parties interested, too soon present it to the deliberate consideration of the legislature and the people. Both the constitutionality and the expediency of the law creating this bank are well questioned by a large proportion of our fellow-citizens, and it must be admitted by all that it has failed in the great end of establishing a uniform and sound currency. Under these circumstances, if such an institution is deemed essential to the fiscal operations of the government, I submit to the wisdom of the legislature whether a national one, founded upon the credit of the government and its revenues, might not be devised, which would avoid all constitutional difficulties, and at the same time secure all the advantages to the government and country that were expected to result from the present bank."

Thus the President had brought up the question of re-charter six or seven years before the expiration of the charter; and yet he berated the directors for applying for a re-charter two or three years later, as being premature!

THE GREAT DEBATE BETWEEN SENATORS HAYNE AND WEBSTER.—THE SOUTH AGAINST THE NORTH.

Early in the first session of the Twenty-first Congress—January, 1830—Mr. Foot, Senator from Connecticut, introduced the following resolution:

"*Resolved,* That the Committee on Public Lands be instructed to inquire into the expediency of limiting for a certain period the sales of the public lands to such lands only as have heretofore been offered for sale and are subject to entry at the minimum price. Also, whether the office of Surveyor-General may not be abolished without detriment to the public service."

There was nothing in the resolution itself which gave it the importance it acquired by the debate to which it gave rise, and, but for its being seized upon as an occasion for the display of sectional animosity and denunciation, it might have been passed and acted on without creating a ripple in the proceedings of the Senate. But the debate which followed its introduction and grew out of it was the most important and memorable, on account of the great principles which were discussed, and the high reputations and eminent abilities of the two principal speakers, that had occurred in Congress since the no less memorable debate upon Jay's treaty, in 1794, when Madison and Fisher Ames were the two great speakers.

Mr. Benton opened the debate in a fierce onslaught not only upon the harmless resolution but upon New England, charging that section of the country with perpetual hostility to the West, mainly in endeavoring to prevent the sale of the public lands and emigration to settle them, and thus to check the growth of the West.

The debate assumed a wide range, and embraced almost every political subject that had agitated the country since the formation of the Constitution. It was eminently of a party and acrimonious character, the members of the two parties, Jackson and Anti-Jackson, attacking and defending with their sharpest weapons, and with a *vim* to which the asperities that grew out of the Presidential election of 1828, and the sweeping proscriptions of those in office which had followed, gave force.

It lasted over two months, and was participated in by nearly all the Senators,—Benton, Barton, Burnett, Foot, Grundy, Holmes, Johnston, Knight, Livingston, Noble, Rowan, Robbins, Smith, and Sprague. Several of the speeches were continued from day to day, some gentlemen occupying the floor at intervals for eight or ten days.

But the great and absorbing interest of this celebrated debate, that which has given it the historical importance which it bears, culminated in the discussion between Mr. Webster and Colonel Hayne of the principles of the Constitution and the character and powers of our government. Under the lead of Mr. Calhoun, South Carolina was then arraying herself against the general government, threatening to resist the execution of the revenue laws, which she denounced as oppressive and unconstitutional. The positions he assumed as the true interpretation of the Constitution were, in fact, *nullification*, afterwards, but not then, avowed. Colonel Hayne and Colonel Benton were in accord in their hostility to New England, and she was assailed by both. This aroused Mr. Webster, who came to the defense of his own section of country, and especially his beloved Massachusetts. Replying to Colonel Hayne, he had incidentally introduced the subject of slavery, and drew a comparison between Kentucky and Ohio,—a slave and a free State.

This aroused Colonel Hayne, who showed impatience to

reply, saying, in opposing the postponement of the debate to accommodate Mr. Webster, who had a case to argue in the Supreme Court, and had just come from that tribunal, that he had a shot to return, and, laying his hand on his breast, that he wished to relieve himself of something that rankled there. Mr. Webster then said, with no little spirit, "Let the debate proceed: I am ready to receive the Senator's shot."

Both gentlemen had spoken, and in doing so had only warmed each other up and sharpened the conflict. They were, respectively, the champions of the sections of the nation they represented and the principles held by their respective sections. The field was even greater than the celebrated "field of the cloth of gold:" it was the floor of the Senate of the United States. They knew that not only the eyes of the sections they respectively represented and championed, but the eyes of the whole nation were upon them. They felt that the questions they were discussing, involving as they did the future fate of the nation, the powers of its government, were the most important that could arise; and they put forth their utmost strength.

Colonel Hayne was a son of South Carolina, of whom the State was justly proud,—the son, too, of the patriot who fell a victim to British cruelty during the Revolution. He was a highly-educated gentleman and lawyer, of refined and fascinating manners, exceedingly amiable and unassuming, with a mellifluous voice, which he knew well how to modulate. What he said of Mr. Webster—"that he had never heard him utter a word in a careless or vulgar style; that he seemed never to forget his own dignity or be unmindful of the character and feelings of others"—may with equal truth be said of him. As pure as a child in morals, he was as simple as a child in manners: he was therefore equally admired and beloved by all who had the happiness to know him. He was of slender form, but lithe and graceful in his movements, and pleasing in his general aspect. He was the polished Saladin of the contest, Webster the ponderous Cœur de Lion.

Mr. Webster was always scrupulously well dressed when he expected to speak in the Senate, and on this occasion particularly so. He was then in the prime of manhood,—forty-eight years of age; his thick, glossy hair black as the raven's wing; his forehead broad and massive, towering above his large, dark, deep-set, wonderfully-powerful eyes; his garb, a blue coat with metal buttons, a buff vest rounding gracefully over his full abdomen; his shoulders broad, his chest deep and capacious. A white cravat encircled his great neck, the support of his ponderous head.

When Mr. Webster consented to receive, then and there, the "shot" which Colonel Hayne expressed a desire to discharge, the latter took the floor, January 21, 1830, and opened his battery. He spoke to a full Senate, and to galleries and lobbies filled to their utmost capacity, chiefly by ladies. Around him gathered the prominent Jackson Senators, who encouraged him by their approving smiles, and sometimes aided him by notes handed to him. Mr. Calhoun never appeared more happy, and frequently sent notes to his friend and pupil, giving him hints, suggestions, and facts. Colonel Hayne did not conclude his speech on the first day, and the Senate adjourned over to the 25th, when he closed. It was a great occasion for the South, and loud were her exultations that he was more than a match for Mr. Webster. The "Telegraph" was especially jubilant.

Colonel Hayne had spoken of Mr. Webster's sleeping on his first speech. Mr. Webster replied, true, he did, and as he had no opportunity to reply instanter, the floor having been given to Colonel Benton, he must sleep on it or not sleep at all. But he had no time to give it a thought till he rose to reply the next day. And now Mr. Webster replied the next day to Colonel Hayne's second two-days' speech. This reply is admitted to be the ablest speech Mr. Webster ever made, one of the greatest ever delivered in Congress, and not surpassed by any in the British Parliament; and yet the only time he had for preparation was from the evening of one day to the morning of the next.

The friends of each of the great orators, or those who concurred with them in their respective views, claimed the superiority in logical argument, beauty of illustration, just deduction, and force and elegance of rhetoric. But, as there was no such test of superiority in this instance as there was in the great race between Eclipse and Henry,—the North and the South,—scarcely less celebrated than the debate, each party could adhere to its own predilection. Posterity has settled the question. Mr. Webster's second speech on that occasion has placed him, as an orator and statesman, in the rank of Demosthenes, Cicero, Chatham, Burke, and Ames.

"That speech did more than make the name of WEBSTER immortal. It achieved more, much more, than a triumph over the Southerner and his heresies. It fired the patriotic heart of the country. It made it rejoice that the country was ours, then and forever. It planted deep, deep, in every true American heart that sentiment so vital to our duty, our honor, our fame, our power, our happiness, our freedom, 'Liberty and Union, now and forever, one and inseparable.'"*

The Senate-chamber on this occasion was literally filled to overflowing. "The press of auditors," says Mr. Niles, "seems to have been unprecedented: grave Senators were lost in the crowd of ladies, every convenient place for sitting or standing, save the Vice-President's seat and the Secretary's table, being occupied by them." The occasion was a memorable one; and though more than forty years have passed away, and every Senator and officer of the Senate then present has gone to his long home, there are still a few persons lingering in Washington who well remember the intense interest felt, and the universal discussion of the merits of the two great orators.

On the day of the delivery of Mr. Webster's speech, the Senate met and transacted some formal business; but all were waiting for the knight who was to break a lance that day,—"the great defender of the Constitution," as he was ever after called. Mr. J. M. Clayton, who had dined with Mr. Webster the evening before, relating the circumstances to me, said, "I kept my eye on the door. Presently in walked, with a slow and stately step, the observed of all observers, dressed with scrupulous care, as he always was on such occasions. As soon as he entered, I left my seat and went so as to meet him, as if by accident. As we met, I asked, in a very low tone, 'Are you well charged?'

* Reverdy Johnson.

'Seven fingers,' in a similar tone, was the reply; and I passed on, as he did, to his seat."

Sportsmen will understand what "seven fingers" meant; it having reference to the charge of a gun,—four fingers being a full charge. It seems by this that Mr. Webster felt that he was well prepared for his task.

"Mr. Webster," he said, "never for an instant hesitated for a word. The most appropriate one for the occasion presented itself the instant it was wanted. His elocution was the steady flow of molten gold. I never heard him speak after that, when the words he required were so completely at his command and so readily presented themselves as on that occasion. The subject to be discussed,—the Constitution of the United States,—true constitutional doctrines to be enforced,—the North to be defended,—the heresies of Nullification to be overturned and scattered to the winds,—these filled and inspired his great patriotic soul, and aroused every mental faculty he possessed. The occasion was a great one, and greatly and triumphantly did he meet it."

Mr. Hayne, in his speech, distinctly asserted the right of a State to nullify an act of Congress distasteful to her. Mr. Webster denied this power, and illustrated its practical operation in a manner so clear and forcible as to carry conviction to every unbiased mind. General Jackson subsequently, in his proclamation called forth by the threatening attitude of South Carolina, maintained the same construction of the Constitution. Still, however, this notion as belonging to *State rights* had taken too strong a hold of the Southern mind to be given up upon argument, as the Rebellion afterwards proved. The heresy had also taken root in some Northern minds, as a part of the Democratic creed. There is hardly a vestige of it now left north of the Susquehanna.

GENERAL JACKSON FIRES A SHOT INTO NULLIFICATION.—HIS CELEBRATED TOAST, "OUR FEDERAL UNION: IT MUST BE PRESERVED."

"The great debate," as that between Mr. Webster and Mr. Hayne was called, took place from the middle to the latter part of January, Mr. Webster's last and great speech being made on the 26th. This debate was the subject of constant comment by Senators and members of the House. It presented two opposite political doctrines: the one the doctrine "that in case of a plain, palpable violation of the Constitution by the general government, a State may interpose" and nullify the law for her own protection. This, no other than *nullification*, was the doctrine of Colonel Hayne. The other doctrine, that of Mr. Webster, was that this government is the independent offspring of the popular will. It is not the creature of State legislatures, and is not obliged to act through State agency. The Constitution has declared that "the Constitution, and laws of the United States made in pursuance thereof, shall be the supreme law of the land, anything in the Constitution or laws of any *State* to the contrary notwithstanding." In other words, it is a *national* government, possessing within itself all the powers necessary to enforce its laws and for its own preservation; and no State, or combination of States, has the power to arrest or prevent the execution of a law of the United States.

In order to give popularity to and strengthen what the nullifiers preferred to call the State's rights doctrine rather than nullification, it was determined to celebrate the birthday (13th of April) of Thomas Jefferson, the apostle of Democracy, by a banquet, to which the President and Vice-President, the Secretary of State, and others should be invited. Of this banquet Colonel Benton gives an account:

"There was a full assemblage when I arrived, and I observed gentlemen standing about in clusters in the anteroom and talking with animation on something apparently serious and which seemed to engross their thoughts. I soon discovered what it was,—that it came from the promulgation of the twenty-four regular toasts, which savored of the new doctrine of nullification, and which, acting on some previous misgivings, began to spread the feeling that the dinner was got up to inaugurate that doctrine and to make Mr. Jefferson its father. Many persons broke off, and refused to attend further; but the company was still numerous and ardent, as was proved by the number of volunteer toasts given—above eighty—in addition to the twenty-four regular toasts, and the numerous and animated speeches delivered. When the regular toasts were over, the President was called upon for a volunteer, and gave it,—the one which electrified the country, and has become historical:

"'OUR FEDERAL UNION: IT MUST BE PRESERVED.'

"This brief and simple sentiment, receiving emphasis and interpretation from all the attendant circumstances, and from the feeling which had been spreading from the time of Mr. Webster's speech, was received by the public as a proclamation from the President to announce a plot against the Union and to summon the people to its defense. Mr. Calhoun gave the next toast; and it did not allay the suspicions which were crowding every bosom. It was, 'The Union: next to Liberty, the most dear: may we all remember that it can only be preserved by respecting the rights of the States and distributing equally the benefit and burden of the Union!'

"The toast touched all the tender parts of the new question,—liberty *before* Union,—only to be preserved,—*State rights,*—inequality of *burdens* and *benefits.* These phrases, connecting themselves with Hayne's speech and with proceedings and publications in South Carolina, unveiled NULLIFICATION as a new and distinct doctrine in the United States, with Mr. Calhoun for its apostle, and a new party in the field, of which he was the leader. The proceedings of the day put an end to all doubt about the justice of Mr. Webster's grand peroration, and revealed to the public mind the fact of an actual design tending to dissolve the Union."

This celebrated toast was not an impromptu one, conceived and brought forth at the table by General Jackson, but one deliberately and carefully concocted at the White House before he left it for the banquet. He had an inkling of the purpose of the banquet, and might have stayed away; but he chose to face the young monster NULLIFICATION and deal him a stunning, if not a death blow. His course was characteristic of him, and by it he did more to strengthen the Union sentiment in the United States than he could have done in any other way.

Besides, he thus met the disunionists or nullifiers face to face, and gave them to understand what they might expect from him.

GEORGIA AND THE CHEROKEES.

Georgia wanted "more room" and more land. She had got rid of the Creeks, and had taken possession of their lands and distributed them by lottery among her citizens. But there was not enough for all, and she therefore took constructive possession of the whole territory occupied by the Cherokees by extending her laws over it and annexing the various parts of it to certain counties, or erecting them into new counties, at the same time abolishing all Indian laws.

Thus threatened, the Cherokees addressed a memorial to Congress. "We are told," they say, "if we do not leave the country which we dearly love, and betake ourselves to the Western wilds, the laws of the State [of Georgia] will be extended over us, and the time, 1st of June, 1830, is appointed for the execution of the edict. When we first heard of this, we were grieved, and appealed to our father the President, and begged that protection might be extended over us. But our father the President refused us protection, and decided in favor of the extension of the laws of the State over us. We dearly love our country, and it is due to your honorable bodies, as well as to us, to make known why we think the country is ours, and why we wish to remain in peace where we are.

"The land on which we stand we have received from our fathers, who possessed it from time immemorial, as a gift from our common Father in heaven. . . . This right of inheritance we have never *ceded*, nor ever *forfeited*." . . .

The Cherokees had at this time made great progress in civilization, in agriculture, and in the arts of domestic life, some of them having very fine, well-cultivated, and well-stocked farms. Some of their chiefs and principal men were highly educated, and exhibited great talents. In this respect they had no superiors among those who were now seeking to rob them of their lands and drive them into the wilderness and back to the savage condition from which they had emerged.

But the fiat had gone forth, and go they must,—as they did, finally, upon military compulsion.

A bill was introduced into Congress providing for the removal of the Cherokees to lands to be assigned them west of the Mississippi River, and, after long and earnest debate in both branches, was finally passed *as a party measure;* for in no other way could a majority in either House have been obtained for it, such was its palpable injustice, and so strong were the sympathy for the Indians and the feeling at the North against it.

The Indians again appealed to Congress in eloquent and beseeching language to be allowed to remain where they were, and to be protected by the government, and issued a touching address to the people of the United States; but their appeals, however pathetic, were in vain, except to increase the sympathy felt for them among religious people, and by all classes at the North generally. Orders were issued for their removal, and they were forced to abandon their homes and farms, some of them desirable residences and estates, where every comfort and many luxuries had been enjoyed.

The Indians endeavored to obtain protection through the Supreme Court of the United States, and with that view employed Mr. Wirt as their counsel. A correspondence took place between him and Governor Gilmer, of Georgia, previous to suit being commenced, which on the part of the latter was imperious in its tone and treated some parts of Mr. Wirt's letter with studied irony.

A suit was brought and argued in the Supreme Court; but the court declined to decide the questions brought before it, deeming them of a political rather than a judicial character. With Mr. Wirt was associated Mr. John Sergeant, of Philadelphia.

An Indian, George Tassels, being charged with committing a homicide in the Indian country after Georgia had extended her laws over it, was arrested, indicted, tried, and convicted before Judge Clayton, who sentenced him to be hung, and declared that should the Supreme Court of the United States issue a writ of error in the case he would pay no attention to it. A writ of error was issued in the case, but was disregarded, and

Tassels was hung. Nothing more was heard of the writ of error.

Great feeling and indignation were excited among the religious people of the United States by the arrest, imprisonment, and brutal treatment, by the authorities of Georgia, of several missionaries in the Indian country.

Mr. Adams had incurred the hostility of Georgia by protecting the Creeks and Cherokees against her impatient and grasping rapacity; General Jackson won her support by yielding to all her demands.

RUPTURE BETWEEN GENERAL JACKSON AND MR. CALHOUN.

I have mentioned how Mr. Calhoun was nominated as Vice-President on the ticket with General Jackson in Pennsylvania, through the instrumentality of his friend Mr. Dallas, with the understanding that General Jackson was to serve but one term and be succeeded by Mr. Calhoun. It was well understood by the leading men of the Jackson party, in March, 1829, when General Jackson was inaugurated, that Mr. Calhoun was to be his successor at the end of four years; though probably the former was in no way committed to this arrangement.

But Mr. Van Buren had not been many months in the cabinet ere there was a change in the political atmosphere, perceived only by those who had an inside view of affairs at Washington.

It was well known, to Southern gentlemen at least, that, though Mr. Crawford and Mr. Calhoun were members of Mr. Monroe's cabinet, there was no friendship between them, but rather the contrary; and Mr. Crawford, believing that Mr. Calhoun in some degree instigated the attack on him by Ninian Edwards in his celebrated "A. B." letters, was desirous to thwart Mr. Calhoun's aspirations.

With this view, probably, Mr. Crawford addressed a letter to Mr. John Forsyth, on the 30th of April, 1830, detailing Mr. Calhoun's acts and propositions in cabinet council in relation to General Jackson's doings in Florida, and particularly stating that "Mr. Calhoun's proposition in the cabinet was that General Jackson should be punished in some form." Of course this letter was intended for General Jackson's eye, and met it, whereupon he immediately addressed a note to Mr. Calhoun, inclosing a copy of Mr. Crawford's letter, calling his attention to it, and demanding an immediate, categorical answer.

As the doings in cabinet council are sacred, to be divulged by no one, the astonishment of Mr. Calhoun at the proceedings being thus reported after a lapse of many years, and the anxiety which this unwarrantable divulgence caused him, knowing as he did the wrath which the discovery of his unfriendly intentions towards General Jackson at the time mentioned would kindle, may be conceived. He replied, however, in a manly tone; and General Jackson rejoined, closing with the words, "Understanding you now, no further communication with you on this subject is necessary." This letter bore date May 30, 1830, and from this date the breach between the President and the Vice-President was complete, though not generally known for a considerable time.*

With this publication the controversy ended, but ended in a total separation of the two high official parties, leaving them irreconcilable enemies. Mr. Calhoun's address to the people of the United States, and the letters published with it, may be found in the fortieth volume of "Niles's Register," from page 11 to page 45. But it is not probable that any one at this day will take interest enough in the quarrel of two men who forty or fifty years ago filled a large space in the public eye and exercised a controlling influence on the public mind to read what was then read with so much avidity.

THE BREAKING-UP OF THE CABINET.

The rupture between General Jackson and Mr. Calhoun was one of the causes, but not the sole cause, of the breaking-up of the cabinet. There had been *social* troubles from the commencement of the Jackson dynasty. General Jackson had

* A writer in the "London Quarterly Review" for July, 1852, says, "Since the Revolution of 1688 there have been very few examples of members of a cabinet divulging its secrets. In some rare cases men have been provoked to such revelations; but the rest, including the best, have forborne under all circumstances and provocations."

declared that he would place Major Eaton where the ladies would be *compelled* to visit his wife.* But, though the general might command an army, he found, as many even more distinguished warriors had found before him, that

> "If women will, they will, you may depend on't;
> And if they won't, they won't, and there's an end on't."

The wives of some of the members of the cabinet would hold no social intercourse with Mrs. Eaton; neither would Mrs. Calhoun, Mrs. General Macomb, Mrs. General Towson, and many others. This was a constant source of irritation. Every possible means was resorted to to induce these ladies to meet her in society, but in vain.

It was understood that Mr. Ingham, Secretary of the Treasury, who rumor said had been forced upon General Jackson by Mr. Calhoun's friends to the exclusion of Mr. Baldwin, the President's choice, was a friend of Mr. Calhoun. Thus con-

* This can hardly be understood by those who are not familiar with the circumstances which created a "tempest in a teapot" in Washington in the winter and spring of 1829, without explanation; and, however unpleasant it is to relate matters such as then disturbed society in the capital, it becomes necessary to do so, as they were the means of bringing about events that must be noted.

Major John H. Eaton, United States Senator, and the special friend of General Jackson, was married to Mrs. Timberlake, *née* O'Neil, in December, 1828. On her return to the city from a wedding-tour, in the early part of January, 1829, Mrs. Eaton called and left cards at Mr. Calhoun's, General Peter B. Porter's, and one or two other places, making a first visit to those who by the laws of etiquette should be first visited by a Senator or his wife. The cards left at Mr. Calhoun's and General Porter's were unnoticed,—the visit not returned. Mrs. Eaton, as Mrs. Timberlake, had been long well known in Washington, and many ladies, among them Mrs. General Towson and Mrs. General Macomb, not only did not, but declared, in no secret manner, that they would not, visit Mrs. Eaton. This created a great hubbub in Washington, in the midst of which General Jackson arrived. Immediately Mrs. Eaton laid her case and complaints before him, when he swore, by the Eternal, that he would place Major Eaton in a position where the ladies would be compelled to visit Mrs. Eaton. Whereupon Mrs. Calhoun, Mrs. Towson, and other spunky ladies replied, according to report at the time, that neither General Jackson nor any other man could, or should, compel them to visit any woman they did not choose to visit. Jupiter took the part of Juno, but could not help her; and her woes and complaints disturbed the cabinet until it was broken up. I have already spoken of this matter; but this further explanation seems necessary.

stituted, there could be no harmony in the cabinet, and its dissolution was inevitable. It soon "went by the board."

Mr. Van Buren, whether by previous concert with General Jackson or not must be left to conjecture, tendered his resignation in a characteristic letter, in which a cause for this step was mistily stated; namely, that he was considered a candidate for the high office of President as General Jackson's successor, and it was therefore improper for him to remain in the cabinet. Why this fact should have such significance at this particular time no one could see. It had long been known that he was an aspirant for the Presidency, but he had not been spoken of publicly as a candidate; and, for aught any one could see, there was as much impropriety in his becoming a member of the cabinet in 1829 as there was in his remaining in it in 1830. But by giving this reason for retiring he announced his purpose of being a candidate to succeed General Jackson.

His resignation was followed by that of Major Eaton, Secretary of War. The other members of the cabinet were informed that an entire reorganization would take place, and that their resignations would be accepted. They were accordingly tendered.

That the refusal of the families of Messrs. Ingham, Branch, and Berrien to invite Mrs. Eaton to their parties or hold social intercourse with her was the real cause of the rupture of the cabinet there can be no doubt. Quite a voluminous correspondence was drawn out on this subject, consisting of letters from Mr. R. M. Johnson, Mr. Berrien, Mr. Ingham, Major Eaton, Mr. Calhoun, and Mr. Blair, which were published, and thus the public were let into the secrets of the cabinet.

Mr. Richard M. Johnson was deputed by the President to call on the refractory members. An interview took place at Mr. Berrien's house. What the purpose was, and what was said, Mr. Berrien afterwards stated in a letter, forced from him by circumstances, addressed to Mr. Johnson. From this letter we learn "that an impression had been made upon the mind of the President that a combination existed between Messrs. Ingham, Branch, and Berrien to exclude Mrs. Eaton from the society of Washington; . . . that this conviction had been produced upon his mind by the fact that those gentlemen had given large parties to which Mrs. Eaton had not been invited; that the President would in the future expect that at least on such occasions (that is to say, when large or general parties were given) Mrs. Eaton should be invited."

In reply to this, Mr. Berrien said "he would not permit the President or any other man to regulate the social intercourse of himself or his family, and that if such a requisition was persevered in he would retire from office."

Mr. Berrien refers to an interview he had with the President, in which "he expressly declined to discuss the question of the truth or falsehood of the reports to which he (the President) referred [reports in regard to Mrs. Eaton]. Without undertaking to decide whether they were true or false, it was his purpose merely to conform to the general sense of the community of which he had become a member, and he could not be induced to change that determination."

Mr. Ingham also made a public statement confirming that of Mr. Berrien. Mr. Branch, in a letter to Mr. Berrien, says, "My recollections of the interview [with Colonel Johnson,—spoken of by Mr. Berrien and Mr. Ingham] will most abundantly corroborate all that you have said."

The resignations of these gentlemen were immediately tendered, and they retired. Major Eaton having issued an address to the people in reference to the break-up of the cabinet, and brought in Mr. Calhoun's name, the latter replied. He said,—

"It is impossible to doubt that the main drift of Major Eaton's address is to hold me up as the real author of all the discord which is alleged to have prevailed in the late cabinet. . . .

"With this view, and in order to give a political aspect to the refusal of Mrs. Calhoun to visit Mrs. Eaton, he, Major Eaton, states that she and myself called in the first instance on him and Mrs. Eaton. . . . Unfortunately for Major Eaton, his statement is not correct. Mrs. Calhoun never called on Mrs. Eaton at the time he states, nor at any time before or since, nor did she ever leave her card for her, nor authorize any one to do so. . . .

"This is not the first time that Mrs. Calhoun has contradicted the statement that she had visited Mrs. Eaton. It was reported at the time that she had visited Mrs. Eaton, and that her card had been left. She then on all suitable occasions contradicted it, as directly and pointedly as she now does."

The real cause of the rupture of the cabinet cannot now be misunderstood. It was then a universal theme for editors, and of talk among the people.

Mr. Van Buren was, immediately after his resignation, appointed minister to England; the post he had coveted under Mr. Adams. Major Eaton was appointed governor of Florida, and Mr. Barry, minister to Spain. Mr. Ingham, Mr. Branch, and Mr. Berrien retired to private life, Mr. Ingham never again to leave it.

Mr. Berrien soon separated himself from the Jackson party, and eventually became a very prominent member of the Whig party.

Up to this time, Mr. Calhoun, who for many years had been an aspirant for the Presidency, was making satisfactory advances towards the glittering object of his ambition. But now had come a frost, a killing frost. The fruit of all his earnest labors to organize and give strength to the Jackson party—to put down Mr. Adams's administration without respect to its measures—was the Sodom apples which had turned to ashes on his lips. He for whose elevation he had zealously and successfully labored was now his implacable enemy and the ardent friend of his more fortunate rival. The Presidential seat was a "dissolving view," floating away beyond his reach for a long, perhaps indefinite, period. It proved to be forever.

A NEW CABINET APPOINTED.

An entirely new cabinet was appointed by General Jackson, consisting of the following gentlemen:

Edward Livingston, of Louisiana, Secretary of State; Louis McLane, of Delaware, Secretary of the Treasury; Lewis Cass, of Michigan, Secretary of War; Levi Woodbury, of New Hampshire, Secretary of the Navy; R. B. Taney, of Maryland, Attorney-General; Amos Kendall, of Kentucky, Postmaster-General.

In most respects each of these gentlemen was superior to

his predecessor, and the cabinet, as a whole, was a very able one.

Mr. Livingston, Mr. McLane, General Cass, Mr. Woodbury, and Mr. Taney had belonged to the old Federal party; though Mr. Woodbury left it in early life.

Mr. Livingston was a man of great learning and eminence as a jurist and publicist, had had great and varied experience in public life, and proved to be a useful counselor to the President in the crisis upon which the country was entering. He had served as aid-de-camp to General Jackson at the battle of New Orleans, and had voted for him for President, as a member of the House, in February, 1825. He was entitled, therefore, to General Jackson's confidence; and he possessed it. Though he had been for many years a citizen of Louisiana, residing and practicing law in New Orleans, he was a native of New York, had represented the city in Congress at the time General Jackson was a member, and had been mayor of New York. In high party times of old he had been a Federalist, and, in regard to the construction of the powers of the general government under the Constitution, was believed to still hold to the Federal doctrines. In view of the doctrine of State rights now advocated by South Carolina and her leading men, this was very important.

Mr. McLane was worthy of the high favor in which he was held by the little State of Delaware, which he had ably represented in both branches of Congress for many years, and was much esteemed by members of both bodies in his private and public character.

"THE KITCHEN CABINET."

At this time it began to be alleged that there was "a malign influence" at work in Washington and brought to bear especially on the President: it was frequently spoken of by the "Telegraph," now the organ of the Calhoun section of the Jackson party. Ere long it was said that a back-stairs or kitchen cabinet had come into existence, where all public measures, appointments, removals, etc., were discussed and determined upon before being submitted to the cabinet proper;

that the Constitutional advisers of the President were mere figure-heads, never really consulted. This came to be pretty generally believed, and the term "kitchen cabinet" was as familiar to the people as a household word.

This inner council, or confidential cabal, was understood to be composed of William B. Lewis, Second Auditor, Amos Kendall, Postmaster-General, Francis P. Blair, editor of the "Globe," lately established, and a few men of less note. The President undoubtedly placed great confidence in these men, than whom three more astute politicians could hardly be found.

The establishment of the "Globe," the rupture with Calhoun, and the breaking-up of the first cabinet had inaugurated a bitter war between the two rival papers, though really between the President and Mr. Calhoun, in consequence of which there were rich revelations made to the public, some of which I have already given.

ANTI-MASONIC NOMINATION FOR PRESIDENT.

The hostility to Masonry, caused by the abduction and murder of Morgan, had extended from New York into Pennsylvania, Vermont, Massachusetts, Rhode Island, Ohio, and other States, to a greater or less extent, and an Anti-Masonic party was the result. It now assumed to be a national party. In Pennsylvania it was composed, in a considerable degree, of original Democrats and Jackson men; and in every State where it took root it cut into both the great parties alike. It seemed to be the only thing that could detach any considerable number of the Jackson men from their party; but the hostility to Masonry—the indignation felt towards a society which could sanction, if not enjoin, such an outrage in a civilized community, as the masses believed the Masonic fraternity had in the case of Morgan—rose to fanaticism. Strong as their feeling had been in favor of Jackson, amounting, as some thought, to infatuation, it was overridden by a still stronger, upon which they now acted.

It was determined by the leaders of this party to nominate candidates of their own for President and Vice-President, to be voted for in 1832. A national convention was therefore called, and held at Baltimore in October, 1831, at which it was intended to nominate John McLean, one of the justices of the Supreme Court, for President. No other individual had been mentioned, or seriously thought of, and the leaders, or some of them, professed to know that Judge McLean would accept the nomination. But on arriving at Baltimore a letter was received from him, then at Nashville, positively declining the nomination.

This was very embarrassing; but Mr. Wirt, then residing and being in Baltimore, was thought of, waited upon, and nominated for President, and Amos Ellmaker, of Pennsylvania, for Vice-President. Of this convention John C. Spencer, of New York, was President, and two gentlemen were members who in after-years enjoyed a high national reputation and exercised an immense influence in national affairs,—William H. Seward and Thaddeus Stevens.

A NATIONAL REPUBLICAN CONVENTION had been designated to meet at Baltimore in December, to nominate Henry Clay for President. Mr. Wirt had been requested to prepare the address of that convention, and was engaged in its preparation when he was sought for by, and consented to accept the nomination of, the Anti-Masons.

This nomination took the country, and especially the National Republicans, by surprise; Mr. Wirt's acceptance of it was a source of regret to many of his and Mr. Clay's friends,—perhaps to Mr. Clay himself, who entertained a high personal esteem for him, which this circumstance did not lessen.

Mr. Wirt deeply regretted, when he came to reflect upon the step he had taken, that he had allowed his name to be thus used, and himself to be put in an attitude of antagonism to his friend Mr. Clay and his political *confrères* of the National Republican party. They sorrowed for him as one who, with the best intentions and the noblest of natures, had erred.

NATIONAL REPUBLICAN CONVENTION.

The National Republican Convention was held at Baltimore, and Mr. Clay and John Sergeant were nominated for President and Vice-President. This was a ticket eminently worthy the support of every American citizen. It seemed superfluous to say that both these gentlemen had long been pre-eminent as statesmen, and identified with the great leading public measures to which the country owed much of its prosperity. The only task the convention had to perform in regard to the candidate for the Presidency was simply to register the will of those they represented. Had they nominated any other than Mr. Clay for President, their action would have been promptly repudiated, and he would have been proclaimed their candidate by those who voted for him.

JOHN SERGEANT.

Mr. Sergeant was a man whose life was as pure as his talents as a lawyer and statesman were eminent. He was one of the few native-born Philadelphians to whom the city felt a warm attachment and of whom she was justly proud. To know was to admire him; to know him intimately, to love him. With what affection and pride did Philadelphians speak of "*our* John Sergeant"! In the recollection of his unassuming deportment, pleasant conversation, the overflow of kindly feeling, and a well-stored mind, spiced not unfrequently with lively humor, it is pleasant to linger over his name,—a green tree in full foliage in the midst of a desert of politics.

But, proud as the Philadelphians were, and the State ought to have been, of him, such was, and ever has been, the indifference of Pennsylvanians in regard to the eminent men of their State—the entire absence of State pride—that there never was a time, probably, during his whole public life, when he could have been elected to the Senate of the United States,—this honor being usually conferred on men of inferior ability, sometimes of marked inferiority. In this respect Pennsylvania has ever presented a striking contrast to Virginia, Massachusetts, South Carolina, and some other States.

FIRST SESSION OF THE TWENTY-SECOND CONGRESS.—MR. CLAY IN THE SENATE.—HIS BILL TO REDUCE REVENUE DUTIES.

The first session of the Twenty-second Congress commenced on the 5th of December, 1831. A great number of questions of vital importance to the country came before that body at this session.

The feeling at the South against the tariff, and especially against the principle of protection, continuing to increase, and the public debt being near a total extinction, Mr. Clay, now a member of the Senate, deemed it a favorable moment to settle the controversy between the friends and opponents of the protective policy upon a more firm basis, by the passage of an act which should reduce the amount of duties collected on foreign merchandise. His plan was to enlarge greatly the list of free articles, consisting of such as were not produced or manufactured in the United States and therefore did not come in competition with any here, and at the same time to levy discriminating duties upon such as were produced or manufactured here.

He introduced the subject by submitting a resolution declaratory of the policy he proposed, and accompanied its introduction by a speech, which, as it was the first he had made after his entrance into the Senate, and the first he had made in eight years in the halls of Congress, together with his high reputation as an orator, and the anxiety to see and hear the man who filled so large a space in the public eye and the hearts of the people, did not fail to fill the galleries to overflowing, especially with ladies. The floor of the Senate was also crowded, members of the House rushing in with eager anxiety to hear the great orator, "Harry of the West."

In speaking of the Sinking-fund act, Mr. Clay paid a just tribute to the memory of Mr. Lowndes, whose reputation as a wise and prudent statesman, a pure, high-minded, honorable man, has come down to the present day. "That act," said Mr. Clay, "was prepared and proposed by a friend of yours [Mr. Calhoun] and mine, whose premature death was not a loss merely to his native State, of which he was one of its brightest ornaments, but to the whole nation. No man with whom I ever had the honor to be associated in the legislative councils combined more extensive and useful information with more firmness of judgment and blandness of manner than did the lamented Mr. Lowndes. And when in the prime of life, by the dispensation of an All-wise Providence, he was taken from us, his country had reason to anticipate the greatest benefits from his wisdom and discretion."

Mr. Clay closed by saying,—

"Sir, I came here in a spirit of warm attachment to all parts of our beloved country, with a lively solicitude to restore and preserve its harmony, and with a firm determination to pour oil and balm into existing wounds, rather than further to lacerate them. . . . I expected to be met by corresponding dispositions, and hoped that our deliberations, guided by fraternal sentiments and feelings, would terminate in diffusing contentment and satisfaction throughout the land. And that such may be the spirit presiding over them, and such their issue, I yet most fervently hope."

Mr. Hayne, of South Carolina, rose, not to reply at this time to Mr. Clay, but to ask how it was possible that they could meet on ground which involved no concession whatever to the views of the South, but which proposed to maintain the protective system in all its rigor. "In the presence of this august body, and before his God," he said, "he would repeat his deep conviction that the consequences to grow out of the adjustment of this great question involved the future destinies of this country, and, in order that we should approach it with wary steps and becoming caution," he moved to postpone the further consideration of the subject till the following Monday; and on that day he replied in a very elaborate and able speech, in which he presented at large the views of the South, examined the character of the protective system, denied its beneficial effects, at least upon the South, held it to be unconstitutional, unjust, and oppressive, and eulogized free trade.

Mr. Hayne was the champion of the South on this occasion, as he had been two years before in the great debate between himself and Mr. Webster, and Mr. Clay stood forth as the advocate and defender of the protective policy, as Mr. Webster then had done as "the great expounder of the Constitution." Both occasions called forth great eloquence and abilities, and a debate in which the whole country took a deep and lively interest. The friends of the respective doctrines and policy upheld and advocated could not have desired or found abler advocates.

Mr. Clay replied to Mr. Hayne in a speech which occupied two days; but the great crowd who attended each day manifested no signs of weariness.

He spoke of the distressed and depressed condition of the country,—the stagnation in business of all kinds; bankruptcies and failures during the period of seven years preceding the passage of the tariff act of 1824, which he designated as the period of the greatest adversity the country had witnessed; claimed that the seven years succeeding the passage of that act was a period of the greatest prosperity; spoke of the present flourishing condition of the country; contended that all the predictions of evil results from that act had proved false, while all the beneficial effects anticipated by its advocates had been more than realized. He referred to the act of 1792, the second act passed by the First Congress, as establishing the principle of protection and adopting the policy as the true one for the country; reviewed the history of the country down to 1816, and spoke of the tariff act of that year; that when he acted with Mr. Calhoun, side by side, with perhaps less zeal than he (Mr. Calhoun) exhibited, he did not understand him then as considering the policy forbidden by the Constitution.

Mr. Calhoun (Vice-President) here interposed, and said the constitutional question was not debated at that time.

Mr. Clay.—"True; but why not? Because it was not debatable,—was never made a distinct, tangible question until 1820." He then spoke of the tariff acts of 1824 and 1828, and said that the latter was made as bad as possible by its enemies in order to render it odious and destroy the system; of the effect of manufactures upon the Western States; of South Carolina refusing, in ill humor, to take the productions of Kentucky; and, finally, of the conciliatory spirit in which he had brought forward this measure.

Colonel Benton, giving an account of this debate, designates this as "Mr. Clay's great speech." It was one of his greatest efforts.

The debate thus opened became one of absorbing interest in

both branches of Congress, nearly every prominent Senator and the ablest speakers in the House sharing in it. It was an irritating subject to the South, and in discussing it the members from that section, especially from South Carolina, indulged in the most intemperate expressions permissible in a deliberative body.

The friends of the protective policy, though less intemperate in their language, were no less firm in their adherence to their traditional policy and earnest in its support.

A BRUTAL ASSAULT ON A MEMBER OF THE HOUSE.

As if to increase the irritation of the public mind to a state of exasperation, a personal assault of a brutal character was made upon a member of Congress, for words spoken in debate, by a personal and political friend of the President. Mr. Stanberry, of Ohio, was assailed and knocked down with a heavy cane by General Houston, of Tennessee. The matter was next day brought before the House by a note addressed to the Speaker by Mr. Stanberry, who was unable to attend in his place in the House. The outrage was perpetrated on the 13th of April, 1832, and the case was not finally disposed of until the 14th of May. Upon the assault being made known in the House, the feeling became intense.

General Vance, the colleague of Mr. Stanberry, submitted a resolution directing the Speaker to issue his warrant to bring Samuel Houston before the House.

Mr. Polk, of Tennessee, opposed it. A warm debate followed.

General Vance put a hypothetical case,—supposing the Executive, for the purpose of defeating a measure, etc., should get some of "his myrmidons" to knock down members, etc.

The House well understood that in this parliamentary form the charge was made against the President of instigating this attack, and that General Houston was one of the "myrmidons" of the Executive.

In the use of this word, and in making this indirect charge upon the President, General Vance but expressed the general feeling, if not of the House, at least of the opposition in and out of it. But the word rankled like a dart, and served only to provoke the friends of Jackson.

Mr. Philip Doddridge, of Virginia, one of the ablest men in the House, and an old member, declared that the measure proposed by General Vance ought to be adopted without discussion, unless gentlemen meant deliberately to give notice to the world that they would permit a band of assassins to waylay and murder as many members as they pleased.

Colonel Drayton, of South Carolina, than whom no one was more respected and beloved,—a very Bayard, *sans peur et sans reproche*,—desired the House should be deeply impressed with the sentiment that when once the day should arrive when freedom of discussion in that hall should be restrained, the pillars of the Constitution would totter, and the fair temple of our liberties must speedily fall. Would any man tell him that freedom of debate could be preserved if a member of that body, for words spoken in his place as a representative, was to suffer personal violence? It was the lawless violence of brutal and infuriated mobs that intimidated and governed the Constituent Assembly of France, and that dictated an unsparing proscription which filled the prisons and reared the guillotine.

Colonel Drayton proceeded at some length in this strain, carrying with him the sympathies of the House, save a few members.

Great excitement prevailed, and the debate became very acrimonious. A few of the Jackson men denied the power of the House to issue the process, and opposed the resolution, which was passed,—145 to 25.

The case went to a select committee for investigation, and before which Mr. Houston appeared with counsel. The committee reported to the House the fact of the unjustifiable assault,—a violation of the privileges of the House,—and a resolution, which was adopted, that Samuel Houston be brought before the bar of the House and reprimanded by the Speaker.

On the day fixed, he was brought in by the Sergeant-at-arms, and a chair set for him in the area in front of the Speaker (Mr. Stevenson).

On being addressed by the Speaker by name, Mr. Houston rose and stood till the Speaker pronounced the reprimand.

He was then discharged; but the feeling created by this transaction was far from being allayed. Members felt that they were in a reign of terror, and liable at any time to be attacked for the part they were taking in the House. A mere reprimand for a brutal assault on a member for words spoken in debate was rather a lame and impotent conclusion, and called forth severe comment.

ATTEMPT OF HEARD TO ASSASSINATE ARNOLD.

That members should have a constant apprehension of violence cannot excite surprise, since on the very day Houston was reprimanded, and after the performance of that ceremony, W. D. Arnold, a member of the House from Tennessee, was attacked while on his way from the House after its adjournment, and in the midst of members.

The following is a portion of the statement of the affair in the "United States Telegraph" of the 15th May:

"*Attempted Assassination.*—After the House of Representatives had adjourned yesterday, as Mr. Arnold, of Tennessee, was descending the steps of the terrace into the street, in advance of other members, he was assaulted by Morgan A. Heard, who had a pistol carrying an ounce ball, which he fired at Mr. A. With a small sword-cane the latter struck the pistol, and thus probably saved his life. He then knocked Heard down: the scabbard flew off his sword, and he was about to pierce Heard, when his arm was arrested by a member.

"The case presents a remarkable interposition of Providence. The House had just adjourned; there were near a hundred members of Congress in the range of the ball, which passed near Mr. Tazewell's head."

Of course the affair was bruited over the city immediately, and added greatly to the feverish state of public feeling here and throughout the country.

Mr. Arnold came into the hall next morning fully armed, and, proceeding to his seat, laid the big Heard pistol on his desk, but retained pocket-pistols in his belt. Members, of course, gathered round him to see the pistol Heard had used. No proceedings were taken in relation to this last assault.

The assaulted member gave notice that he wanted no protection from the House; that he could protect himself.

YOUNG MEN'S NATIONAL CONVENTION.

On the 7th of May, 1832, a national convention of young men assembled at Washington, and organized by electing William Cost Johnson, of Maryland, its President; Charles James Faulkner, of Virginia, William Pitt Fessenden, of Maine, and George W. Burnet, of Ohio, Vice-Presidents. The convention, of which I was a member, consisted of three hundred and sixteen delegates, representing almost every State. Politically, it was a National Republican convention, but was dubbed, facetiously, "Clay's Infant-School." But, "infant" or adult "school," it was made up of the very *élite* of the nation, and numbered among its delegates not a few young men of highly cultivated minds, brilliant talents, and captivating oratorical powers, of which they gave proof in speeches made in the convention. A considerable number of these young men afterwards filled high positions in public life, as governors, Senators and Representatives in Congress, ministers abroad, judges, etc. Among the most brilliant speakers of the convention were Brantz Mayer, of Baltimore, Edward G. Prescott, of Boston, Messrs. Duer and Graham, of New York, Mr. Hanna, of Philadelphia, Messrs. Cost Johnson and Bradford, of Maryland, Mr. Faulkner, of Virginia, Mr. Kinnicut, of Massachusetts, and Mr. Wm. Pitt Fessenden, of Maine.

The object of the convention was simply to confirm and approve the action of the National Republican Convention which had nominated Henry Clay and John Sergeant as candidates for the Presidency and Vice-Presidency.

Near the close of the session of the convention, which sat several days, Mr. Clay was invited to be present and address that body, and, having consented, a committee waited upon and accompanied him to the convention, when he was welcomed in a neat address by Mr. Charles James Faulkner, vice-president, in the absence of the president (Cost Johnson), and addressed the body in his usual felicitous manner, on the topics of the day.

Before adjourning, the convention appointed a committee of

one from each State represented, and one from the District of Columbia, to wait upon the venerable Charles Carroll, of Carrollton, to express to him the high sense of the members of the convention of the virtues of himself and associates, and of their labors in the great cause of national union and independence.

The committee assembled at Baltimore, and, in discharge of the duty assigned them, waited, by appointment, on Mr. Carroll, whom Mr. Brantz Mayer, as chairman of the committee, addressed in a short but touching speech.

Mr. Carroll was highly gratified by this expression of the feelings of the young men of the United States, and hoped they might enjoy through life, and transmit to posterity, the noble institutions of this happy land.

But few of the "young men" who constituted that body are now living; and the few who are, are now venerable grandfathers and great-grandfathers, but they have not, I am sure, forgotten the scenes and incidents of that day. They will not have forgotten the zeal and activity of "Bobby Horner" in taking care to provide funds for expenses, and in making all arrangements for visiting Mount Vernon. They cannot have forgotten the burst of applause which Brantz Mayer brought out when speaking of "the battle of New Orleans, that springboard from which General Jackson vaulted into the Presidential saddle!" They cannot have forgotten the visit of Henry Clay to the convention, when many of them for the first time saw face to face, and took by the hand, him whom they had long admired. They cannot have forgotten their visits to Mr. Adams, Mr. Webster, and Mr. Calhoun, of whom they had heard so much, but whom many of them had never seen; nor the very eloquent and feeling address to them of one of their members, —Mr. Bradford (one of the few survivors), late Governor of Maryland,— after their return from Mount Vernon.

REJECTION OF THE NOMINATION OF MR. VAN BUREN AS MINISTER TO ENGLAND.

I have, in its proper place, noticed the appointment of Mr. Van Buren as minister to England. His nomination as such now came before the Senate for confirmation, and met decided opposition, on the ground, chiefly, of the instructions given to Mr. McLane, as minister to England, in regard to the West India trade.

The following are extracts from Mr. Van Buren's instructions to which exceptions were taken:

"The opportunities which you have derived from a participation in our public councils, as well as other sources of information, will enable you to speak with confidence of the respective parts taken by those to whom the administration of this government is now committed, in relation to the course heretofore pursued upon the subject of the colonial trade. Their views upon that point have been submitted to the people of the United States, and the counsels by which your conduct is now directed are the result of the judgment expressed by the only earthly tribunal to which the late administration was amenable for its acts. It should be sufficient that the claims set up by them, and which caused the interruption of the trade in question, have been explicitly abandoned by those who first asserted them, and are not revived by their successors. . . . To set up the acts of the late administration as the cause of forfeiture of privileges which would otherwise be extended to the people of the United States, would, under existing circumstances, be unjust in itself, and could not fail to excite the deepest sensibility. . . . You cannot press this view of the subject too earnestly upon the consideration of the British ministry.

* * * * * * * *

"I will add nothing as to the impropriety of suffering any feelings that find their origin in the past pretensions of this government to have an adverse influence upon the present conduct of Great Britain."

The speeches of the leading Senators in opposition to the confirmation of this nomination, though severe in their comments upon these instructions, were of a manly, patriotic character. Mr. Van Buren was not assailed, but his official acts as Secretary of State,—the begging as a boon to the party now just come into power what the government had for many years justly demanded as a *right*, and styling those demands "claims" and "pretensions." It was his lack of national feeling which called forth the condemnation of Senators. In addressing the Senate against the confirmation of the nomination, Mr. Webster declared that the pervading topic through the whole letter of instructions is, not *American* rights, not *American* defense, but denunciations of past "*pretensions*" of our own country, reflections on the past administration, and exultation and a loud claim of merit for the administration now in power. "Sir," said Mr. Webster, "I would forgive mistakes; I would pardon the want of information; I would pardon almost anything, where I saw true patriotism and sound American feeling; but I cannot forgive the sacrifice of this feeling to mere party. I cannot concur in sending abroad a public agent who has not conceptions so large and liberal as to feel that in the presence of foreign courts, amidst the monarchies of Europe, he is to stand up for his country, and his whole country; that no jot or tittle of her honor is to come to harm in his hands; that he is not to suffer others to reproach either his government or his country, and far less is he himself to reproach either; that he is to have no objects in his eye but *American* objects, and no heart in his bosom but an *American* heart; and that he is to forget self, to forget party, to forget every sinister and narrow feeling, in his proud and lofty attachment to the republic whose commission he bears."

Mr. Clayton said, "Our minister did as he was ordered to do. He 'entreated,' and 'appealed,' and 'begged,' and 'prayed,' and 'regretted,' and 'solicited,' and 'hoped to be excused,' and confessed *we had been in the wrong*, instead of repelling with dignity the insolence and sarcasm of the British ministry, until the contemptible boon was 'granted' and the national character effectually degraded.

* * * * * * * *

"Let us say to the British government this day, by our vote, that we never consented to the disgrace which has befallen us, and that we prefer to recall the minister who has dishonored us, to all the pretended benefits of this miserable negotiation."

Mr. Clay, after commenting upon the instructions characterizing our position in the controversy under former administrations as "*pretensions*," "*claims explicitly abandoned*," proceeded:

"On our side, according to Mr. Van Buren, all was wrong; on the British side, all was right. We brought forward nothing but *claims* and *pretensions;* the British government asserted, on the other hand, a clear and incontestable RIGHT. We erred in too tenaciously and too long insisting upon our *pretensions*, and not yielding at once to the force of their *just* demands. And Mr. McLane was commanded to avail himself of all the circumstances in his power to *mitigate* our *offense*, and to dissuade the British government from allowing their feelings, justly incurred by the past conduct of the party driven from power, to have an adverse influence towards the American party now in power. Sir, was this becoming language from one independent nation to another? Was it proper in the mouth of an American minister? Was it in conformity with the high, unsullied, and dignified character of our previous diplomacy? Was it not, on the contrary, the language of an humble vassal to a proud and haughty lord? Was it not prostrating and degrading the American eagle before the British lion?"

The American people have for forty years past heard much of the "spoils" of the enemy being the right of "the victors;" a sentiment first announced in the Senate by Mr. Marcy, of New York. The speech in which this doctrine or rule was announced was a part of this debate. Mr. Marcy, in replying to Mr. Clay and defending Mr. Van Buren, said,—

* * * * * * * *

"The occasion which rendered it proper that he should say something had arisen in consequence of what had fallen from the honorable Senator from Kentucky [Mr. Clay]. His attack was not confined to the nominee; it reached the State which he [Mr. Marcy] represented in this body. One of the grounds of opposition to the minister to London taken by the Senator from Kentucky was the pernicious system of party politics adopted by the present administration, by which the honors and offices were put up to be scrambled for by partisans, etc., a system which the minister to London, as the Senator from Kentucky alleged, had brought here from the State in which he formerly lived and had for so long a time acted a conspicuous part in its political transactions. I know, sir, that it is the habit of some gentlemen to speak with censure or reproach of the politics of New York. Like other States, we have contests, and, as a necessary consequence, triumphs and defeats.

* * * * * * * *

"It may be, sir, that the politicians of the State of New York are not so fastidious as some gentlemen are, as to disclosing the principles on which they act. They boldly preach what they practice. When they are contending for victory they avow their intention of enjoying the fruits of it. If they are defeated, they expect to retire from office. If they are successful, they claim, as a matter of right, the advantages of success. They see nothing wrong in the rule, that TO THE VICTOR BELONG THE SPOILS OF THE ENEMY."

This last sentence has given more *éclat* to Mr. Marcy's name than all else he ever wrote or did. As Governor of New York, as Secretary of War, and as Secretary of State, he and all his sayings and doings may be forgotten, if they have not been already; but as the Senator who first proclaimed that the offices of the government were the "spoils" for which the two parties contended,—virtually declaring that principles, or government policy, were of no moment,—his name will go down to posterity.

Mr. Webster called attention to the fact that Congress itself had sanctioned what Mr. Van Buren denominated our "pretension," by the act of March 1st, 1823, for which the Senator from Maryland (Mr. Smith), who had defended the minister, and Mr. Van Buren himself, voted. How the latter could have overlooked or forgotten this act, he could not conceive.

Mr. Van Buren was defended by his friends, but the nomination was rejected by the casting vote of the Vice-President (Mr. Calhoun), being designedly so arranged by the anti-Jackson Senators.

MOVEMENT TO BRING GENERAL JACKSON OUT FOR A SECOND TERM.

It being understood by General Jackson's supporters from the beginning that he was opposed to a President's holding the office for more than one term, it became necessary for his friends who desired his election for a second term to take some steps to have it appear that *the people* demanded his re-election. It has been stated by Wm. B. Lewis, General Jackson's most trusted friend, that before the close of 1829 the general had made up his mind to do all that in him lay to elect Mr. Van Buren as his successor to the Presidency; and with that object in view he wrote a letter to his friend Judge Overton, of Tennessee, the secret purpose of which the judge never knew, but which was to be explained, if circumstances should require the use of the letter, by Mr. Lewis. At that time General Jackson's health was infirm, and it was doubted by himself whether he would live to the end of his first term. But he did; and he, Mr. Van Buren, and their confidential friends saw that the country was not ready to make Mr. Van Buren General Jackson's successor, and therefore Mr. Van Buren insisted on the general's running a second time.

But how was he to be brought on the course? Mr. Lewis was equal to the occasion. On the 11th of March, 1830, he addressed a letter to Colonel L. C. Stambaugh, of Harrisburg, Pennsylvania, in which he says, "With regard to General Jackson's serving another term it would be improper in me, perhaps, situated as I am, to say anything; but, my dear sir, almost every friend he has, I mean *real friend*, thinks with you that there is no other way by which the great Republican party, who brought him into power, can be preserved. Clay's friends are beginning to hold up their heads again; their countenances are brightening because of the anticipated split between the friends of those who aspire to succeed the present chief magistrate.

* * * * * * * *

"I do not think it would be proper for General Jackson to avow at this time his determination to serve another term, nor do I think it would be prudent for his friends *here* to take the lead in placing his name before the nation for re-election. According to the general's *own* principles (always practiced on by him), he cannot decline serving again if called on by the people.

"I am not authorized to say that he would permit his name

to be used again, but, knowing him as I do, I feel *confident* that if he believed the interests of the country required it, and it was the wish of the people he should serve another term, he would not hesitate one moment. If, then, it is the desire of your State that he should serve another term, *let the members of her Legislature express the sentiments of the people upon that subject.* But let it be done in such a way as not to make it necessary for him to *speak* in relation to the matter. Such an expression of public sentiment would come with better grace from Pennsylvania than any other quarter, and would have a powerful effect,—because of her well-known Democratic principles, and because she has always been the general's strongest friend. *If anything is done in the business, the sooner the better.*

"Yours sincerely,

"W. B. Lewis."*

Inclosed in this letter was one drawn up by Mr. Lewis, dated Harrisburg, March 20, 1830, addressed to "*His Excellency Andrew Jackson, President of the United States*," intended to be signed by the members of the Legislature of Pennsylvania, and which was signed by sixty-eight members. This address to General Jackson, thus signed, was immediately published in the Harrisburg "Pennsylvania Reporter." Of course it made a great sensation in the political world, as up to that time General Jackson was considered irrevocably committed to a single term.

Mr. Lewis himself relates† that this first movement towards bringing the general out for a second term was followed up by the Legislatures of New York and Ohio principally on his suggestions and advice to the friends of the administration in those States, and that he wrote many letters urging the absolute necessity of such a step as the most effectual way of defeating the machinations of Mr. Calhoun and his friends, who were resolved on forcing General Jackson from the Presidential chair after one term.

He goes on to explain that Mr. Calhoun's second term as

* Parton's Life of Jackson.

† See Parton's Life of Jackson.

Vice-President was drawing to a close, that it would not do to run him for a third term, and that his friends did not wish him to retire to private life for four years; they therefore resolved to get rid of the general on the ground that it was understood, during the canvass, that in case he should be elected he would serve but four years.* It was to defeat this project of the Vice-President, Major Lewis says, that this movement was made. "The scheme," he says, "succeeded admirably, and in a few months the hopes of Mr. Calhoun and his friends were completely withered."

And thus was Mr. Calhoun paid for abandoning Mr. Adams, going over to General Jackson, and laboring with such extraordinary zeal to overthrow Mr. Adams's administration. NEMESIS was ever on his track.

BALTIMORE JACKSON NATIONAL CONVENTION.—NOMINATION OF MR. VAN BUREN AS VICE-PRESIDENT.

Thus was General Jackson already in the field as candidate for President for a second term. But it was necessary to hold a national convention, not only formally to nominate him, but to nominate a candidate for Vice-President. This convention was held at Baltimore on the 21st of May, 1832, and it was well known that it was General Jackson's pleasure that Mr. Van Buren should be the candidate. Besides this, Mr. Van Buren's nomination as minister to England had just been rejected by the Whigs and Calhoun men,—by Calhoun's own casting vote,—reasons enough why he should be thus nominated; and he was accordingly placed on the ticket with General Jackson. But in two States, namely, Pennsylvania and South Carolina, he was so unpopular that neither would vote for him.

The anti-Jackson men in the Senate, including Mr. Calhoun and Mr. Hayne, believed, and expressed their belief, that the exposure of the humiliating and anti-American instructions of Mr. Van Buren to Mr. McLane in regard to the West India controversy would seriously injure his hold on the American

* General Jackson at this very time recommended in his annual messages the alteration of the Constitution so as to prevent a President from being re-elected.

people. But it is quite certain that it did not affect him to the amount of a single vote. He had always been obnoxious to Pennsylvania; and in South Carolina, considered, as he was, the enemy of Mr. Calhoun, he could look for support only from the anti-Calhoun party. But Jackson's popularity was sufficient to overcome all objections among his supporters elsewhere and triumphantly elect him. This fondness of "the old hero" for "the little magician," as he was termed, gave rise to many amusing caricatures and squibs and much doggerel. The President was represented as an old granny with the little pet in his lap, feeding him with a pap-spoon, fondling and soothing him, granny-like.

But all efforts to cast ridicule upon him and the President he could afford to treat with scorn. "Let him laugh who wins." All such attempts only seemed to endear him the more to "the old hero," whose confidence and favor he knew well how to win and preserve.

Mr. Van Buren's good nature and complacency could scarcely be moved by any amount of sarcasm, wit, pasquinade, caricature, or ridicule. All such missiles fell upon him as harmless as water upon a duck's back. He possessed a happy philosophy which enabled him to laugh as heartily at all such attempts to injure him as if they were not aimed at him. This self-control, amiability, and imperturbable composure undoubtedly constituted his strength, and enabled him to navigate successfully the troubled waters of politics when others, possessing more talent but less *tact*, were wrecked or engulfed. His object was success; and whether this was to be attained by supporting this measure or that, or this man or that, was a question to be decided by weighing all the probabilities, pro and con. He could not say, as Mr. Clay did, "I had rather be right than be President," and probably could hardly conceive that Mr. Clay could be sincere in such a declaration.

"The evil which men do lives after them."

He brought the corrupting practice, described by Mr. Marcy as prevailing in New York, to Washington, where it soon took deep root, and still flourishes.

It seems to have been the wish of General Jackson, as early as 1830, before Mr. Van Buren departed on his mission to England, that he should be the candidate of the party for Vice-President on the ticket with him; and Mr. Lewis, the adroit manager of party movements, was the contriver of the plan by which the desired object was effected.

DISTRIBUTION OF THE PROCEEDS OF THE PUBLIC LANDS.

As it was customary for the committee on manufactures of the Senate, forty years ago, to have charge of all tariff questions, and as Mr. Clay was the great champion of the protective policy, on entering the Senate he was placed on that committee, at the head of which was Mr. Dickinson, of New Jersey, a Jackson tariff man.

At this time the public debt was nearly or quite extinguished; the receipts from the customs were large, and from the sales of the public lands unusually so. The treasury was, consequently, full, and a large surplus over and above the expenses of the government was accumulating. Under this condition of the finances, it became a puzzling question what should be done with the public lands. It was a question of immense importance, but one which all desired to avoid handling, as it was supposed that no plan could be devised to dispose of them that would not bring down upon its author the hostility either of the West and Southwest, or of the North, East, and Atlantic Southern States.

In this dilemma, the Jackson men in the Senate, being in the majority, bethought them of a smart piece of strategy, namely, to refer the subject of the public lands to the committee on manufactures! The proposition was resisted by the members of that committee, and the National Republican Senators generally, as absurd. It was asked what this committee had to do with the public lands. How could it be expected that they should know anything about them, especially as Mr. Clay was the only man from the West on the committee, and he was not from a State having public lands? Why not refer the subject to the committee on public lands, which was made up, with a single exception, of Senators from those States where these lands were situated, and who were supposed to be familiar with the subject?

As it was the purpose of this movement to embarrass Mr. Clay, these arguments had no weight whatever. The subject was forced upon that committee and upon Mr. Clay, and he took it up, resolved to master it. His report upon it, which he presented to the Senate in due time, elicited high and universal commendation in every part of the United States. This was a result which his political opponents in the Senate had not counted on or dreamed of. Instead of compelling him to injure himself with this two-edged weapon they had thrust into his hands, they had unwittingly done him a very great favor, and got themselves into a bramble-bush from which they could extricate themselves only by backing squarely out, thus acknowledging their stupidity and evil design, and making themselves ridiculous.

The conclusion to which the committee came is comprised in a bill accompanying the report, entitled "A bill to appropriate for a limited time the proceeds of the public lands of the United States."

The title of the bill indicates the plan of the committee to relieve the plethoric treasury of the United States of its accumulating surplus. It provided that the proceeds of the sales of the lands should be distributed to the different States in the ratio of their respective federal representative population. To this plan neither the new nor the old States objected. But Mr. King, of Alabama, chairman of the committee on public lands, some weeks after the report had been made, gave notice that he should embrace the first opportunity to move that the bill reported be referred to the committee on public lands, in order that a fair report might be made!

Subsequently he spoke at length on the subject. But when it was known that Mr. Clay was to reply to him on this subject, the galleries were, as usual, filled to overflowing, a considerable portion of the audience being ladies. When, at the proper time, Mr. Clay moved to take up the subject, Mr. Forsyth interposed a motion, seconded by Mr. Tazewell, that the Senate should go into executive session. But, to the credit of that body, the motion was promptly and almost unanimously negatived. This manœuvre was noticed by Mr. Clay, who said that, "in rising to address the Senate, he owed, in the first place, the expression of his hearty thanks to the majority, by whose vote, just given, he was indulged in occupying the floor on this most important question. . . . Their decision demonstrated that feelings of liberality and courtesy and kindness still prevailed in the Senate; and that they would be extended even to one of the humblest members of the body, as he was."

Alluding to the extraordinary reference of the subject of the public lands to the committee on manufactures, he remarked, "I have nothing to do with the motives of honorable Senators who composed the majority by which the reference was ordered. The decorum proper in this hall obliges me to consider their motives to have been pure and patriotic. But still I must be permitted to regard the proceeding as very unusual. The Senate has a standing committee on the public lands, appointed under long-established rules. The members of that committee are presumed to be well acquainted with the subject; they have, some of them, occupied the same station for many years, are well versed in the whole legislation on the public lands, and familiar with every branch of it,—four out of five of them come from the new States.

"Yet, with a full knowledge of all these circumstances, a reference was ordered by a majority of the Senate to the committee on manufactures,—a committee than which there was not another standing committee of the Senate whose prescribed duties were more incongruous with the public domain. It happened, in the construction of the committee on manufactures, that there was not a solitary Senator from the new States, and but one from any Western State. The committee earnestly protested, but in vain. I will not attempt an expression of the feelings excited in my mind on that occasion. Whatever may have been the intention of honorable Senators, I could not be insensible to the embarrassment in which the committee of manufactures was placed, and especially myself. Although any other member of that committee would have rendered himself, with appropriate researches and proper time, more competent than I was to understand the subject of the public lands, it was known that, from my local position, I alone was supposed to have any particular knowledge of them. Whatever emanated from the committee was likely, therefore, to be ascribed to me. If the committee should propose a measure of great liberality towards the new States, the old States might complain. If the measure should seem to lean towards the old States, the new might be dissatisfied. And if it inclined to neither class of States, but recommended a plan according to which there would be distributed impartial justice among all the States, it was far from certain that any would be pleased.

"Without attributing to honorable Senators the purpose of producing this personal embarrassment, I felt it, as a necessary consequence from their act, *just as much as if it had been in their contemplation.*

"The report and bill were hardly read in the Senate before they were violently denounced, and they were not considered in the Senate before a proposition was made to refer the report to that very committee of the public lands, to which, in the first instance, I contended the subject ought to have been assigned. It was in vain that we remonstrated against such a proceeding as unprecedented, as implying unmerited censure on the committee on manufactures. . . . In spite of our remonstrances, the same majority, with but little, if any, variation, which originally resolved to refer the subject to the committee on manufactures, determined to commit the bill to the land committee."

As a specimen of a cool, calm, caustic parliamentary rebuke, and of severe criticism, this speech has few equals.

The bill was finally referred to the committee on public lands; but it availed them nothing, for it passed the Senate at this session, and the House of Representatives at the next, although the committee on public lands, through their chairman, Mr. King, made a vigorous counter-report.

THE TARIFF BILL OF 1832 AGAIN.

Two other important measures were brought forward at the first session of the Twenty-second Congress, namely, a tariff bill, and the "Enforcement," or "*Force bill.*" The tariff bill, introduced early in the session by Mr. Clay, underwent a most elaborate and heated discussion in both branches of Congress, but especially in the House, where the language of Mr. McDuffie and other Southern members was violent and denunciatory. It would hardly be worth while to repeat this language at the present day. The bill passed, only to be repealed by the "Compromise act" at the next session.

The subjects which were brought before the Twenty-second Congress during the first and second sessions were many and of the greatest importance. Of two of these, namely, the tariff bill and the Land Distribution bill, I have spoken; but the application by the president and directors of the Bank of the United States for a re-charter, the bill introduced for that purpose, the debate thereon, its passage by the two Houses, and its veto by the President, were of absorbing interest to the whole country.

THE CASE OF THE CHEROKEES AGAIN.

The State of Georgia, as we have already seen, extended her laws over the country occupied by the Creek Indians; she also extended them over the country occupied by the Cherokee Indians within the borders of that State as defined by the charter from the King of England. She claimed that these lands belonged to her, and that she had a right to disregard the laws and usages of the Cherokees and assume jurisdiction and authority over them and all others in that territory. Among her laws was one, recently passed, making it a misdemeanor for any white person to reside in what was called the Cherokee nation without a license from that State. Two persons, missionaries to the Indians, were residing in the Cherokee country at the time this law was passed, and had been residing there for several years. As they did not recognize the right of Georgia thus to extend her laws and assume jurisdiction over a country which never had belonged to her, they did not heed the law, and were consequently arrested, indicted, convicted, sentenced to the State prison, and imprisoned. They then, by their counsel, Mr. Sergeant and Mr. Wirt, appealed to the Supreme Court of the United States, before which tribunal the case was ably argued, exciting the deepest interest not only at the capital and in the court, but throughout the whole country. Chief-Justice Marshall delivered the opinion of the court, which was long and exhaustive, reversing the opinion of the Georgia court, and declaring the recent acts of that State, taking possession of the Cherokee country and providing for the punishment of persons residing therein without the license of the governor, etc., to be contrary to the Constitution, laws, and treaties of the United States, and therefore null and void. The Supreme Court then ordered the prisoners, Samuel A. Worcester and Elizur Butler, to be released.

The Chief-Justice reviewed the origin of the European title to lands in America upon the ground of discovery. This right, he demonstrated, was merely conventional among European governments, and in no respects changed, or affected to change, the rights of the Indians as the occupants of the soil. They were treated as nations capable of holding and ceding their territories, capable of making treaties and compacts, and entitled to all the powers of peace and war, not as conquered or enslaved communities. They had always been considered as distinct, independent political communities, retaining their natural rights as the undisputed possessors of the soil from time immemorial. The very term "nation," so generally applied to them, means a people distinct from all others. The United States had so treated them, and had made many treaties with them. The Chief-Justice spoke especially of the treaty of Hopewell between the Cherokees and this government, negotiated July, 1791, which recognizes them as a nation, which fixes the boundaries between the two contracting powers, and solemnly guarantees on the part of the United States the peaceable possession of all their lands not conveyed by this treaty. This relation of the Cherokees to the United States had been solemnly recognized by Georgia down to the year 1829.

This celebrated case is fully reported in Peters's Reports, to which the reader is referred.

The decision was, that the acts of Georgia are repugnant to the Constitution, laws, and treaties of the United States.

The decree of the court was that the prisoners should be released. Will it be believed, at this day, that the State of Georgia refused to obey the mandate of the court, that the President of the United States refused to execute it or to order its execution, and that it never was executed, but was treated not only as a nullity, but with scorn and derision?

The President, on this occasion, set up the extraordinary pretension that he was not bound by the decision of the Supreme Court; that he was an independent, co-ordinate department of the government, and had a right to execute the Constitution as HE UNDERSTOOD IT, and not as any court understood it. Can it be believed that such was the fealty of party, such the habit of declaring, if not believing, that "the old hero" could neither do nor say anything wrong, that his partisans at once adopted the dogma, and boldly claimed that he was as much the judge of what was constitutional or unconstitutional as the Supreme Court, of which he was perfectly independent? Such was the ground taken by the government paper at the capital, others, among them the "Albany Argus," following its lead.

Strong as was once the feeling, especially among the Friends, Methodists, and other religious sects, in the United States, in regard to the treatment of the Cherokees and the imprisonment of the missionaries by the Georgians, there are few now living who have any recollection of the matter or any knowledge of those transactions; and the monstrous claim of the President, which grew out of the decision of the court and the reluctance of General Jackson to fall out with Georgia, is as completely forgotten as if it had been asserted a hundred years ago.

This extraordinary claim of General Jackson and his partisans for him received its quietus from the Supreme Court of the United States in the case of Amos Kendall, Postmaster-General, *vs.* the United States, *ex relatione* Stockton, Stokes & Co., reported in 12th Howard's Reports. The opinion of the court was the production of Mr. Justice Smith Thompson. That opinion, as read in court, contained the following paragraph:

"It was urged at the bar that the Postmaster-General was alone subject to the direction and control of the President with respect to the duties imposed upon him by this law, and this right of the President is claimed as growing out of the obligation imposed upon him by the Constitution to take care that the laws be faithfully executed. This is a doctrine that cannot receive the sanction of this court. It would be vesting in the President a dispensing power which has no countenance for its support in any part of the Constitution, and is asserting a principle which, if carried out in its results to all cases falling within it, would be clothing the President with a power entirely to control the legislation of Congress and paralyze the administration of justice."

After the reading of the opinion, Mr. Butler, Attorney-General, rose and said that in that opinion it had been stated that the obligation imposed on the President to see the laws faithfully executed implied a power to forbid their execution. He disclaimed such a doctrine, and felt it to be a duty he owed to himself and the station he occupied to repudiate such a doctrine as contrary to his long-established opinions; and he hoped the court would either expunge this part of the opinion or so modify it as to exonerate him from the imputation of having asserted such a principle.

Mr. Justice Thompson said he had endeavored to state faithfully and impartially the arguments of counsel, but if he had fallen into error he was willing to correct it. The opinion had been submitted to all the judges in conference, and no one had intimated that the argument had been misapprehended.

Mr. Justice Baldwin had paid much attention to the argument, and said there was no mistake or misapprehension in the statement of it.

Mr. Justice McKinley had also listened with much attention, and had no hesitation in saying that the doctrine attributed to counsel was not only enunciated, but it constituted the drift of the whole argument.

Mr. Justice Wayne's understanding of the argument of counsel was in accordance with that stated in the opinion, and he had heard the doctrine enunciated with equal astonishment and indignation.

The "National Intelligencer" of October 14, 1854, to which I am indebted for the statement of this case, says that the opinion was modified in conformity with Mr. Butler's request; but the original opinion, as read, will be found in the handwriting of Mr. Justice Thompson, among the archives of the Supreme Court, and still shows how it stood before the alteration.

"Thus," says the editor, "in the tribunal of the highest resort under the Constitution, were the prerogative claims and arbitrary constructions of his own power by President Jackson stamped with the seal of condemnation, decisively, irreversibly, now and forever."

THE BANK OF THE UNITED STATES.—APPLICATION FOR A RE-CHARTER, ETC.

In his first annual message to Congress, in December, 1829, President Jackson informed that body that "the charter of the Bank of the United States expires in 1836, and its stockholders will probably apply for a renewal of their privileges. In order to avoid the evils resulting from precipitancy in a measure involving such important principles and such deep pecuniary interests, I feel that I cannot, in justice to the parties interested, too soon present it to the deliberate consideration of the legislature and the people. . . . It must be admitted by all that it has failed in the great end of establishing a uniform and sound currency." The President also called attention to the subject in several subsequent messages. Three years after this the bank directors applied for a renewal of the charter, when a hue and cry was set up that the application was *premature.*

Mr. Dallas, in presenting the memorial, said *he had been requested to present the memorial,* but intimated very strongly that it would have been better to delay the application.

In a conversation I had with Mr. Biddle, president of the bank, in regard to Mr. Dallas's remark, he stated that it had not been the intention of the directors to intrust Mr. Dallas with the memorial, nor, of course, with the management of the interests of the bank in Congress, but to put them into other hands,—Mr. Webster's, I think; that, hearing of this, Mr. Dallas addressed him a letter remonstrating against it, as it would be virtually saying to the world that his ability or his disposition to aid in obtaining a re-charter was doubted; that, being himself a citizen of Philadelphia, where the bank was located, he should feel greatly hurt to be thus passed over. In consequence of this letter, Mr. Biddle said, Mr. Dallas was intrusted with the presentation of the memorial and the management of the interest of the bank in the Senate.

Instead, therefore, of being "*requested*" to present the memorial, he *sought* the office or duty.

When the bank directors applied for a renewal of its charter, its bills were preferred to specie in every part of the United States, Mexico, and South America,—preferred, because they were more convenient to carry, and could be easily transmitted to any distance by mail, and commanded specie everywhere. The Germans of Pennsylvania hoarded them, as they formerly had hoarded silver, and large sums were thus laid up by that proverbially cautious, industrious, thriving people. They were current in Europe, and in almost every part of the civilized world.

During the existence of the bank, the exchanges between the Northern commercial cities, New York, Philadelphia, Boston, etc., and the Southern and Western, were from one-quarter to one-half per cent.; seldom, in any case, exceeding three-fourths per cent. Drafts of the bank on its branches in these cities, or of its branches on it or on each other, could at all times be obtained at these rates; so that the transmission of funds back and forth was a matter of little difficulty and of comparatively small expense.

The memorial of the bank directors was presented in the Senate by Mr. Dallas, and in the House by Mr. McDuffie. In the Senate it was referred to a select committee, in the House to the committee of ways and means. The application for a re-charter at once met with very determined opposition, and the bank was fiercely assailed,—in the Senate by Colonel Benton, and in the House by many leading Southern and Eastern men. It found able defenders and advocates in Mr. McDuffie and Colonel Drayton, of South Carolina, Mr. Wilde, of Georgia, and others.

After some days' warm discussion, it was ordered that a special committee be appointed to whom the subject should be referred, and who should proceed to Philadelphia and make a thorough investigation of the affairs of the institution. The committee consisted of Messrs. Clayton, of Georgia, R. M. Johnson, of Kentucky, F. Thomas, of Maryland, C. C. Cambreling, of New York, McDuffie, of South Carolina, Adams, of Massachusetts, and Watmough, of Pennsylvania: the four first named opposed to the bank, the three last in favor of it.

The committee visited Philadelphia, and made a thorough examination of the affairs of the bank, and three reports: a majority report, being a long indictment against the institution; a minority report, favorable to it; and a report by Mr. Adams alone. These changed not a vote or an opinion: those opposed to the bank opposed it still, and those who advocated its re-charter continued to do so with none the less zeal.

MR. ADAMS'S REPORT.—THE NEW HAMPSHIRE INTRIGUE EXPOSED.

Like all other papers or documents upon important subjects emanating from Mr. Adams's pen, his report on the bank was a most elaborate and exhaustive production. He brought forward the fact, before unknown, that the controversy between the bank and the friends of the administration began in 1829, almost immediately after General Jackson's inauguration, by an attempt on the part of Mr. Woodberry, Isaac Hill, and other well-known politicians of New Hampshire, to compel the bank to remove Jeremiah Mason from the presidency of its branch at Portsmouth, New Hampshire, because, "as a *politician*, he was not very acceptable to the majority in Portsmouth and the State;" that is, he was not a Jackson man.

Mr. Woodberry, then Senator of the United States from New Hampshire, addressed a letter to the Secretary of the Treasury, complaining that "The new president, Jeremiah Mason, is a particular friend of Mr. Webster; and his political character is doubtless well known to you. Mr. Webster is supposed to have had much agency in effecting the change. . . . The objections to the continuance of Mr. Mason in office are twofold: first, the want of conciliatory manners and intimate acquaintance with our business men; and, secondly, the fluctuating policy pursued in relation to both loans and collections at the bank, together with the partiality and harshness that accompany them." Mr. Woodberry also states that the salary had been greatly increased upon the change of president of that branch.

This letter was transmitted by the Secretary of the Treasury to Mr. Biddle, president of the bank at Philadelphia, who replied, —first, that the president of the branch bank was not changed; that Mr. Shapley, the late president, declined serving any longer, and Mr. Mason was appointed to fill his place. Second, that the salary of the new president was not increased a dollar. Third, that Mr. Webster had not the slightest agency in obtaining for Mr. Mason the appointment; the nomination was made without the knowledge of Mr. Webster or Mr. Mason. Mr. Webster, however, was requested to endeavor to prevail on him to serve.

Mr. Biddle states also in his letter to the Secretary that on the day Mr. Woodberry wrote to him, the Secretary, he addressed a letter to himself, and in reply he requested Mr. Woodberry to state the objections to Mr. Mason. In his answer, Mr. Woodberry said, "From the confidential character of this letter, it is due in perfect frankness to state that the president of the present board, as *a politician,* is not very acceptable to the majority in this town and State. But it is at the same time notorious that the charges against him, in his present office, originated exclusively with his political friends." On this Mr. Biddle remarks, "It appears, then, from Mr. Woodberry's own statement, that so far from employing the influence of the bank *with a view to political effect,* it is a notorious fact that the complaints are made by Mr. Mason's own political friends: so that, in truth, if there be any politics in the matter, it is a question between Mr. Mason and politicians of his own persuasion; that is to say (for, after all, I suspect it will result in this), that Mr. Mason has had the courage to do his duty whether he offends his political friends or not. He may have done his duty too rigidly; that is a fit subject of examination, and shall be examined; but Mr. Woodberry's own declaration to me seems to be irreconcilable with his letter to you."

Mr. Biddle adds, "It is the settled policy of the institution, pursued with the most fastidious care, to devote itself exclusively to the purposes for which it was instituted; to abstain from all political contests; to be simply and absolutely a *bank*, seeking only the interests of the community and the judicious employment of the funds intrusted to its management, and never for a moment perverting its power to any local or party purposes. The affairs of the bank and all its branches are thoroughly imbued with this spirit, knowing, as they do, that their interference in political contentions would be highly offensive to the general administration of the institution." There is much more of a like import in this letter, but what I have given will suffice. It must be remembered that this letter was written six months before General Jackson's first annual message was delivered; before it was known what were his views, if he had any then, in regard to the bank; and before it could have been surmised that a conflict was to follow.

Among other letters brought to light by Mr. Adams, relating to, and constituting a part of, this New Hampshire attempt to turn the bank into a political engine for the benefit of the operators, was a letter from Isaac Hill, then Second Comptroller of the Treasury, addressed to two well-known Jackson men in Philadelphia, inclosing a petition, "subscribed," he says, "by about sixty of the most respectable members of the New Hampshire Legislature, *naming suitable persons* for directors at Portsmouth." He says, "THE FRIENDS OF GENERAL JACKSON in New Hampshire have had but too much reason to complain of the management of the branch at Portsmouth."

These letters Mr. Adams declared were more deserving the attention of Congress and of the nation than any other of the papers commented upon in the report of the majority of the committee.

That a control, for *party* purposes, was attempted to be exercised over the operations of the Bank of the United States by certain prominent members of the Jackson party, who were known to exercise much influence at Washington, and even at the Executive mansion, no one can doubt. Had they succeeded in obtaining the control sought for, and in making a political engine of the bank, favorable to the administration, does any one suppose that its re-charter would have been resisted by what was subsequently known as "the kitchen cabinet," or that we should ever have heard of "the Bank Veto Message"?

In that case the institution would have been an instrument of monstrous political power in their hands. Fortunately, the bank was in the hands of a president and directors possessing firmness and honesty enough to resist all attempts to warp it into the current of corrupting influence or make it subservient to the views and interests of unscrupulous politicians. Baffled as they were in their purpose, it was quite natural they should seek to destroy that which they could not control. Hence the various intimations, by the President in his messages, of his hostility to the institution.

Mr. Adams declared that the bank had been conducted with as near an approach to perfect wisdom as the imperfection of human nature permitted.

The majority report was the production of Mr. Clayton, of Georgia, the chairman of the committee. It was very long, and glaringly exhibited his utter ignorance of the science and true principles of banking, and exposed him to the keen shafts of grave ridicule, which Mr. Adams did not hesitate to use, to the great amusement of the House. Mr. Adams said there was not a paragraph in it in which he could concur, and that one member of the committee, Colonel R. M. Johnson, had signed it out of good nature, without knowing anything that it contained, merely to enable the chairman to make a majority report. One member of the committee (Mr. Clayton), Mr. Adams said, had addressed one hundred and sixty-one questions to the president of the bank never submitted to the committee, and even drawn up after the committee had closed their examinations at Philadelphia, and after he, Mr. Adams, had returned to his post here in the House. He had found many of them, upon perusal, passing his powers of comprehension, and the skeleton of a profound dissertation upon coins, currency, paper, credit, circulation, and banking. He could not withhold his admiration from the comprehensive views and profound knowledge of the subject discovered in those inquiries, and he believed that satisfactory answers to them might form a very useful, sound, though somewhat larger volume than the Legislative and Documentary

History of the Bank of the United States compiled by the indefatigable research and industry of the Clerk of the House of Representatives and his associate. [The volume referred to is a large folio of six or seven hundred pages.] But a large portion of the questions might with more propriety be addressed in a circular to the presidents of all the banks in the four quarters of the globe than to the president of the Bank of the United States, and it may be doubted, of many of the inquiries, whether a convention of all the bankers in the world would not be reduced to the necessity of leaving them as they found them, to be solved only by the ingenuity or sagacity of their author.

Colonel Benton has been candid enough to inform us what was the character of the warfare waged by the Jackson men against the United States Bank. "Seeing," he says, in his "Thirty Years' View," "that there was a majority in each House for the institution, and not intending to lose time in arguing for it, our course of action became obvious, which was to attack incessantly, assail at all points, display the evil of the institution, rouse the people, and *prepare them to sustain the veto*. . . . We determined to have a contest in both Houses, and *to force the bank into defenses which would engage it in a general combat and lay it open to side-blows as well as direct attacks.*"

THE VETO OF THE BANK BILL.

After a long and heated discussion, the bill to re-charter the bank passed in the Senate by a vote of 28 ayes to 20 noes; in the House by 106 ayes to 84 noes.

The President, however, sent a message to the Senate vetoing it.

It is impossible to exaggerate the excitement which this produced in every part of the country. Those who favored the veto went wild with exultation. Meetings were everywhere held; crowds of excited people attended, were addressed by sober-minded and by impassioned speakers; and the meetings gave vent to their feelings in resolutions and anathemas. Meetings of "original Jackson men" were called in almost every city and important town to denounce the President and openly declare their secession from the Jackson party.

Many leading papers in different parts of the country which

had supported Jackson from the beginning wheeled around, denouncing him as false to all his former professions and avowed principles, and accusing him of being under the control of a "kitchen cabinet." The "Courier and Enquirer," of New York, and the "Inquirer," of Philadelphia, were among the most prominent of these journals. The former, especially, at once opened a tremendous fire upon the President, creating great excitement in New York, and bringing down the ire of Tammany upon the head of the fearless editor, Colonel J. Watson Webb.

In the Senate, Mr. J. M. Clayton, Mr. Clay, Mr. Webster, and other Senators assailed the veto message with great power and vehemence, while it was as earnestly sustained by Colonel Benton and by Mr. White, of Tennessee,—the latter a man of sterling worth, ability, and purity of character, esteemed alike by those who concurred and those who differed with him in public affairs.

The message was drawn up with great *political* skill and tact. As Colonel Benton once coarsely said of a resolution offered to the Senate, "it contained a stump-speech in its belly." It was adroitly calculated to confound the foolish, if it could not convince the wise. It cunningly placed the President in the attitude of an honest, patriotic Hercules contending single-handed with "a monster" dangerous to the *people*, for whose sake he was resolved to destroy it at every hazard; and this idea took wonderfully with the ignorant, simple-minded, who knew no guile and dreamed of none in others. The bank was denounced as "a great monopoly," "a gigantic *moneyed* institution," dangerous to the liberties of the *people;* it was "*aristocratic*," and therefore the enemy of the *democracy*.

The President said, "It is maintained by the advocates of the bank that its constitutionality in all its features ought to be considered as settled by precedent and by the decision of the Supreme Court. To this conclusion I cannot come."

After speaking of the precedents, namely, of the establishment of the bank in 1791, the failure of Congress to re-charter it in 1811, and the chartering of the present bank by Congress in 1816, he says,—

"If the opinion of the Supreme Court covered the whole

ground of this act, it ought not to control the co-ordinate authorities of this government. The Congress, the Executive, and the Court *must, each for itself, be guided by its own opinion of the Constitution.* Each public officer who takes an oath to support the Constitution swears that he will support it *as he understands it, and not as it is understood by others.* . . . The opinion of the judges has no more authority over Congress than the opinion of Congress has over the judges; and on that point *the President is independent of both.*"

This is the same monstrous assertion that was made by the President in the Cherokee case.

Scarcely less extraordinary than the passages I have quoted is the following:

"Had the Executive been called upon to furnish the project of such an institution, the duty would have been cheerfully performed." Notwithstanding he had again and again declared that such an institution was *unconstitutional!*

I have had occasion to speak of the fact that the President had, in his first annual message, December, 1829, called the attention of Congress to the circumstance that the charter of the bank would expire in 1836; that it was proper to bear the fact in mind; and that he again reminded Congress in a subsequent annual message, intending, doubtless, that the subject should not be lost sight of; yet *now* he makes it an objection to the bank that its directors did not wait till the charter had expired before applying for a renewal of it. He says,—

"As the charter had yet four years to run, and as a renewal now was not necessary to the successful prosecution of its business, it was to have been expected that the bank itself, conscious of its purity and proud of its character, would have withdrawn its application for the present, and demanded the severest scrutiny into all its transactions."

Mr. Clay addressed the Senate on the veto message, and in the course of his remarks he said, "The friends of the President, who have been for near three years agitating this [bank] question, now turn around upon their opponents who have supposed the President quite serious and in earnest in presenting it for public consideration, and charge them with prematurely agitating it, and that for electioneering purposes. The other side understands perfectly the policy of preferring an unjust charge in order to avoid a well-founded accusation."

He then noticed and commented on the various points of the message in his usual bold, vigorous, and eloquent style, and especially the extraordinary assumption that all who take an oath to support the Constitution swear to support it "as they understand it." He closed by saying,—

"We are about to close one of the longest and most arduous sessions of Congress under the present Constitution; and when we return among our constituents, what account of the operations of their government shall we be bound to communicate? We shall be compelled to say that the Supreme Court is paralyzed, and the missionaries retained in prison in contempt of its authority and defiance of numerous treaties and laws of the United States; that the Executive, through the Secretary of the Treasury, sent to Congress a tariff bill which would have destroyed numerous branches of our domestic industry and led to the final destruction of all; that the veto has been applied to the Bank of the United States, our only reliance for a sound, uniform currency; that the Senate has been violently attacked for the exercise of a clear constitutional power; that the House of Representatives has been unnecessarily assailed; and that the President has promulgated a rule of action for those who have taken the oath to support the Constitution of the United States that must, if there be practical conformity to it, introduce gradual nullification, and end in the absolute subversion of the government."

Mr. Webster closed a very able speech, delivered with earnest solemnity, in the following language:

"As far as its power extends, either in its direct effects, or as a precedent, the message not only unsettles everything which has been settled under the Constitution, but would show, also, that the Constitution itself is utterly incapable of any fixed construction or definite interpretation; and that there is no possibility of establishing by its authority any practical limitations on the powers of the respective branches of the government.

"When the message denies, as it does, the authority of the

Supreme Court to decide on constitutional questions, it effects, so far as the opinion of the President and his authority can effect, a complete change in our government. It does two things: first, it converts constitutional limitations of power into mere matters of opinion, and then it strikes the Judicial Department, as an efficient department, out of our system.

* * * * * * * *

"Mr. President, we have arrived at a new epoch. We are entering on experiments with the government and the Constitution of the country hitherto untried, and of fearful and appalling aspect. This message calls us to the contemplation of a future which little resembles the past. Its principles are at war with all that public opinion has sustained, and all which the experience of the government has sanctioned. It denies first principles; it contradicts truths heretofore received as indisputable. It denies to the Judiciary the interpretation of law, and demands to divide with Congress the origination of statutes. It extends the grasp of Executive pretension over every power of the government. But this is not all. It presents the chief magistrate of the Union in the attitude of *arguing away* the powers of that government over which he has been chosen to preside, and adopting, for this purpose, modes of reasoning which, even under the influence of all proper feeling towards high official station, it is difficult to regard as respectable. It appeals to every prejudice which may betray men into a mistaken view of their own interests, and to every passion which may lead them to disobey the impulses of their understanding. It urges all the specious topics of State rights, and national encroachment, against that which a great majority of the States have affirmed to be rightful, and in which all of them have acquiesced. It sows, in an unsparing manner, the seeds of jealousy and ill will against that government of which its author is the official head. It raises a cry that *Liberty is in danger*, at the very moment when it puts forth claims to powers heretofore unknown and unheard of. It affects alarm for the *public freedom*, when nothing so much endangers that freedom as its own unparalleled pretenses. This, even, is not all. It manifestly seeks to influence the poor against the rich;

it wantonly attacks whole classes of the people for the purpose of turning against them the prejudices and the resentments of other classes. It is a state paper which finds no topic too exciting for its use, no passion too inflammable for its address and its solicitation. Such is this message."

AN EXCITING SCENE IN THE SENATE.

In the course of this debate, which was characterized by great heat on both sides, a scene occurred between Mr. Clay and Colonel Benton which had, for a time, an intense interest. Mr. Benton, having the floor, in reply to Mr. Clay's speech, charged him with the use of language discourteous and disrespectful to the chief magistrate.

Mr. Clay rose, and, after some explanations touching his remarks about a tariff bill being sent to Congress by the Executive, by his officer the Secretary of the Treasury, he said, "The Senator from Missouri has adverted to the fact of crowded galleries. But if, impelled by curiosity, the galleries are sometimes filled when some Senators are to speak, no member knows better than the honorable gentleman that, when some others rise, the galleries are quickly emptied."

Mr. Clay observed that he had been accused of want of courtesy and decorum towards the chief magistrate in his remarks upon his veto message. He had felt it his duty to discuss that message, examine and weigh all the arguments and extraordinary propositions it contained, and in doing so he appealed to the Senate if he had not treated the President and his message with all the respect consistent with the occasion and with the high responsibility under which every member of the body was bound to act.

In some past transactions, well known to the public,* he (Mr. Clay) had been furnished with just cause for resentment; but the present was not the occasion, nor the Senate the place, for indulging such feelings: they had high duties to perform here, which should be performed under a deep sense of the obligations they owed to the country.

* Mr. Clay alluded to General Jackson's charge against him and Mr. Adams of bargain and corruption.

"But, Mr. President," said Mr. Clay, "I cannot allow the Senator from Missouri to instruct me in etiquette and courtesy and how I shall deport myself towards an exalted personage." Mr. Clay made allusions to several incidents in Mr. Benton's life of a not very exalted character, which would not now be understood, but which were barbed darts that irritated and stung. He then proceeded: "I never had any personal rencontre with the President; I never promulgated a bulletin on any such rencontre; I never complained of the President beating a brother of mine after he was prostrated and lying apparently lifeless.* Nor did I ever make a prophecy of events which would ensue from the elevation of the President, as the public press ascribes to the Senator from Missouri."

Colonel Benton replied that it was true he and General Jackson had a personal conflict; they had fought, and, he hoped, like men; and with the cessation of their conflict ceased their enmity. [But not until it was evident that Missouri would support Jackson.] There was no adjourned question of veracity between them. [Alluding to a former controversy between Mr. Clay and Mr. Adams in regard to the fisheries and the negotiations at Ghent.] As regards the *prophecy*, he pronounced it *an atrocious calumny*, and he was now no longer in doubt as

* The allusions here were to a very desperate fight—one long remembered on account of the parties engaged, and its savage ferocity—which took place at a hotel in Nashville, between General Jackson and his friend Colonel Coffee, on the one side, and the two Bentons, Thomas H. and his brother Jesse, on the other; all being armed with pistols and other weapons commonly used in desperate personal conflicts. In this fight Jackson was wounded in the arm by Colonel Benton, fell and feigned to be dead, to avoid being killed. Jesse Benton was also wounded, and while lying apparently lifeless, according to the statement of Colonel Benton next day, was savagely beaten. The only wonder was that, considering the ferocity and murderous intent of the parties, and the weapons they used, no one was killed. General Jackson carried Colonel Benton's ball in his arm until after his second election as President, when it was extracted by Dr. Jackson, of Philadelphia.

Colonel Benton and General Jackson became friends; but Jesse Benton was the enemy of Jackson to the last, and never forgave his brother for becoming a Jackson man.

The day after the fight, Colonel Benton issued a ferocious bulletin giving an account of it, denouncing Jackson and Coffee as murderous assassins, etc.

Soon after this famous fight, Colonel Benton left Tennessee and settled at St. Louis, Missouri.

to who had indorsed it, at least in the Senate, and had thus become responsible for it.

Mr. Clay, referring to Mr. Benton's denial of the statement that he had made a prophecy as to what would happen in case General Jackson should be elected,* pausing a moment, and looking Mr. Benton in the eye, asked, "*Can* the Senator from Missouri look me in the face and assert that he never used language similar to that imputed to him?"

Mr. Benton, looking and pointing at Mr. Clay, said "he could, he could."

Mr. Clay.—"I again ask, *Can* that man presume to look me in the face and deny it?"

Mr. Benton repeated his answer, in a loud, defiant tone.

Mr. Clay, looking at him with astonishment, resumed his seat.

Mr. Benton then said he had already pronounced the charge an atrocious calumny; he now pointed out the author, in the Senator; he would pin it to his sleeve, and there it would stick,—*stick*,—STICK.

Mr. Clay rose in an excited manner, and said he returned the charge of calumny to the Senator from Missouri.

The Chair (Mr. Tazewell) said the debate could not longer be suffered,—the Senator from Kentucky must take his seat.

Mr. Clay.—"I wish to explain."

The Chair.—"No further explanation will be heard from the gentleman from Kentucky."

Mr. Clay, in an *imperial* manner, such as no man but himself, and he only when greatly excited, could assume,—in a commanding tone of voice, with erect position and flashing eye,—said, "I tell the President I MUST be heard, and I *demand* to know the point of order."

The Chair.—"The Senator was out of order in the language used to the Senator from Missouri."

Mr. Clay.—"Then I make another point of order. Was not the language of the Senator from Missouri out of order?"

The Chair.—"The present occupant of the chair was not in it when the debate began."

* It was that if General Jackson should be elected President, members of Congress would have to legislafe with pistols by their side.

Mr. Poindexter, who had been in the chair, rose to explain, when Mr. Benton rose and said an apology was due from him, and he made it to the Senate, but not to the Senator from Kentucky.

Mr. Clay.—"To the same tribunal I also offer an apology, but none to the Senator from Missouri."

Here the *scene* ended. During its continuance, the galleries as well as grave Senators were intensely moved.

The vote was then taken on the question whether the bill (bank) should pass, the President's reasons to the contrary notwithstanding; and, a majority, but not two-thirds, of the Senate voting for it, it was lost. And thus ended the Bank of the United States, so far as legislation was concerned.

THE EFFECT OF THE VETO ON PARTIES.

In the Northern and Eastern States especially, the question of re-chartering the bank had been thoroughly discussed by the people, and its re-charter was earnestly desired and advocated by almost the entire portion of the business men. In Pennsylvania, it was claimed to be a *Pennsylvania* measure—a great *Pennsylvania* interest—by all parties, and the only contest about it was which party were the most earnest friends of the institution. The Jackson papers charged the National Republicans with foully slandering the President in accusing him of hostility to the bank and predicting that he would veto the bill to re-charter it. They declared that General Jackson had great regard for Pennsylvania interests, and would never do an act so injurious to those interests as would be the vetoing of that bill.

While the bill was undergoing discussion in the Senate, the United States Circuit Court held a session at Williamsport, on the West Branch of the Susquehanna. It was the practice of the Jackson marshal to summon as jurors to this court the leading politicians of his own party in different parts of the State, thus getting together at the cost of the government a political State convention, which lent its aid in perfecting the plans of the party to carry the election in the fall.

As a Presidential election was to take place this year, the marshal had been careful to gather together, *as jurors*, many of the most sagacious and influential politicians of the Jackson school, who held a meeting and passed a series of resolutions, among which were two or three of the character I have mentioned, that it was a slander upon General Jackson to say that he would veto the bank bill if passed, and claiming him as the friend of Pennsylvania interests. Having done this, and spread their doings over the whole State, they adjourned, as the court did also, and sought their several homes, well satisfied with their important labors and their *pay* as *jurors*.

But who can tell what a day or an hour may bring forth, or what unexpected events may occur! Before some of these *iurors*—the ardent friends of the bank, the great sticklers for Pennsylvania interests, the devoted friends of General Jackson, who became indignant at the *slanders* cast upon him by alleging that he would not sign the bill—reached their homes, the veto message stared them in the face! Of course they felt indignant, and abandoned "the old hero;" of course they stood by what they had said of the bank, its usefulness, importance, etc. They could not turn back upon themselves, unsay all they had said, and present themselves to the world as a poor, craven, subservient, party-ridden set, deserving only the scorn and contempt of all honorable, independent men!

Ay, but they did;—all but three or four of them, who had manliness and independence and pride enough to stand by what they had said. Of these honorable exceptions, I remember William Frick, of Munson, and —— Bull, of Towanda. All the others became at once the most rancorous enemies of the bank, professing to have been convinced by the veto message that the bank was a dangerous institution, and the president and directors a corrupt set of men!

An anti-bank meeting was called in Philadelphia, in which appeared Henry Horn, member of Congress from the first district of Pennsylvania, who was made chairman of the meeting, although *he had voted for the bank bill.* Having done so, he now *apologized* for his vote, saying that he voted, as he supposed, in accordance with the general feeling in his State; thereby admitting that he had no opinion of his own, but only followed what he thought was the majority.

It is no easy task to give the people of the present day the faintest idea of the condition of the currency of the country at the time of the establishment of the United States Bank, and shortly after. There was no specie to be seen; bank-notes and "shinplasters," as the small notes were called, constituted the currency; and the "shinplasters" were issued by States, manu facturing companies, merchants, individuals having the reputation of being "well off," and turnpike companies.

Mr. Ingham, in the letter from which I have quoted, said, "The BANK has purified one of the worst currencies that ever infested any country or people. It consisted of mere paper, of no definite value, accompanied by worthless tickets, issued from broken banks, petty corporations, and partnerships, in almost every village. Instead of this, the United States Bank has given us the best currency known among nations. It supplies a medium equal in value to gold and silver in every part of the Union. . . . Yet General Jackson would destroy this institution, and expose the country to all the evils from which it has so happily but just recovered!"

SOUTH CAROLINA.—NULLIFICATION.—THE PRESIDENT'S PROCLAMATION, ETC.

The tariff act of 1832, while it considerably reduced the revenue and the rate of duties on many imported articles, retained the principle of *protection*, and was therefore obnoxious to the free-traders of the South, those of South Carolina especially, who kept up their clamor and war preparations, or preparations for resisting the collection of custom duties in that State by the United States.

The Legislature was convened by the governor, and passed an act providing for holding a State convention, which was held on the third Monday of November. The convention adopted an "ORDINANCE," 24th of November, 1832, declaring the tariff act null and void, and declaring it also unlawful for the State officers or the United States officers to enforce the collection of duties in that State. The courts were prohibited from allowing appeals to be taken to the Supreme Court of the United States, and clerks of the courts from furnishing papers for such appeals. All public officers were required to take an oath to obey the ordinance and all laws passed in accordance therewith.

"If the government of the United States shall attempt to enforce the tariff laws, by means of its army or navy, by closing the ports of the State, or preventing the ingress or egress of vessels, or in any way obstruct the foreign commerce of the State, South Carolina will no longer consider herself a member of the Federal Union, and will thenceforth hold herself absolved from all further obligation to maintain or preserve her political connection with the people of the other States, and will forthwith organize a separate government, and do all other acts and things which a sovereign and independent State may of right do."

The ordinance was to take effect on the first day of February, 1833.

This was followed by a bellicose proclamation by Governor Hayne, warning the people of South Carolina against all attempts to seduce them from their "*primary* allegiance to the State," and earnestly exhorting them to disregard the vain menaces of military force which the President had put forth. This proclamation was issued on the 31st of December, 1832.

Upon its reaching Washington, the President sent a special message to Congress, asking an increase of executive powers, to enable the government, if necessary, to close ports of entry, remove custom-houses, and do sundry other acts.

The Legislature of South Carolina met soon after the convention adjourned, and passed a series of laws to carry into effect the provisions of the ordinance, and providing for the new state of affairs,—among other things, the purchase of ten thousand stand of arms and the requisite amount of munitions of war.

Such was the attitude of South Carolina towards the government of the United States—an attitude of armed defiance—on the 1st of January, 1833. At once the President put forth a proclamation,* that stirred the people of the whole country like the boom of the first gun at Fort Sumter. South Carolina

* Written by Edward Livingston, Secretary of State.

bravado had no terrors for him. He met threats by cool firmness, and an ostentatious display of military preparations by prompt and decisive action.

The proclamation was an extraordinary paper: extraordinary in its ability, and extraordinary in the doctrines it promulgated, considering the source whence it emanated. It was drawn up with great clearness and logical precision. Its exposition of the powers of the Federal government was in entire accord with the doctrines laid down by Mr. Webster in his celebrated speech in reply to Mr. Hayne, delivered in the Senate some two years and a half before. Indeed, that speech seemed to be the text-book whence the doctrines of the proclamation were drawn. It was a bomb which blew "State rights," as asserted by South Carolina, Virginia, and other States, into a thousand fragments.

The following extract will show what were the doctrines put forth in this celebrated paper:

. . . "We are ONE PEOPLE. . . . The Constitution of the United States forms a GOVERNMENT, not a *league;* and whether it be formed by compact between the States, or in any other manner, its character is the same. . . . To say that any State may at pleasure secede from the Union, is to say that the United States are not a NATION."

MOVEMENTS OF THE GOVERNMENT AGAINST THE NULLIFIERS.

The horizon at this time looked dark and portentous. No one could foretell the result of the conflict should it come to a clash of arms; but the thought of a civil war was saddening. How it was to be avoided no one could see.

The President's proclamation was received in South Carolina with a shout of derision and defiance: had the State been a powerful empire, the leading men—the Haynes, the McDuffies, the Hamiltons, the Hammonds, the Pickenses, the Rhetts, and others—could not have shown more confidence in their own power, or contempt for that of the national government.

There were prominent men, however, in the State who deprecated and opposed the course of the nullifiers, and gave public expression to their views. They designated themselves "Unionists," and were headed by Judge William Smith, formerly a Senator in Congress.

With a view to counteract the purposes of the nullifiers of South Carolina, the Secretary of the Treasury addressed a letter to the collector at Charleston, placing two revenue cutters under his orders, to enable him to levy and collect duties on all vessels arriving at that port, and instructing him, should it become necessary, to remove the custom-house to Castle Pinckney, where his duties could not be interfered with by the State authorities. The collector was directed to require all vessels arriving at that port to be boarded and examined by a revenue cutter.

Meantime, the Secretary of War ordered troops to Charleston, with guns and munitions for Castle Pinckney. General Scott was sent to Charleston to take command, with instructions to "take no step, except what relates to the immediate defense and security of the posts, without the concurrence" of the collector of the port and the district attorney. Should a crisis arise, when the ordinary power in the hands of the civil officers should not be sufficient for the enforcement of the laws, the President would then determine what course should be taken.

The navy department also dispatched several vessels of war to rendezvous at Charleston and make that port their headquarters while cruising up and down the coast. The nullifiers were thus effectually flanked.

Colonel Hayne having resigned his seat in the Senate and accepted the office of governor, Mr. Calhoun was elected to fill the vacancy. He was present when the President's special message to Congress, asking for additional powers, was read, and replied to it with earnestness, vindicating himself as one conscious that he was considered the prime mover of the nullification programme and the great criminal of these treasonable proceedings.

A bill was immediately introduced, giving the President the additional powers asked for, which, after much sharp and spirited debate, became a law, and was known as the "Force Bill" and "Bloody Bill." It had the support of Mr. Clay, Mr. Webster, and the Whigs generally, except those of the South.

Mr. Calhoun and his friends opposed it with unusual vehemence. Circumstances about to occur prevented the necessity of using the extraordinary power conferred by it upon the government.

The proclamation of Governor Hayne had fixed the first day of February as the date when the nullifying ordinance was to take effect. The day came, and passed; yet the President heard of no act being done under that ordinance by South Carolina to which exception could be taken. It was known that he stood ready, firmly resolved that upon the receipt of intelligence that armed opposition had been made to the laws or lawful authority of the United States, he would seize Mr. Calhoun, and perhaps other South Carolinians, on the charge of high treason.

But there occurred no overt act of treason. Perhaps the nullifiers deemed discretion the better part of valor. At any rate, a meeting of some of the leading men of South Carolina was held at Charleston, where it was concluded and resolved that they would for the present postpone the nullification of the revenue laws until it could be seen what Congress should do in regard to certain bills then before that body to reduce the duties on imports.

VERPLANCK'S BILL.

In accordance with the President's message recommending a reduction of the tariff, a bill was prepared by the Secretary of the Treasury, and presented to the House by Mr. Verplanck, which became known as Verplanck's bill. This bill struck a death-blow at protection, throwing the system back, as Mr. Clay said, to its starting-point, 1816. It caused a protracted debate in the House. "The immediate friends of the administration," says Colonel Benton, "seemed to be the only ones hearty in support of the bill; but they were no match in numbers for those who acted in concert against it,—spinning out the time in sterile and vagrant debate."

Viewing the alarming state of the country at that time with the eye of a statesman and the anxious concern of a patriot,—seeing South Carolina arraying herself in a defiant attitude against the Federal government, and the President fully resolved to crush nullification by military force should the nullifiers dare to oppose the execution of the revenue laws, as they were threatening to do,—seeing Mr. Calhoun and other South Carolinians liable to be arrested and imprisoned on the charge of treason,—seeing also the danger his favorite protective system was in of being destroyed by the passage of the Verplanck bill,—Mr. Clay set himself the task of preparing a measure which, in his own words, "should effect the double purpose of saving the protective policy from destruction and saving the Union from the horrors of civil war." This "healing and tranquillizing measure," as he called it, was the bill known as Mr. Clay's Compromise bill, which he asked leave of the Senate to introduce on the 12th of February, 1833.

On asking leave, Mr. Clay addressed the Senate explanatory of his motives and the purposes of the bill. His first object, he said, looked to the tariff, which, he was compelled to say, after the most mature deliberation, stood in imminent danger. History could produce no parallel to the extent of the mischief which would be produced by the sudden overthrow of the various branches of manufacturing which had sprung up under the protective system. He believed this system to be in the greatest danger, and that it could be placed on a better and safer foundation at this session than at the next.

The bill provided for the moderate annual reduction of duties till they should come to twenty per cent. in 1842.

Mr. Calhoun at once announced his readiness to support the bill, and Mr. Forsyth, of Georgia, spoke of it as a project to harmonize the people. The object of the bill, he said, would meet with universal approbation, and it could come from no better source than the Senator from Kentucky.

The bill struck the manufacturers with alarm, and they rushed to the capital to stop it. But they soon found cause to change their minds; at least many of them, who saw that it secured them the benefits of protection for nine years. At home, they could not perceive the danger the protective system was in; here, they saw the precipice upon which they stood, and gladly accepted the only escape that could be found.

Unfortunately, Mr. Clay and Mr. Webster, usually so harmonious in their views of public measures, could not unite on this; and the difference arose from the different stand-points from which each viewed the conflict with South Carolina, and its probable consequences if not arrested. Mr. Clay looked upon this threatened conflict with alarm: he knew the temper of the President, and felt sure that if blood were once shed the consequences would be terrible at best, and no one could see what they might not be. General Jackson, it was known, would, in case of armed resistance in South Carolina to the execution of the revenue laws, immediately arrest Mr. Calhoun on the charge of treason, and possibly put his threat of hanging into execution.

Mr. Clay also deemed his favorite protective system in imminent danger of being overthrown. Speaking of this, and of his being called the father of this system, he said, "I have, indeed, cherished it with parental fondness, and my affection is undiminished. But in what condition do I find this child? It is in the hands of the Philistines, who would strangle it. I would save it if possible."

Mr. Webster did not view the threatening attitude of South Carolina with the same apprehension that Mr. Clay did. He could not believe that that State would go to the extremity she threatened; and if she did, he believed the power of the government was sufficient to coerce her into obedience at once. Nor could he believe that Virginia, Georgia, Mississippi, and perhaps other Southern States, as had been said, would interpose in her behalf, should it come to force. He opposed the bill moderately but firmly. He could not agree with the Senator from Kentucky that the tariff was in imminent danger; that if not destroyed this session, it could not hope to survive the next. "This may be so, sir. This may be so. But, if it be so, it is because the American people will not sanction the tariff; and if they will not, why, then, sir, it cannot be sustained at all."

Mr. Webster delivered his opinions of the proposed measure in a series of carefully-drawn resolutions. He paid a glowing tribute to the purity, zeal, and ability of the Senator from Kentucky, for whom he had long entertained the highest respect, and to elevate whom to a situation where his talents might be still more beneficial to his country he had zealously labored. He also complimented the talents and services of the Senator from South Carolina (Mr. Calhoun), for whom he had a high regard. He then reviewed his own course in relation to the tariff, referring to his former opposition to the protective policy. But, that policy having been adopted and become the settled policy of the country, New England adapted herself to it, and turned all her natural advantages and wealth and industry into the new channel thus marked out for her.

In reply, Mr. Clay paid a high tribute to the patriotism and purity of the Senator from Massachusetts, and expressed his deep regret that he had now to differ with him. Mr. Webster had spoken of the bill having originated in panic. Mr. Clay replied that he was as little sensible to fear as any one, and therefore the remark could not affect him. But he went on to show the causes and circumstances then existing which should at least excite apprehension if not alarm, and which he deemed it wise to provide against.

After the Compromise bill had been some days discussed in the Senate, Mr. Clay proposed an amendment, which was, that from and after the 30th day of June, 1842, the duties required to be paid on foreign merchandise shall be assessed upon the value thereof at the port where the same shall be entered. This was denominated "the home-valuation clause," and met with strong opposition from Mr. Webster and Mr. Calhoun.

In advocating this amendment, Mr. Clay said that his object in introducing this bill was conciliation; to give nine years of peace and tranquillity to the country; and if it was not to be considered permanent for that period of time,—if any gentleman should say he would vote for it and take it for what it is worth now, with the intention of disturbing it next session to get a better measure,—it would lose all its value in his eyes, and he would vote against it.

Mr. Calhoun regretted exceedingly that the Senator from Kentucky had felt it his duty to move the amendment. According to his present impressions, the objections to it were insurmountable; and unless these were removed, he should be compelled to vote against the whole bill, should the amendment be adopted.

Mr. J. M. Clayton declared his determination to vote against the bill unless the amendment should be adopted. He had been anxious to do something for the relief of South Carolina from her present perilous situation; though he had never been driven by the taunts of Southern gentlemen to do that which he now did for the sake of conciliation. "I vote for this bill," said Mr. Clayton, "only on the ground that it may save South Carolina herself."

Mr. Calhoun entreated the Senator to believe that South Carolina had no fears for herself.

Mr. Clayton replied, "I will vote for this measure as one of conciliation and compromise; but if the clause of the Senator from Kentucky is not inserted, I shall be compelled to vote against it. The protective system never can be abandoned; and I, for one, will not now, or at any time, admit the idea."

Much warm discussion followed for two days, when Mr. Calhoun, seeing that the passage or defeat of the bill depended upon his course, finally yielded, voted for it, and it was passed,—26 to 16.

ANECDOTE OF MR. CALHOUN AND MR. SIMMONS.

Some time in 1844, Mr. Simmons, of Rhode Island, while addressing the Senate, took occasion to allude to Mr. Calhoun's vote for the Compromise bill. Upon his doing so, Mr. Calhoun rose and begged leave to correct the Senator, who had stated that he had voted for that bill. "The Senator from Rhode Island is mistaken," he said, "as I did not vote for that bill."

Mr. Simmons said he thought he was not mistaken; his recollection was that the Senator from South Carolina did vote for that bill.

Mr. Calhoun.—"No, sir, I did not vote for it, as I considered some of its provisions unconstitutional."

Mr. Simmons proceeded, but after awhile again alluded to that vote.

Mr. Calhoun again rose, and said he was surprised that the Senator from Rhode Island should persist in saying that he (Mr. Calhoun) voted for that bill. He did not vote for it; he could not have voted for it, as he considered the "home-valuation clause" unconstitutional.

Mr. Simmons again said that he was present when the vote was taken, and thought he could not be mistaken in his recollection.

"Well, then," said Mr. Calhoun, "since the Senator will be convinced by nothing short of the journal, I will refer to that." Calling for the journal, and turning to the passage recording the yeas and nays, he read,—

"Those who voted in the affirmative were Messrs. Bell, Black, Bibb, Calhoun——" Here Mr. Calhoun paused, apparently confounded.

Mr. Simmons.—"I hope the Senator from South Carolina is satisfied."

Mr. Calhoun.—"I remember now, I voted for the bill under protest."

Mr. Clay.—"There's no protest on the record."

Mr. Calhoun.—"No; as no one has a right to enter a protest of record. But I did it under protest, nevertheless."

I was not present at this scene, but the circumstances were related to me by Judge Mangum, who then occupied the chair as President of the Senate, and said he was much surprised and concerned that his friend Mr. Simmons should be so persistent in representing that Mr. Calhoun voted for the bill against his denial of the fact; presuming that Mr. Calhoun must, of course, remember how he voted on so important a measure as that was. But when Mr. Calhoun read from the journal his own name in the affirmative, his surprise amounted to astonishment, and that feeling pervaded the Senate.

On relating this to Mr. John M. Clayton, some ten years after it had occurred, and six or eight years after Judge Mangum had related it to me, he said, with a good deal of warmth, "Yes, he did vote for the bill, and *I made him do it.* I wish I had been present at the time; I should not only have told him that he voted for the bill, but that I *compelled* him to do so." Mr.

Clayton then related to me the circumstances connected with it, as follows:

He said he considered the bill as one mainly for the relief of South Carolina and of Mr. Calhoun himself; that the South Carolina Senators were anxious that it should pass, but did not want to vote for it; that he was determined they should, or that they might fight it out with "Old Hickory" (the President) as they could. Accordingly, he got a majority of Senators to agree to vote to lay the bill on the table unless the Senators from South Carolina would agree to vote for it. Mr. Clay came to him and begged him to let them off. His reply was, "No, sir, I will not. I know, in your magnanimity, you would let them off; but I will not. If they can't vote for a bill that is to save their necks from a halter, their necks may stretch. They *shall* vote for it, or *it shall not pass.*"

Mr. Clayton said that Mr. Miller, Mr. Calhoun's colleague, came to him as the vote was about to be taken, and said *he* would vote for the bill, but he wanted Mr. Calhoun should be let off. "The very man," answered Mr. Clayton, "of all others who *must* vote for it if it passes. And now," said Mr. Clayton, taking out his watch, "at the end of fifteen minutes I shall move to lay the bill on the table unless within that time you inform me authoritatively that Mr. Calhoun will vote for it."

"He came," said Mr. Clayton, "in about ten minutes, and said Mr. Calhoun would vote for it. 'Very good,' I replied; 'you have saved your necks from a halter.' I was master of the situation on that occasion, and not Mr. Calhoun nor Mr. Clay."

Colonel Benton has given a more detailed account of the circumstances attending the passage of the Compromise bill, and also Mr. Calhoun's brief remarks upon voting for it; but there is no variation of facts in his account from Mr. Clayton's statement of them to me. He says Mr. Clay's motive was the saving of the protective policy and preserving the support of the manufacturers; and Mr. Calhoun's, that of saving himself from the perils of his situation.

HOW THE VERPLANCK BILL WAS KILLED AND THE COMPROMISE BILL PASSED IN THE HOUSE.

Colonel Benton, in his "Thirty Years' View," gives us an account of the passage of the Compromise bill in the House. Speaking of Verplanck's bill, he says, "The 25th of February had arrived, and found the bill still afloat upon the wordy sea of stormy debate, when, all of a sudden, it was knocked over, run under and submerged, and lost in a new one which expunged the old one and took its place. It was late in the afternoon of that day, and within a week of the end of Congress, when Mr. Letcher, of Kentucky, the friend of Mr. Clay, rose in his place and moved to strike out the whole Verplanck bill, except the enacting clause, and insert a bill offered in the Senate by Mr. Clay, since called the 'Compromise.'

"The bill was offered without previous notice just as the House was about to adjourn, and while some members were putting on their overcoats to walk home. Some were taken by surprise, and asked for delay. But this was refused, and the bill went through with a speed no less surprising than the time and manner of its entrance,—ayes, 119; noes, 85; the Southern members generally voting for it, as did many Northern men, even Mr. Verplanck himself.

"In the Senate the debate had thus far been on the motion for leave to introduce the bill. That which had passed the House now came to the Senate and took the place of the one which Mr. Clay had asked leave to introduce. It was now before the Senate, and underwent elaborate debate, with the result already mentioned.

"Undoubtedly the reason why the bill was so promptly passed by the House was the threatening attitude of General Jackson to Mr. Calhoun. Mr. Letcher had seen the President and sounded him on the subject of a compromise; the President would have no negotiation, but would execute the laws. Subsequently, Mr. Josiah S. Johnson, Senator from Louisiana, came to Mr. Letcher's room in the night, and informed him that he had just learned that General Jackson would admit of no further delay, and was determined to take at once a decided course with Mr. Calhoun (an arrest and trial for treason being understood). Mr. Johnson urged Mr. Letcher to go to Mr. Calhoun immediately and apprise him of his danger. He went, found Mr. Calhoun in bed, was admitted, and informed him. He was evidently disturbed." *

AN EPISODE IN THE SENATE.—MR. WEBSTER.—MR. POINDEXTER.

In the course of the debate on the Force bill, which met such fierce opposition from the Southern men, Mr. Poindexter, of Mississippi, irritated, probably, by Mr. Webster's support of that measure, took occasion to allude to the course of the latter during the War of 1812, on which he commented with great severity, and compared it with the conduct of Mr. Calhoun. Mr. Webster declined all explanations, and treated the unjustifiable attack with dignified indifference. He said, however, that the Senator from South Carolina was a member of the House with him at the time alluded to, and if *that* Senator desired any explanation of his course at that time, he should pay the most cheerful and respectful attention to his request; but he did not feel himself called upon to take any notice of the remarks of the gentleman from Mississippi. Stung by this contemptuous treatment, which was apparent to and attracted the attention of the galleries as well as of Senators, Mr. Poindexter hastily rose, and, in a voice of passion, said, "*I have the most perfect contempt for the Senator from Massachusetts.*"

This was one of those unpleasant, painful scenes which sometimes, but rarely, occur in the Senate, where, formerly at least, the members bore themselves towards one another with such urbane, refined courtesy, and where self-respect, as well as respect for the body, forbade all coarse, vituperative language, —scenes greatly to be deprecated at all times. These *scenes*, however, are enjoyed immensely by a certain portion—and that usually a large one—of the galleries, who come there for excitement and to luxuriate on a sensation.

A few days after this occurred, Mr. Clay assumed the office of peacemaker. He rose and said, "An incident occurred a few days ago which gave me very great pain, and I am quite

* Colonel Benton's Thirty Years' View.

sure that the whole Senate participated in the feeling." He then spoke of what had occurred between the two Senators, and expressed his confidence that it arose out of a misunderstanding and that zeal and warmth which both the gentlemen felt,—the one to carry, the other to defeat the measure. He then paid a glowing compliment to the speech which Mr. Poindexter made against the bill at the time; but said that in concluding his able speech, it appeared to him and to others, and doubtless to the Senator from Massachusetts, that there was something personal and peculiarly harsh in his language. Acting on the feeling which this would naturally produce, the Senator from Massachusetts, in the course of his observations, also used language which may have seemed unnecessarily harsh; but, from the sense in which he (Mr. Clay) understood the language of the Senator from Mississippi, the Senator from Massachusetts might have found some justification.

Mr. Clay said he was sure that both Senators entertained a high respect for each other, and there could be no cause for permanent estrangement. He said he should feel deep regret and pain if the two honorable Senators should be separated by hostile feelings thus originating, and he did not doubt that the Senate shared with him in his regret. After speaking in this conciliatory strain for some time, he resumed his seat, when Mr. Poindexter rose, and in some very appropriate remarks expressed his sincere regret at what had occurred. The Senator from Massachusetts, he said, well knew the respect and kindness he (Mr. P.) bore for him; and he assured him it was not his intention to reflect either upon his personal or political character, or to trespass on his feelings.

Mr. Webster then rose and said it was not more a matter of regret to the Senator from Mississippi than to himself that the misunderstanding had occurred; their intercourse had been on a footing of kindness and courtesy ever since they had met, and there was no Senator towards whom he was less inclined to manifest any want of decorum. He thought the Senator's remarks had a strong personal bearing on himself, and that they were so intended. He was very happy to hear the honorable Senator disavow such intention. On his part, after further remarks, he disavowed any intention to offer any personal disrespect in his answer to the remarks of the Senator towards him.

Mr. Poindexter again rose, and said that the disclaimer of the Senator from Massachusetts called for a further explanation from him. He admitted that he used expressions in reply to Mr. W. which were harsh, and might appear to be a violation of the respect which ought to be preserved between members of that body. He now, with great pleasure, retracted those expressions, hastily used on the impulse of the moment, and tendered his hand to the honorable Senator in perfect sincerity and cordiality.

The two Senators then advanced towards each other, met, and shook hands, to the great gratification of the whole body and themselves.

CHAPTER IV.

The President makes a Tour to the Eastern States.—Great Attention and Respect paid him.—Black Hawk.—The Cherokee Missionaries.—An Exciting Scene in the Senate between Mr. Clay and Colonel Benton.—The Past raked up.—The Bank Bill vetoed.—Effect upon Parties.—Nullification in South Carolina.—President's Proclamation.—Governor Hayne in Reply.—South Carolina in an Attitude of Resistance.—Movements of the Government against South Carolina.—Removal of the Public Deposits from the Bank of the United States.—First Session of the Twenty-third Congress.—The "Panic Session."—Mr. Clay's Resolutions condemning the Removal of the Deposits.—Proceedings thereon in the Senate.—The National Republican takes the Name of the Whig Party.—Great Numbers of Memorials and Delegations sent to Congress and the President.—The Country greatly excited.—Mr. Binney.—The President's Protest against Clay's Resolutions, passed by the Senate, censuring him.—The Virginia Resolutions.—Great Commotion from a Small Cause: the Figure-Head of Jackson on "Old Ironsides" sawed off.—A Change in the Cabinet: Taney succeeds Duane in the Treasury Department.—The "Pet Banks."—A Gold Currency promised.—The Death of Five Distinguished Men.—The Muse of History recording the Doings of the House of Representatives.—Unfriendly Relation with France.—Attempted Assassination of the President.—Mr. Calhoun's Report on Executive Patronage, and Debate thereon.—A Pleasant Interpellation: Mr. Buchanan and Mr. Clay.—Mismanagement of the Post-Office Department.—William Cost Johnson backs down the Hot-headed Champions of the Postmaster-General.—Presidential Candidates nominated.—The National Convention of the Jackson Party held at Baltimore; nominates Mr. Van Buren for President, and Colonel R. M. Johnson for Vice-President.—Delegates "fresh from the People," self-appointed.—Mob to put down Abolitionism in Boston.—Expunging Resolution.—Death of Chief-Justice John Marshall.—Distribution of the Surplus Revenue.—The Mania of Speculation.—The Moon Hoax.—First Session of the Twenty-fourth Congress.—Abolition Petitions.—Stirring Scenes in the House of Representatives.—Mr. Adams's Extraordinary Speech.—Mr. Wise's ditto.—Scathing Replies to Mr. Adams by Mr. Harlan and Mr. George Evans.—United States Bank re-chartered by the Pennsylvania Legislature.—Rebellion and Revolution in Texas.—The Massacre of Colonels Fannin and Ward, and their Men, at Goliad.—The Massacre of Colonel Crockett at the Alamo.—The Bloody Battle of San Jacinto: Santa Anna defeated and taken Prisoner.—Seminole War.—The Specie Circular.—Its Effect on the Country.—A Protracted and very Exciting Scene in the House.—A Gloomy Day in the Senate.—The Expunging Resolution passed.—Chancellor Kent's Letter to Mr. Clay.—The Expungers have a Royal Feast at the White House.—General Jackson's Administration closes, and he returns to the Hermitage.—A Sketch of him.—His Death.

MARCH 4, 1833.—GENERAL JACKSON'S SECOND INAUGURATION.

THE Twenty-second Congress ended on the 3d of March, 1833, and General Jackson was inaugurated for a second term on the 4th.

The Compromise act having put nullification to rest, and the House of Representatives having declared it safe to continue the deposits of the public funds in the Bank of the United States, there seemed to be nothing to agitate the public mind, or to prevent the period between the adjournment of the last and the assembling of the next Congress from being as calm as the preceding year had been tempestuous. There was, to the ordinary eye, no cloud on the horizon; all looked clear and calm.

BURNING OF THE TREASURY.

An incident occurred in Washington after the adjournment of Congress, which caused great sensation there, and attracted the notice of the country; namely, the burning of the treasury building, on the night of the 30th or morning of the 31st of March. The fire was not generally supposed to have been *accidental.* It commenced in a room in which were papers the destruction of which was supposed to be highly desirable by certain parties, and which were destroyed. This was the second time in thirty-three years, Mr. Niles stated, that a destructive fire had occurred in that department.

The President immediately directed the Secretaries of State, Treasury, and War, and the Attorney-General and Postmaster General, to investigate the matter and report. They did so, but were unable to obtain any satisfactory account of the origin of the fire. Many books and papers were destroyed, chiefly old records and files; but, on the whole, the fire did not involve the government in a very heavy loss, except the building.

THE PRESIDENT'S TOUR.

During the early part of the summer of 1833 the President took a tour North and East, passing through Baltimore, Philadelphia, New York, Providence, Boston, and Portsmouth, where his tour ended, or rather at which point he retraced his steps, though it had been his intention to go at least as far as Portland, Me.

At every place on his way he was received with the respect due to the chief magistrate of the nation by all parties, and by his special friends or partisans with great *éclat* and enthusiasm, making himself agreeable to all by that dignified suavity and lofty courtesy which he could display when not chafed or in bad humor.

In no place was the demonstration of respect to the President more marked than in Boston, a city most decidedly opposed to him and his policy, but whose enlightened citizens could lay aside their hostility to the man when called upon to pay respect to the office and its occupant.

Ill health was the cause given for his suddenly facing about and hastily returning to Washington.

BLACK HAWK.

I have omitted to mention in its proper chronological place what was called "the Black Hawk war," a war waged by the noted Indian chief of that name; and I should not now refer to it except that Black Hawk, having, with his family and some of his subordinate chiefs, been taken prisoner and brought to Washington, became an object of much curiosity and sympathy with the people of the East. Indeed, he was a "hero" in their eyes, as was shown by their attentions to him, and by the crowds that gathered round him and sometimes impeded his progress altogether.

After being kept at Washington for some weeks, he and his followers, including his son, were released and permitted to proceed homeward, to the Mississippi River, Wisconsin, with an agent. They went by the way of Baltimore, Philadelphia, New York, Albany, etc.; and it so happened that he arrived at Philadelphia nearly at the same time that General Jackson arrived, so that the city had two heroes within her bounds at the same time. It may be considered invidious to say that the hero of "Bad Axe" attracted greater attention and was followed by far greater crowds than the "hero of New Orleans;" yet so it was.

On the arrival of the boat at the wharf at New York, on board of which was this Indian chief, such was the immense crowd gathered to see him that it was more than an hour before he could land, and it was almost impossible to make way for him to the quarters he was to occupy. A somewhat similar scene occurred at Albany. At Baltimore, so immense were the numbers who crowded to see him and his followers, that it was found necessary to quarter them in Fort McHenry to avoid the crowd.

PRESIDENTIAL ELECTION, 1832.

The Presidential campaign of 1832 was an earnest one. The events of General Jackson's administration had kept the country greatly excited, and caused party spirit to run high. The two parties were exceedingly exasperated against each other.

The National Republicans opposed the re-election of General Jackson, on the ground that he had, while seeking the office, proclaimed that no man ought to hold that high office for more than a single term, but was now a candidate for a second term; that he had violated, or disregarded, every principle he himself had announced previous to his election. Foremost of these was the declaration that members of Congress ought not to be appointed to office during the term for which they were elected, and for two years thereafter, and that if such continued to be the practice, corruption would become the order of the day; whereas, in the face of this declaration, which won him great popularity with the people, he had himself appointed more members of Congress to office during the first six months of his administration than had been appointed by his predecessors from the commencement of the government down to his time. They charged him, also, with coming into office with the promise of retrenching the expenses of the government, whereas he had more than doubled them. They charged him, further, with recommending to Mr. Monroe the patriotic course, in selecting his cabinet, of disregarding *party* lines, and thus "to destroy the monster, party;" that the President should be the head of the nation, and not of a party; whereas he had, in violation of this precept, been more proscriptive on party grounds than any one had ever been,—acting upon what had been denominated "the spoils system." They charged him, moreover, with manifesting an unreasonable hostility to the United States Bank, and of doing the country great injury by trying "experiments" upon the currency; of appointing bad men to office; of exhibiting a fierce and irascible temper; of encouraging bullies to attack members of Congress for words spoken in debate; and of disregarding and refusing to have executed the decision and decree of the United States Supreme Court, claiming an equal right with that tribunal to judge of the constitutionality of a law.

On the other hand, the Jackson men denounced the United States Bank as a monster, and *Nick Biddle* as "Old Nick" himself; justified all the measures and acts of the President; promised the people a gold and silver currency instead of "Clay's rag money;" dwelt with delight upon "the yellow boys," the "Jackson currency," and "Benton mint-drops,"—though no one, except now and then an office-holder, ever saw a gold coin. Their presses teemed with charges of "bargain and corruption,"—the old calumny against Mr. Clay,—freely indulging in the use of the epithets of "Federalists," "Blue Lights," "Hartford Conventionists," etc., delighting, at the same time, to laud the President as "the hero of New Orleans," "the old Roman," and applying to him the affectionate sobriquet of "Old Hickory." But their most effective mode of promoting their cause and stirring the enthusiasm of their followers was the raising of hickory poles, the emblem, of course, of "Old Hickory." These hickory poles, or hickory-trees trimmed so as to leave no limbs or foliage except a bunch at the top, were to be seen everywhere: every city ward had its hickory pole at the head-quarters of the party; every town, village, hamlet, and cross-roads was decorated with them. They were cut and trimmed in the woods and hauled and raised amidst enthusiastic "hurrahs for Jackson," always by comparatively large crowds,—not all as sober as deacons,—sometimes with much ceremony, oratory, music, and a procession.

M. Chevalier, the French traveler, then in this country,

speaks thus of a Jackson procession he witnessed in New York: "It was nearly a mile long. The Democrats marched in good order, to the glare of torches; the banners were more numerous than I had ever seen them in any religious festival: all were in transparency, on account of the darkness. On some were inscribed the names of the Democratic societies or sections; others bore imprecations against the Bank of the United States: *Nick Biddle* and *Old Nick* here figured largely. . . . From farther than the eye could reach came marching on the Democrats. The procession stopped before the houses of the Jackson men to fill the air with cheers, and halted at the doors of the leaders of the opposition to give three, six, or nine groans. These scenes," says M. Chevalier, "belong to history and partake of the grand; they are the episodes of a wondrous epic which will bequeath a lasting memory to posterity."

This was on the occasion of a hickory-pole raising.

Such displays as are here mentioned beget enthusiasm, and do more to win a certain class than all the arguments and all the printed matter that ever flowed from the lips or was poured forth from the press, as our experience taught us in 1840. This was emphatically "THE HICKORY-POLE CAMPAIGN."

The election took place, and from the result one would have inferred that there had been no serious opposition.

Maine, New Hampshire, New York, New Jersey, Pennsylvania, Virginia, North Carolina, Georgia, Alabama, Mississippi, Louisiana, Tennessee, Ohio, Indiana, Illinois, and Missouri gave their entire votes for General Jackson, and Maryland gave him three. The same vote was given for Van Buren for Vice-President, except that of Pennsylvania, cast for William Wilkins. The votes of Massachusetts, Rhode Island, Connecticut, Delaware, Kentucky, and five votes of Maryland were cast for Clay and Sergeant; that of Vermont, for Wirt and Ellmaker. South Carolina threw her vote away upon Floyd and Lee.

For President.		*For Vice-President.*	
Jackson	219	Van Buren	189
Clay	49	Sergeant	49
Wirt	7	Ellmaker	7
Floyd	11	Lee	11
		Wilkins	30

THE CHEROKEE MISSIONARIES.

When I last spoke of the Cherokee missionaries, Revs. S. A. Worcester and Elizur Butler, it was in reference to the decision of the Supreme Court which declared the act of Georgia, under which they were convicted and imprisoned, unconstitutional, and contrary to the laws and treaties of the United States. They were then in prison; but the President, assuming to be independent of the Supreme Court, and to have the same right to judge of the constitutionality of a law as that tribunal had, refused to order its mandate to be executed, which was, that the prisoners should be released: consequently they remained in prison until, upon their petition to Governor Lumpkin, of Georgia, for release, he *graciously* pardoned and released them! Their *crime*, it will be remembered, was residing in the Cherokee territory, by permission of the President of the United States, without license from his *Excellency* the Governor of Georgia.

Immediately upon the close of Congress, a few days after the passage of the Compromise and Force bills, Mr. Calhoun departed for South Carolina, and, hastening to Columbia with all speed, arrived there in time to meet the State convention, which stood adjourned to meet immediately after the close of Congress, to await what might be done to satisfy their demands. Some of the hottest of the Hotspurs were dissatisfied with the Compromise, as being an insufficient measure; but Mr. Calhoun's explanations and influence were enough to induce the convention cordially to approve his course and to repeal the ordinance of nullification; thus restoring things in that State to their normal condition,—the two parties in the State, the Nullifiers and the Unionists, abandoning their respective organizations and forgetting past differences.

Mr. Calhoun's neck had been rescued from the halter with which he was threatened by the President, by Mr. Clay's "healing and tranquillizing measure," the "Compromise;" and from this time until he went back to the Democratic party, in 1837, he acted harmoniously with the Whigs.

In some parts of the country Mr. Clay was lauded to the echo for what he had done. In other parts, and especially in

Pennsylvania, he was consigned to the bottomless pit. But what right had Pennsylvania to complain of Henry Clay for abandoning, as she alleged, his own great American system? What claim had she upon him? When did she ever lay him under obligation to her by her support? Clamorous always for the protection of her manufactures, and loudest in her professions of attachment to those measures of which he had always been the most distinguished champion and consistent supporter, she had at all times shown her appreciation of him by opposing him whenever she had an opportunity to do so; and she consistently continued her opposition, even at the sacrifice of her favorite measures, not only opposing him, but industriously heaping calumny upon his name, down to the day of his death.

The energetic course pursued by General Jackson towards South Carolina raised him to the zenith of his popularity. Mr. Webster also largely increased the high estimation he was held in, by his prompt and able support of the President's proclamation and the "Force bill."

Simultaneously with the vehement debate in the Senate upon the Force bill, Mr. Calhoun introduced a series of "resolutions on the powers of the government," involving the doctrine of nullification. The first declared that the people of the several States are united as parties to a constitutional COMPACT; that the Union, of which the said *compact* is the bond, is a union between the *States* ratifying the same.

The second declared that the people of the several States thus united created a general government, to carry into effect the objects for which they were formed, and delegated certain definite powers, to be exercised jointly; the residuary mass of powers to be exercised by its own government; and that whenever the general government assumes the exercise of powers not delegated by the *compact*, its acts are unauthorized and of no effect; and that in such case each State, without any common judge, has an equal right to judge for itself, as well of the infraction as of the mode and measure of redress.

The third resolution is negative; denying every doctrine asserted by Mr. Webster in his speech in reply to Colonel Hayne, and put forth in the proclamation.

Mr. Calhoun sustained these resolutions in a thoroughly studied metaphysical speech, characteristic of his peculiar abilities.

In reply to these resolutions, Mr. Webster presented in four brief, compact propositions his views of the nature of our Federal government, as being a UNION instead of a LEAGUE, and as acting upon INDIVIDUALS, in contradistinction to STATES:

"1. That the Constitution of the United States is not a league, confederacy, or compact between the people of the several States in their sovereign capacities, but a government proper, founded on the adoption of the people, and creating direct relation between itself and individuals.

"2. That no State authority has power to dissolve these relations; that nothing can dissolve them but revolution; and that, consequently, there can be no such thing as secession without revolution.

"3. That there is a supreme law, consisting of the Constitution of the United States, acts of Congress passed in pursuance of it, and treaties; and that in cases not capable of assuming the character of a suit in law or equity, Congress must judge of, and finally interpret, this supreme law, so often as it has occasion to pass acts of legislation; and in cases capable of assuming and actually assuming the character of a suit the Supreme Court of the United States is the final interpreter.

"4. That an attempt by a State to abrogate, annul, or nullify an act of Congress, or to arrest its operation within her limits, on the ground that, in her opinion, such law is unconstitutional, is a direct usurpation on the just powers of the general government and on the equal rights of other States, a plain violation of the Constitution, and a proceeding essentially revolutionary in its character and tendency."

Mr. Webster sustained these propositions by an elaborate argument, peculiarly Websterian. But they have since been established beyond peradventure by the War of the Rebellion, which at the same time killed all such heresies as the propositions of Mr. Calhoun. No State would now for a moment assert the right to judge of the binding force of an act of Congress, or the right to secede from the Union. Such fallacies are of the past, of days never to return. The first gun at Fort Sumter blew nullification and secession into thin air.

REMOVAL OF THE DEPOSITS FROM THE UNITED STATES BANK.

During the summer of 1833, Mr. McLane was transferred from the Treasury to the State Department, as the successor of Mr. Livingston, appointed Minister to France; and Mr. William J. Duane, of Philadelphia, was appointed Secretary of the Treasury.

General Jackson had determined to remove the public deposits from the United States Bank, but well knew that Mr. McLane was opposed to this measure and could not be induced to perform the act as Secretary of the Treasury; he was therefore transferred to the State Department, and one who was supposed to be more pliant to the wishes of the President was appointed his successor. But it turned out, as we shall see, that Mr. Duane was no less unwilling to be made the instrument to do what he could not approve than was Mr. McLane.

The President had, in his annual message of 1832, recommended an inquiry into the condition of the bank, in order to allay "the apprehension that it is no longer a *safe* depository of the money of the people." Upon this suggestion, Mr. McLane, Secretary of the Treasury, appointed as agent to make the investigation Mr. Henry Toland, a Jackson man, who performed the duty faithfully.

Mr. Toland reported that the liabilities of the bank amounted to	$37,296,950.20
And the funds to meet them, to	79,593,870.97
Showing an excess of	$42,296,920.77

over liabilities in its vaults.

He therefore reported that of the security of the public moneys and the solvency of the bank there could not, in his opinion, be a doubt.

The House of Representatives, upon this showing, and after an investigation by the committee of ways and means, resolved, by a vote of more than two-thirds, "That the government deposits may, in the opinion of this House, be safely continued in the Bank of the United States."

This, however, did not stop the efforts of its assailants to create the belief that it was insolvent and unsafe. Something must be done to operate on public opinion. Some stirring sensation must be produced; some unquestionable demonstration of the truth of their allegations must, if possible, be effected. How should it be done? A happy thought suggested itself: namely, to break one of the branch banks, of which there were ten or twelve, situated in different commercial cities. If any *one* of these branch banks could be broken, the public would at once take the alarm and believe the whole concern rotten; and so the idea was at once adopted, the scheme put into the hands of a shrewd operator in Wall Street to be carried into effect, and the branch at Savannah selected as the one to be the victim.

Savannah was then far distant from the commercial centres, New York and Philadelphia, and the business of the bank was comparatively small, consisting chiefly in drafts upon cotton sales, requiring very little specie, of which there was a small amount, no way comparable to the amount of its bills in circulation, kept in its vaults. It was an easy matter, therefore, for the broker in New York employed to carry the nefarious scheme into effect to secure a vastly larger amount of the bills of the bank than there was usually specie in its vaults; and if it could only be caught napping, if a large amount of its bills could be obtained and presented for redemption before the bank should suspect the plot laid for it, the thing would be accomplished, its bills protested, its doors closed. "The plot was a very good plot." But let us see how it turned out.

In the parlor of the mother-bank, in Philadelphia, sat "Nick Biddle," "calm as a summer's morning," reading the weekly reports made to him by the presidents of the several branch banks. "Of course," says one who has told the story very amusingly, "Old Nick was constantly on the alert for his cunning and powerful foes. Like a spider in the centre of his net, he watched sharply to see where and how it was threatened. Studying over the usual weekly returns one day, he observed in the return from one branch, 'We return you less than our average of Savannah branch notes.' This was not calculated to arrest any special attention. But when other branches, the next and for several successive weeks, made the same return, it may be supposed that the wary president did not fail to note these significant signs.

"Just what it all meant he could only guess; but he guessed right. So, keeping his own counsel, he quietly shipped two hundred thousand dollars of specie to the Savannah branch, with a letter of caution and advice to the president."

Meantime, the operator in New York, having secured some one hundred and fifty to one hundred and seventy-five thousand dollars of the bills of the Savannah Branch Bank, departed southward, confident of closing her doors.

Arriving safely at Savannah, he wended his way next morning to the bank. Expressing a wish to see the president on important business, he was shown into his room and politely received. He soon informed the president that he was a broker from New York; that he had a quantity of his bills which he had brought for redemption, and that the amount was probably much larger than was usually presented at any one time. This did not at all surprise or disconcert that officer, who said he should be happy to give him drafts on New Orleans or New York for the amount. These were, however, declined, and the specie demanded. The president said he could have the specie or the drafts in New York, and thereby save transportation and insurance. But no: the specie he must have then and there; and so it was counted out, keg after keg. But when a hundred or a hundred and twenty-five thousand dollars had been counted, and still the kegs came rolling out, Mr. Broker began to think he might as well accept drafts on New York, and kindly offered to do so. It was too late, however: the president told him he wished to get rid of the specie, and was much obliged to him for relieving him of it. So he had the satisfaction of shipping the specie to New York, and paying freight and insurance thereon, when he might have had drafts. Thus "Old Nick" baffled this cunningly-devised scheme to break one of his branch banks and create a money panic.

The proposed measure of removing the public deposits from the Bank of the United States was General Jackson's own. It was well known that neither Mr. McLane, Mr. Duane, General Cass, nor any one of the cabinet proper, favored the measure, except Mr. Taney, and that Mr. Van Buren and William B. Lewis were also averse to it. But it was earnestly urged by Mr. Kendall, Mr. Blair, Mr. Taney, and probably Colonel Benton.

This opposition induced the President to assume the entire responsibility of the measure, which he did in a paper read to his cabinet on the 18th of September, giving his reasons for the act. After admitting that "the power of the Secretary of the Treasury over the deposits is unqualified," he says, in his closing paragraph, "The President again repeats that he begs his cabinet to consider the proposed measure as his own, in the support of which he shall require no one of them to make a sacrifice of opinion or principle. Its responsibility has been assumed after the most mature deliberation and reflection, as necessary to preserve the morals of the people, the freedom of the press, and the purity of the elective franchise."

This paper was drawn up by Mr. Taney. General Jackson tried every means to induce Mr. Duane to give the order for the removal; but his efforts proved fruitless. Mr. Duane firmly refused to perform the act unless Congress should so order. General Jackson therefore removed him on the 23d of September, and Mr. Taney was appointed his successor immediately after. On the 26th, three days after this change in the cabinet, the public deposits were removed.

The sensation produced by this extraordinary act in commercial, financial, and business circles in every part of the United States was unprecedented. The banks in every part of the country, but especially in the commercial cities, were compelled to call in their loans and curtail their circulation; trade and commerce became embarrassed; distrust and uncertainty everywhere prevailed, putting a stop to enterprise; produce was reduced in value, and was unsalable; manufactures were checked, laborers thrown out of employment, failures and bankruptcies of daily occurrence, and general financial distress pervaded the country. Thousands were stricken down from wealth to poverty, overtaken, as it were, in a serene and cloudless day by a sweeping and destructive tornado.

The country felt the storm from centre to circumference. Meetings were everywhere held; many of the friends, as well as the opponents, of the administration, gave vent to their disapprobation of this act, and united in remonstrances against it. The press teemed with denunciations of the measure; and it seemed as if the President, obstinate and stubborn as he was known to be, could not resist the general clamor and the influence brought to bear upon him.

The hostility thus exhibited against the bank, now deprived of the public funds, rendered it imperatively necessary that it should protect itself by curtailing its discounts and accommodations, and this of itself aggravated the prevailing commercial distress.

But, of course, it was charged by the government presses with creating and doing all in its power to increase the public distress, and with making all the mischief to revenge itself for being deprived of the deposits.

FIRST SESSION OF THE TWENTY-THIRD CONGRESS; CALLED THE PANIC SESSION.

On the assembling of the Twenty-third Congress, the President in his annual message spoke of what had been done *by the Secretary of the Treasury*, with his approval, and dealt some blows at the bank, accusatory of its doings as *reported by the government* directors, by way of justifying his extraordinary proceeding towards that institution. The Secretary also, in his report to Congress, gave his reasons for removing the public funds from the bank, and thus the matter had come before Congress for its action.

It had been anticipated, since the dismissal of Mr. Duane, that the approaching session would be a very stormy one: it could not be otherwise; the whole country was in a high state of excitement and ebullition; banks were failing, bankruptcies daily taking place, business broken up, and confidence shaken.

In the Senate there was a small anti-administration majority, reckoning Mr. Calhoun and his few friends adverse to the administration, as he and they now were.

In the House, Stevenson, administration, was re-elected Speaker by 142 to 75. The war of the giants soon opened. At the commencement of the session the President nominated to the Senate, as government directors of the bank, James A. Bayard, Peter Wager, H. D. Gilpin, John T. Sullivan, and Hugh McEllery. The nomination of Mr. Bayard was confirmed; that of the other nominees, who had maintained a very hostile attitude to the bank for some time past, was rejected,—25 to 20.

With his wonted determination not to be thwarted in his purposes, the President immediately re-nominated those who had been rejected, who were as promptly again rejected,—30 to 11.

MR. CLAY'S RESOLUTIONS CONDEMNING THE REMOVAL OF THE DEPOSITS.

Mr. Clay led off in the Senate against the recent acts of the President and Secretary. On the 11th of December he called for a copy of the paper read by the President to his cabinet, which was refused. He then, on the 26th, presented the two following resolutions:

"1. *Resolved*, That the President, in the late executive proceedings in relation to the public revenue, has assumed upon himself authority and power not conferred by the Constitution and laws, but in derogation of both.

"2. That the reasons assigned by the Secretary for the removal are unsatisfactory and insufficient."

Mr. Clay followed up these resolutions by one of his masterly speeches, of two days' length: great it truly was, for great was the occasion, and great he felt must be the effort to resist what he deemed high-handed executive usurpations and assumptions of power. As usual when he was expected to address the Senate, the galleries were packed, and every avenue to the chamber where his voice could be heard, although he could not be seen, was densely crowded. He opened his speech by saying, in a solemn and impressive tone that reached the heart of every hearer, "Mr. President: We are in the midst of a revolution; bloodless as yet, but rapidly tending towards a total change of the pure republican character of the government, and to the concentration of all power in the hands of one man. The powers of Congress are paralyzed, except when exerted in conformity to his will, by the frequent and extraordinary exercise of the executive veto.

* * * * * * * *

"The judiciary has not been exempt from the prevailing rage for innovation. Decisions of the tribunals, deliberately pronounced, have been contemptuously disregarded, and the sanctity of numerous treaties openly violated."

In the paper read to his cabinet by General Jackson, a copy of which he refused to send to the Senate upon its call, he said, "The President begs his cabinet to consider the proposed measure as his own. *Its responsibility is assumed.*"

Commenting on this, Mr. Clay said,—

"Sir, is there a Senator here who will tell me that this removal was not made by the President?"

In that paper the President had said, and Mr. Clay read, "In the remarks he has made on this all-important question, he *trusts* the Secretary of the Treasury will see only the frank and *respectful* declarations of the opinions which the President has formed on a measure of great national interest, deeply affecting the character and usefulness of his administration; and *not a spirit of dictation*, which the President would be as *careful to avoid* as ready to resist."

"Sir," said Mr. Clay, "how kind! how gentle! The Secretary was told by the President that he had not the slightest wish to dictate,—oh, no; nothing is further from the President's intentions. But, sir, what was he told in the sequel? 'If you do not comply with my wishes, you must quit office.'"

The famous "paper" reads, "Its responsibility has been assumed, after the most mature deliberation and reflection, *as necessary to preserve the morals of the people, the freedom of the press, and the purity of the elective franchise.*"

"The morals of the people!" exclaimed Mr. Clay. "What part of the Constitution has given to the President any power over 'the morals of the people'?" And he proceeded to remark upon this paragraph of the "paper" with scorching sarcasm.

But enough has been quoted to give an idea, though a very faint one, of this most eloquent speech. Let another, a patriot and life-long Democrat,—an original Jackson man,—speak of it.

Governor Erastus Root, of Delaware County, New York, writing to Mr. Clay on the 12th of January, 1834, asks,—

"When will the mad career of the 'military chieftain' be checked? or is it never to meet with a check? Will a thoughtless multitude, led on or encouraged by knavish politicians, always sing pæans of praise to the usurpations of a despot, if emblazoned with military renown?" . . .

Chief-Justice Ambrose Spencer, of New York, in a private letter written within a few days of this time, says, "I feel, as I did when I saw you, most desponding at the prospect before us; and yet, were I called to act, I would, if possible, nerve myself for the contest, and fight the battle on the last inch of ground left."

Mr. Benton replied, defending the President and Secretary, and justifying the acts of both. From this discussion arose what was termed "the independent, or sub-treasury," now in existence.

Mr. Calhoun supported Mr. Clay's resolutions. He said, "The Senator from Kentucky read a striking passage from Plutarch, descriptive of Cæsar forcing himself, sword in hand, into the treasury of the Roman commonwealth. We are in the same stage of our political revolution, and the analogy between the two cases is complete, varied only by the character of the actors and the circumstances of the times. That was a case of an intrepid, bold warrior seizing forcibly the treasury of the country. The actors in our case are artful, cunning, and corrupt politicians. They have entered the treasury with the false keys of sophistry, as pilferers, under the silence of midnight. . . . The Senator said truly, and, let me add, philosophically, that 'we are in the midst of a revolution.'"

On the 5th of January, 1834, Mr. Webster, from the committee on finance, made an elaborate report on the removal of the deposits, embracing Mr. Clay's second resolution, namely, "that the reasons assigned by the Secretary for the removal were unsatisfactory and insufficient." Upon the recommendation of the committee, the resolution was adopted,—ayes 28, noes 18.

The other resolution occupied the Senate and underwent debate from time to time till the 28th of March, 1834, when it passed, 26 to 20, in the following form:

"*Resolved*, That the President, in the late executive proceedings in relation to the public revenue, has assumed upon himself authority and power not conferred by the Constitution and laws, but in derogation of both."

This is the famous resolution which was afterwards *expunged*.

VIRGINIA RESOLUTIONS.

Many State Legislatures took up the subject of the removal of the deposits, and passed resolutions expressive of their views thereon. Among the first to do this was the General Assembly of Virginia, which adopted a series of eight or ten resolutions, couched in strong, clear, decisive language. The first resolution declared the removal of Mr. Duane because he would not do an act he deemed wrong, at the bidding of the President, to be a palpable usurpation of power. Another read thus: "*Resolved*, That the recent removal of the Federal deposits from the Bank of the United States and its branches, at the instance and upon the responsibility of the President of the United States, is regarded as an alarming usurpation of power, and a breach of the public faith."

These resolutions having been transmitted to Congress, as well as to the Senators and Representatives in Congress from that State, Mr. Rives, a Jackson Senator, immediately resigned his seat in the Senate, and was succeeded by Benjamin Watkins Leigh, who concurred with the Assembly.

THE NATIONAL REPUBLICAN BECOMES THE WHIG PARTY.

The excitement created by the removal of the deposits, instead of abating, continued to increase during the winter and spring of 1834. As the pressure in the money-market grew more stringent, business became more deranged, and failures multiplied in commercial cities. There was a financial panic; and large meetings were held, memorials to Congress signed by tens of thousands, without distinction of party, and these memorials sent to Congress by large committees composed of men of the highest character, wealth, and influence in the respective localities from which the memorials emanated. The opponents of the administration charged that the government had become a "one-man power;" that the President had usurped powers not belonging to him, and that he was arbitrary, tyrannical, imperious, dictatorial, and regardless of the Constitution and laws, trampling both under foot whenever they obstructed his will.

A number of gentlemen were about to publish a tri-weekly political paper, to be called the "Star-Spangled Banner," and I suggested to one of the writers (Joseph McIlvaine, recorder of Philadelphia) that we had better drop the name by which we were then designated, and assume one that appealed to the patriotic feelings and sympathy of the masses. "But," said Mr. McIlvaine, "unfortunately, we have no such name." I replied, I thought we had; that the term "*Whig*" was such a one; that it was the name by which the patriots of the Revolution were known; that it was synonymous with a friend of liberty and an opponent of arbitrary government.

After discussing the subject, Mr. McIlvaine concurred in my proposition, and at his suggestion I wrote an article proposing this change, which appeared in the first number of the "Star-Spangled Banner," on the eleventh day of February, 1834; from which time that paper designated the opposition party as *Whigs*, using no other term. The paper was sent to every anti-Jackson member of Congress of any prominence during the session, and soon the term *Whig* was generally adopted.

MEMORIALS AND DELEGATIONS.

Many delegations were sent from the cities, towns, and counties in the Northern, Middle, and Eastern States with memorials to Congress, and instructed to call personally on the President, represent the state of the country to him, and remonstrate with him. These delegations performed the duty assigned them, held interviews with Senators and members of Congress, returned home, reported to public meetings called for the purpose, and many of their reports were made public and spread broadcast over the country.

The delegation from Philadelphia to the President was the first in order, and the first whose report was published. The delegation was composed of some fifteen or twenty of the most respectable citizens, headed by Elihu Chauncy; its report was drawn up by Joseph McIlvaine, and made to a large meeting held at the Exchange. The report was quite elaborate, giving an account of their interview with the President. I give a very brief synopsis of it: "The chairman had hardly announced the general nature of our mission, when the President interrupted him, and proceeded in a vehement discourse of more than twenty minutes to announce to us his opinions and his determinations in reference to the restoration of the deposits. Application for relief must be made to the United States Bank, not to him. Whatever distress existed was caused by the bank, to crush the State banks and compel the government to abandon its policy. The present directors had violated its charter. He regarded the bank as a monster of corruption. The law creating the bank was unconstitutional. Having made up his mind irrevocably in regard to the bank and deposits, *Andrew Jackson* never would restore the deposits, nor re-charter that 'monster;' he would undergo the tortures of the Spanish Inquisition before he would do either. He declared his purpose to continue the present system of collecting the revenue by State banks, until the *experiment* had been fully tried. The President admitted that considerable distress had followed the action of the government; he had never doubted that brokers and stock speculators, and all who were doing business on *borrowed capital*, would suffer severely; but all such *ought to break*."

The interview, the delegation say, lasted about an hour, and during that time it had been impossible for the delegates, without unpardonable rudeness to the chief magistrate of the nation, to explain to him their business and their wishes.

A delegation from Baltimore also called upon the President. They say in their report that when they made known their mission,—that they came to ask relief,—"Relief, sir!" interrupted the President, greatly excited; "come not to me for relief; go to the *monster*. Did not Nick Biddle come here, sir, and on his oath swear before a committee that with six millions in his vaults he could meet the wants of the whole people? and now, when he has wrung more than ten millions from the people, he sends you to me."

A delegation of a similar character from New York came to Washington and waited on the President for a similar purpose. It was headed by James G. King. The members of the delegation having been each introduced, Mr. King began, in a dignified manner, to inform the President of the object of their visit. He had uttered but a few words when the President broke in upon him with,—

"Mr. King, you are the son of Rufus King, I believe?"

"Yes, sir."

"Well, sir, Rufus King was always a Federalist, and I suppose you take after him. Insolvent? What do you come to me for, then? Go to Nicholas Biddle. We have no money here. He has millions in his vaults, and yet you come to *me* to save you from breaking."

He continued denouncing Biddle and the bank for fifteen minutes, working himself into a high excitement, walking up and down the room, and finally declaring his unchangeable purpose not to restore the deposits.

The same language was the reply to other delegations.

Memorials continued to pour in to the Senate and House from every section of the country,—from the East, the North, the West, and the South; some few from the supporters of the President, but mostly from Boards of Trade, from Chambers of Commerce, from immense meetings of mechanics, from merchants,—indeed, from every class of people. Great meetings, too, were held, and addressed by able and ardent speakers, —one especially at Castle Garden, New York, composed of mechanics; one in Philadelphia, which was attended by the various guilds, trades, associations, and companies, headed by their officers and respective banners,—forty thousand said to be present; one at Wilmington, Delaware, and one near Philadelphia, both of which were composed of great multitudes.

The latter was addressed by Mr. McDuffie and other Southern gentlemen, in their accustomed animating style.

Mr. Poindexter, Mr. Preston, Mr. McDuffie, and other Southern gentlemen visited Philadelphia and New York, where they were fêted and listened to with great enthusiasm by multitudes, to whom their fiery oratory was a novelty.

It was something new to see these anti-tariff, nullification orators, so lately denounced by Northern people, cheered to the very echo, both in Philadelphia and in New York, as they poured forth their scathing words against their former chief.

Speaking of this state of public feeling, Colonel Benton says, "It will be difficult for people in after-times to realize the degree of excitement, of agitation, of commotion, which was produced." He speaks of it as a *frenzy*.

HOUSE OF REPRESENTATIVES.

I have thus far noted only the doings of the Senate at this session of Congress, for the reason that there the stirring measures which occupied that body and the House, and moved the country, commenced and absorbed attention. Formerly the House was the scene of the greatest attraction, as in that body the debates were more animated and took a wider scope than in the Senate. In the latter body, like that of the House of Lords, a sense of decorum prevented any lofty flights into the regions of imagination and eloquence,—grave argument and a subdued tone being, in primitive times, deemed strictly senatorial, as was a full-dress, knee-breeches and buckles, shoe-buckles, clubbed hair, ruffled shirts, etc.,—a style of dress to which Mr. Rufus King and Mr. Gaillard adhered so long as they were in the Senate.

But with the transfer of Mr. Webster, Mr. Clay, Mr. Calhoun, Mr. Forsyth, and Mr. Grundy to the Senate, an entire change took place, and that body became more popularized, and assumed a leading part in the doings of Congress, becoming the attractive and objective point of the Capitol. Its contracted galleries were almost constantly crowded, and quite frequently jammed to overflowing. When the Senate-chamber was first completed, it was without galleries, as no one attended the debates, if such they might be called, in that body, which was too sedate, dignified, and dull to attract spectators. The introduction of more popular speakers and a different style of debate changed this, and forced the erection of galleries.

Day after day, week after week, and month after month, memorials came up from the people, were presented to the House, and called forth discussion. Mr. Benton says, in his "Thirty Years' View," "Every morning for three months the presentation of these memorials, with speeches to enforce them, was the occupation of each House," and he quotes from many of the speeches made on the occasion. The memorials, he says, were "lugubrious," and, he might have added, represented a very distressed state of the country, especially its financial, commercial, and industrial affairs.

In delivering a very inflammatory speech on this subject, in reply to those who depicted the sad condition of trade, commerce, credit, and the finances of the country, Mr. Beardsley, from Utica, New York, exclaimed, in thundering tones, "Perish credit! perish commerce! perish trade! rather than the country shall be ruled by this moneyed monster!"

He was from this time familiarly known as "Perish-Credit Beardsley."

Mr. Beardsley, however, in the above only reiterated the sentiment of the President, uttered about the same time, namely, that "all who traded on borrowed capital ought to break."

In addressing the House on the removal of the deposits, having occasion to speak of the directors of the bank, Mr. Binney characterized them as "men who, from earliest youth to their present mature age, have been beloved, respected, and honored by all around them, and who are as much the standard of all the virtues, private, social, and patriotic, as the coins of your mint are the standard of your currency." In thus describing these men, Mr. Binney described himself, every word of his high encomium being as applicable to him as to any one of the Board of whom he truthfully spoke.

No man in either branch of Congress was more profoundly respected, or deserved to be. He was no politician, in the ordinary sense of the term; he was no partisan. He discussed all public questions as a statesman anxious only for the good of the country. In closing one of his model speeches in the House, he declared—and in doing so every one could bear testimony to the truth of his declaration—"that he had not, consciously, uttered a sentiment in the spirit of mere party politics; and he invoked the same spirit from others. The great interests of the country, and the discussion of them," he said, "should be above the influence of mere party. The question of the bank is one of public faith; that of the currency, one of national prosperity; that of the constitutional control of the treasury, one of national existence. It is impossible that such momentous interests shall be tried and determined by those rules and standards which, in things indifferent in themselves, parties usually resort to."

There was no occasion for his disclaiming the conscious utterance of a sentiment in the spirit of mere party politics: it was not his wont to do so at any time; his remarks were ever characterized by an elevation of tone and a propriety and dignity of manner admired by all, but followed by few.

Alluding to the depressed condition of business, the alarm and anxiety everywhere prevailing, Mr. Binney said, "If any man is so blind to the realities around him as to consider this but as a theatrical exhibition, got up by the bank, or the friends of the bank, to terrify and deceive the nation, he will still be blind to them, until the catastrophe of the great drama shall make his faculties as useless for the correction of the evil as they now seem to be for its apprehension."

Mr. Binney served but a single term in Congress, positively refusing a re-election. He felt out of place in the House of Representatives. Acting, as he always did, under a high sense of obligation to perform faithfully all the duties devolving upon him in whatever public station he had been placed by his fellow-citizens, he was exceedingly annoyed and disgusted at the frequent absence from the House of members when important votes were to be taken, and at the indifference shown by such derelict members when remonstrated with. As an example: Robert Letcher, of Kentucky, contested in the House the seat of Thomas P. Moore. The contest was a severe one, and occupied the House for a long time. Mr. Binney had charge of the case as one of the committee on elections, and, in a masterly argument, endeavored to show that Mr. Letcher was entitled to the seat. He labored in the investigation and argument of the case as he would in an important cause in court. He felt confident that the claimant would obtain, as he thought he ought to obtain, his seat. The vote was taken, and Mr. Letcher came within three votes of obtaining his seat; at the same time some five or six members were absent who would have voted with Mr. Binney had they been present, some of them having spoken in favor of Mr. Letcher's claim. Happening to be at Washington at this time, and having a conversation with Mr. Binney, I found he was deeply chagrined at the result, which sent Mr. Letcher back for a new contest before the people, when it would have been otherwise had the absent members duly appreciated the obligation resting upon them to attend to and perform their duties.

Mr. Binney would have been an ornament to the Senate, as would his most cherished friend, John Sergeant; but Pennsylvania never honored herself by sending either to that body.

THE PRESIDENT'S PROTEST.

Soon after the passage of Mr. Clay's resolution censuring the President in regard to the removal of the deposits, the President sent to the Senate his protest against the action of that body in the premises. It was no sooner read in the Senate than it created vehement excitement. It was denounced as a breach of privilege, as an indignity to the Senate, and as unfit to be received.

Mr. Benton took the occasion to give notice of his intention to move to expunge Mr. Clay's resolution from the journal, and to renew the motion from time to time till it should prevail, or so long as he should be a member of the Senate. These matters tended to increase the bitterness of the feeling between the friends and the opponents of the President, which was already in a highly feverish and irritable condition.

The debates which this protest elicited in the Senate were of a more than ordinarily vehement and acrimonious character, and at the same time the public press teemed with articles partaking of the same spirit. The President was exceedingly wroth at the refusal of the Senate to receive and enter his protest on its journal; and the vigorous denunciations poured upon him by his opponents in that body still further chafed and irritated him. Mr. Clay, Mr. Webster, Mr. Calhoun, Mr. Ewing, Mr. Clayton, and other Senators spoke of the protest, and of the haughty arrogance which prompted such a paper, in the most indignant terms. He was, of course, ably defended by his friends, Mr. Benton, Mr. Wright, Mr. Grundy, and the trenchant "Globe."

The conflict arising out of the protest partook more of a personal character than usual; it was, in fact, a *war* between the President and the Senate,—a war *à l'outrance.* No quarter was given, none asked or expected. Each party considered the other as the aggressor, and as guilty of unwarrantable interference and unjustifiable accusation. There could be little moderation on either side under such circumstances. The Senate declared the protest a breach of the privileges of that body,—that the President had no right to send a protest to the Senate,—and refused to receive it.

Mr. Calhoun addressed the Senate on the 5th of May against the reception of the protest, with more than his usual earnestness and power. In opening, he said, "that in order to have a clear conception of the nature of the controversy in which the Senate finds itself involved with the President, it will be necessary to pass in review the events of the last few months which have led to it.

"Their history may be very briefly given. It is well known to all that the act incorporating the Bank of the United States made that institution the fiscal agent of the government, and that, among other provisions, it directed that the public money should be deposited in its vaults. The same act vested the Secretary of the Treasury with the power of withholding the deposits, and, in the event of withholding them, required him to report his reasons to Congress. The late Secretary, on the interference of the President, refused to withhold the deposits, on the ground that satisfactory reasons could not be assigned for the act; for which the President removed him, and appointed the present incumbent in his place, expressly with a view that he should perform the act his predecessor had refused to do. He accordingly removed the deposits, and reported his reasons to Congress, and the whole transaction was thus brought up for our approval or disapproval. . . . We could not hesitate. The subject was accordingly taken up, and after months of deliberation, in which the whole transaction was fully investigated and considered, and after the opinions of all sides, the friends as well as the opponents of the administration, were fully expressed, the Senate passed a resolution disapproving of the reasons of the Secretary, who was but the agent of the President in the transaction. . . .

"It is impossible for the most careless observer to read this paper without being struck with the extreme solicitude which the President evinces to place himself in a position between the Senate and the people. He tells us again and again, with the greatest emphasis, that he is the immediate representative of the American people. HE *the immediate representative of the American people! . . . What effrontery! What boldness of assertion! The immediate representative! Why, he never received a vote from the American people. He was elected by electors,* elected either by the people of the States or by their Legislatures; and of course is at least as far removed from the people as the members of this body. . . .

"But why all this solicitude on the part of the President to place himself near to the people, and to push us off to the greatest distance? Why this solicitude to make himself their sole representative, their only guardian and protector, their only friend and supporter? The object cannot be mistaken. It is preparatory to further hostilities,—to an appeal to the people; and is intended to prepare the way in order to transmit to them his declaration of war against the Senate, with a view to enlist them as his allies in the war which he contemplates waging against this branch of the government. . . .

"Having secured this important position, as he supposed, he next endeavors to excite the sympathy of the people, whom he seeks to make his allies in the contest. He tells them of his wounds,—wounds received in the war of the Revolution; of his patriotism; of his disinterestedness; of his freedom from avarice or ambition; of his advanced age; and, finally, of his religion; of his indifference to the affairs of this life, and of his solicitude about that which is to come. Can we mistake the object? Who does not see what was intended? . . . He first *seized upon the public money, took it from the custody of the law, and placed it in his own possession, as much so as if placed in his own pocket.* The Senate disapproves of the act, and opposes the only obstacle that prevents him from becoming completely master of the public treasury. To crush the resistance which they interpose to his will, *he seeks a quarrel with them*, and, with that view, *seizes on the resolution in question as the pretext.* He sends us a protest against it, in which he resorts to every art to enlist the feelings of the people on his side, preparatory to a direct appeal to them, with the view to engage them as allies in the war which he intends to carry on against the Senate till they submit to his authority.

* * * * * * * *

"I am mortified (said Mr. C.) that in this country, boasting of its Anglo-Saxon descent, any one of respectable standing, much less the President of the United States, should be found to entertain principles *leading to such monstrous results;* and I can scarcely believe myself to be breathing the air of our country, and to be within the walls of the Senate-chamber, when I hear *such doctrines vindicated.* It is proof of the *wonderful degeneracy of the times,—of a total loss of the true conception of constitutional liberty.* But in the midst of this degeneracy I perceive the symptoms of regeneration. It is not my wish to touch on the party designations that have recently obtained, and which have been introduced in the debate on this occasion. I, however, cannot but remark *that the revival of the party names of the Revolution, after they had so long slumbered, is not without a meaning,*—not without an indication of a return to those principles which lie at the foundation of our liberty.

* * * * * * * *

"Gentlemen *ought to reflect* that the extensive and sudden revival of *these names* could not be without some adequate cause.

Names are not to be taken or given at pleasure; *there must be something to cause their application to adhere.* If I remember rightly, it was Augustus, in all the plenitude of his power, who said that he found it impossible to introduce a new word. What, then, is that something? What is there in the meaning of WHIG and TORY, and what in the character of the times, which has caused *their sudden revival, as party designations, at this time?* I take it that the very essence of Toryism—that which constitutes a Tory—is to sustain prerogative against privilege,—to support the executive against the legislative department of the government, and to lean to the side of power against the side of liberty; while the Whig is in all these particulars of the very opposite principles. *These are the leading characteristics of the respective parties,* WHIG and TORY, and run through their application in all the variety of circumstances in which they have been applied, *either in this country or Great Britain.* Their sudden revival and application at this time ought to admonish my old friends who are now on the side of the administration that there is something in the times, something in the existing struggle between the parties, and in the principles and doctrines advocated by those in power, which has caused so sudden a revival and such extensive application of the terms."

This speech sounded like a tocsin, and produced great sensation at the South, which was now stirred with unusual excitement.

But, though the lion roared in the White House at these fierce assaults upon him, and the clamor of the whole country, he was as far from yielding to them as the rock of Gibraltar to the waves constantly dashing against it.

Judge Bibb, a Senator from Kentucky, an original Jackson man, spoke forcibly against the protest and the assumption of powers by the President. "I feel no pleasure," he said, "in resisting this protest. I gave to General Jackson a zealous, and early, and continued support against fearful odds in the circle in which I moved. . . . But I am not content, as a tribute of gratitude to his military services, that he shall be master over the Constitution and liberties of his country.

* * * * * * * *

"And what have we come to in these days? A single person, intrusted with the execution of the laws, with the command of the army and the navy, has laid claim to the custody and management of the public revenue and the public property. He now manages the public treasury, which is continually replenishing under a permanent enactment of taxes, by a system of his own; by the power of his veto, the voice of two-thirds of each House of Congress is necessary to repeal the taxes or take the custody and management out of his hands, or to enact any system against his will.

* * * * * * * *

"The great interests of the country have been deeply affected, disordered, and broken in upon by the mere act of the Executive. The multitudes of sufferers, writhing under the torture thus inflicted, attest this representation by their memorials day after day presented to Congress. And yet I see no remedy. The withering influence of the Executive power is still exerted."

A large portion of the Senators participated in this very heated debate. Mr. Wright, Colonel Benton, Mr. Forsyth, Mr. Grundy, and others defended the President, while on the other side, besides those named, were Mr. Ewing, Mr. Chambers, William C. Preston, Mr. Southard, Mr. Frelinghuysen, and Mr. Poindexter.

The debate lasted for many months, and called out the ablest men in the Senate. And such a Senate! Every man of them, I believe, has passed away; but I instinctively, and with profound respect, bow to their shades, as they rise and stand before me.

Though in the paper read by General Jackson to his cabinet he assumed the whole responsibility of removing the deposits, in his message to Congress, dated 3d of December following, he said,—

"Since the last adjournment of Congress, the *Secretary of the Treasury* has directed the money of the United States to be deposited in certain State banks designated by him, and he will immediately lay before you *his* reasons for this direction."

18

AN EPISODE.—A FIGURE-HEAD SAWED OFF.—A GREAT COMMOTION FROM A SMALL CAUSE.

In the excess of his loyalty and devotion to General Jackson, Commodore Elliott, in command of the navy-yard at Charlestown, had had a figure-head—an image, or bust, of Jackson—made and placed on the frigate Constitution, then lying at that navy-yard.

In the then state of feeling, this called forth great public indignation: it was considered an act of extreme flattery and homage, and a desecration of the noble "Old Ironsides." Great was the outcry against it; but those whom it offended had no redress, as the commodore could disregard or set at defiance the denunciations heaped upon him.

But one rainy morning the offensive figure-head was gone, or rather the head had been removed, leaving a headless bust. Great was the commotion at the navy-yard and on shipboard upon this discovery; great, also, were the excitement and rejoicing in Boston on the occasion. The commodore was terribly exercised, and his wrath was fearful, though he knew not upon whom to expend it. A strict scrutiny was instituted: everybody was examined, but no clue to the perpetrator, or to the means by which the deed had been done, could be obtained. A reward of a thousand dollars for the culprit who had cut off the head of Jackson was offered; but in vain: neither the criminal, nor any information concerning him, or how he did it, could be got. The news soon spread over the whole country, and had the living Jackson's head been cut off it could hardly have caused a greater sensation.

Who did it? and how was it done? It was done by a young man named Samuel H. Dewey, an eccentric, resolute, determined fellow, somewhat of a sailor, who resolved that "Old Ironsides" should not bear the obloquy of carrying such a figure-head. I had from himself a relation of the circumstances of the accomplishment of the feat.

Having determined, if possible, to relieve the ship of her burden, he cogitated a good deal as to how it could be done. The ship lay between two seventy-fours. The only way to reach her was by water. He looked around and found where a small boat was kept that would answer his purpose and was at hand; and then he waited for a favorable night, that is, a dark, rainy one. Taking advantage of such a one, he got into the boat late at night, paddled noiselessly alongside of the Constitution or under her bow, fastened his boat, clambered, by some means not now recollected, up her side, listened for the footstep of the sentinel as he walked fore and aft, kept still and out of sight when the sentinel approached, but crept along upon his retreat, until, finally, he got under the figure-head, where, lying upon his back, he went to work with the saw he had brought with him, first boring a hole through the head with an auger he had brought for the purpose, passing a rope through it and making it fast above. The rain poured in torrents, thus favoring him by drowning the noise of his saw. His progress was necessarily slow, and he was several hours in accomplishing what he had undertaken; but near daybreak he had severed the head, and, securing it from falling into the water, twenty-five feet below, let himself down into his boat by the rope by which he had let the head down, rowed himself silently away, landed, fastened the boat where he found it, took the head, in a large pocket-handkerchief, in his hand, and went his way to his boarding-house, meeting several early risers on that rainy Sunday morning in the streets.

Thus it was accomplished. Some laughed, some swore, some rejoiced, some were indignant; but for weeks, perhaps months, no one could guess who did it, or how it was done. It was a mystery.

Some months after, young Dewey, with his famous trophy, appeared in New York, being apprehensive of arrest at Boston, made himself known, and became quite a lion, being frequently entertained at supper-parties, where he greatly amused the guests by relating, as he did, in a quaint, graphic manner, his adventures and hair-breadth 'scapes. From New York he came to Philadelphia, where he was also fêted and had a jolly good time of it. He then went to Baltimore, and finally to Washington, calling on the Secretary of the Navy and relating to him all the circumstances of the transaction, and drawing from the grave Secretary a hearty laugh instead of a stern rebuke.

CHANGES IN THE CABINET.

Meantime, changes had taken place in the cabinet. The nomination of Mr. Taney as Secretary of the Treasury was withheld until it had become a subject of just complaint that the Secretary was the officer of the President, and not of the constitutional appointing power. But it was finally sent to the Senate and rejected, to the surprise of no one. Mr. Woodbury was then appointed Secretary of the Treasury; Mr. Mahlon Dickerson, of the Navy, in the place of Mr. Woodbury; and William Wilkins, Senator from Pennsylvania, minister to Russia. Mr. McLane resigned the office of Secretary of State, which was filled by Mr. Forsyth, of Georgia, and Mr. Butler, of New York, was made Attorney-General. From this time Mr. McLane disappeared from the arena of politics. He had for eight or nine years been among the friends of Jackson, but not of them; that is to say, he did not approve of all of Jackson's measures,—of the removal of the deposits, the war upon the bank, the proscription of Federal officers, or what was called "reform," "rotation in office," etc.

"THE PET BANKS."

When the public deposits were removed from the United States Bank, they were placed in certain favored or selected State banks, which were thence denominated "Pet Banks."

In order to relieve the stringency of the money market consequent upon the disturbance of the currency by the removal of the deposits, these banks were directed by the Secretary of the Treasury to extend facilities to merchants and others by liberal loans. Desirous to increase their profits, they scarcely needed this suggestion, and they now discounted freely: consequently money became more plenty, or easy to be obtained. Besides this increase in the circulating medium of the country, a large number of new banks were chartered, almost every State granting new charters, avowedly to fill the gap likely to be created by the going out of existence of the United States

Bank. Of course these new institutions were desirous of doing a fair share of business, and therefore discounted liberally. But, though money began to be plenty, the currency was in a bad condition; little silver, and no gold, was seen; small bills, or "shinplasters," as they were called, took the place of silver change; the bills of the banks of one State were at a large discount in an adjoining State, and at a still greater as the distance from home increased. The uniform currency furnished by the United States Bank, and by its controlling power over the State banks, was gone, and "the better currency" that had been promised by the Jackson presses proved to be but a miserable substitute.

GOLD CURRENCY.

It was evident to sagacious, observing men that this "pet bank" system, or "EXPERIMENT," would prove a failure; and during the summer of 1834, Colonel Benton and others began to talk of an exclusive metallic or gold currency. The "Globe" took the hint, and expatiated on the grand idea of "a constitutional" or metallic currency. A bill which favored this idea was introduced in the House, and became a law, equalizing the value of gold and silver. Another bill brought forward as an accompaniment to that, namely, legalizing the tender of foreign coins of gold and silver, also became a law, after much debate in both branches of Congress. But though the "Globe" and its "affiliated presses" were daily singing pæans to the "gold currency," which it emblazoned in big capitals from day to day, and set forth the manifold virtues of this "Jackson money," still, the people saw little of it.

Expatiating on the glorious times the people were to enjoy from an abundance of gold, the "Globe" broke forth in the following ecstatic strain of prophecy:

"A great stream of GOLD will flow up the Mississippi from New Orleans and diffuse itself all over the great West. Nearly all the GOLD COINAGE of the New World will come to the United States. This will fill the West with doubloons and half-joes, and in eight or nine months from this time [July 16, 1834] every substantial citizen will have a long silken purse of fine, open net-work, through the interstices of which the YELLOW

GOLD will shine and glisten. Every substantial man, and every substantial man's wife and daughter, will travel upon GOLD. The satellites of the bank alone, to show their fidelity to their liege monarch, will repine at the loss of paper."

In another issue the editor said, "There is no longer a plea for Federal bank-notes; GOLD is a good enough currency for the republicans of the United States." And again, "Already GOLD is glittering in the pockets and glittering in the hands of the people."

Some pieces of the new gold coinage, eagles and half-eagles, having made their appearance, they were exultingly hailed by the "Globe," which availed itself of the occasion to invoke the gratitude and support of the people, thus:

"JACKSON MONEY—THE BENTON YELLOW JACKETS.—All laboring men and farmers who get it [gold] in actual payment for their labor or products may sleep soundly on their pillows, without fear of banks breaking. And will they not sustain the statesman who gives *gold* to his country and *lead* to her enemies?" And much more of this sort.

After the passage of the acts above mentioned, gold came rapidly into the country from Europe, and the mint was kept actively employed coining the "Benton Mint-Drops," or "Jackson Yellow Boys." At the same time, great pains were taken to get the gold into circulation: still, very little of it shone "through the interstices of the farmers' silken purses."

"The instinctive feelings of the masses," says Mr. Benton, "told them that money which would *jingle* in the pocket was the right money for them,—that hard money was the right money for hard hands. Upon these instinctive feelings gold became the avidious demand of the vast operative and producing classes."

THE DEATH OF FIVE DISTINGUISHED MEN.

Five eminent men identified with American affairs passed away during this period: namely, Charles Carroll, of Carrollton, the last of the signers of the Declaration of Independence, November 14, 1832; John Randolph, in the summer of 1833;

William Wirt, on the 18th of February, 1834, Lafayette, on the 20th of May, and Wm. H. Crawford, in September, 1834.

The death of these notable men was the occasion of many eulogies in various parts of the country, the most marked for ability being those by John Quincy Adams, delivered at the request of the House of Representatives in its hall; by Edward Everett, in Boston, and by the venerable Peter S. Duponceau, in Philadelphia, a youthful companion of Lafayette, the patriarchal Bishop White, one of the chaplains of the Congress of 1776, being present.

THE MUSE OF HISTORY RECORDING THE DOINGS OF THE HOUSE OF REPRESENTATIVES.

Over the entrance to the old hall of the House of Representatives is a beautiful model of a clock and a statue of the Muse of History, symbolic of the passage of time and the recording of the doings of the House as history. The Muse of History is represented in a car, with her pen and tablet in hand, looking down upon the actors below and recording their acts. The wheel of the car forms the dial of the clock, and its hands note the passage of time. The whole design is classic, chaste, and beautiful.

A resolution having been offered by Mr. Everett, that the House should order a certain number of copies of the first three volumes of Gales and Seaton's "Register of Debates," the same order to be extended to the volumes to be thereafter published, Mr. Polk opposed the resolution, and Mr. Adams advocated its passage, as the work was important as an aid to the history of the country. Much of the national history must of course depend on what passed in that House.

"What is the meaning, Mr. Speaker," said Mr. Adams, "of that beautiful marble statue over your clock at the entrance of this hall? Sir, it is the Muse of History in her car, looking down upon the members of this House, and reminding them that as the hour passes she is in the attitude of recording whatever they say or do upon this floor,—an admonition well worthy of being remembered. The reporters at the sides and in the rear of your chair are the scribes of that Muse of

History; and this publication, for which the resolution before you proposes a subscription, is the real, I might say the living, record of that historic Muse. The publication is well known to be the best and most accurate report existing of the debates in Congress, and so long as it shall be continued, and especially so well executed as it has been hitherto, I most earnestly hope that the subscription for the volumes, as they succeed each other, will not be refused."

The resolution, after much opposition and being amended, was passed.

POSTERITY thanks those to whom we are indebted for Gales and Seaton's admirable and valuable "Debates."

UNFRIENDLY RELATIONS WITH FRANCE.

From the date of the treaty by which we acquired Louisiana, down to the abdication of Napoleon I., France had continued to commit unprovoked aggressions upon our commerce and to make unwarranted seizures of our vessels and cargoes. For these a large amount of claims had accumulated, and, though France had been urged to settle these claims, no treaty could be obtained engaging her to do so until the 4th of July, 1821, when she stipulated to pay the United States nearly five millions of dollars in full satisfaction for these depredations.

But up to the meeting of Congress, December, 1834, the French Chambers had unwarrantably neglected to make provision for the payment of the sum due us. The President, in his annual message at that time, brought the subject in an emphatic manner to the notice of Congress and the nation, and went so far as to recommend the passage of a law authorizing reprisals to be made upon French property in case provision should not be made for the payment of the debt at the approaching session of the French Chambers.

This recommendation, and the well-known disposition of the President to resort to coercive measures, created a lively sensation in diplomatic circles, in Congress, and the country at large. The tone of his message was generally approved by the people, who had not forgotten the unprovoked aggressions on our commerce for a long series of years, against which we had again and again remonstrated, and for which we had been, as yet, unable to obtain redress. But, in truth, the American people, like the English, admire pluck, and are not slow to back their government in demanding their rights and compelling other nations to respect them, as in "the Alabama claims" on England.

In consequence of the attitude assumed by the President, apprehensions were entertained among mercantile and commercial men of a rupture between the two nations, which would seriously affect their interests. In this state of affairs, Mr. Clay, as chairman of the committee on foreign relations, took up the subject, it having been referred to that committee, and in due time made an elaborate report upon the relations existing between the United States and France, reviewing them in all their bearings, and closing with recommending the adoption of a resolution, "That it is inexpedient, at this time, to pass any law vesting in the President authority for making reprisals upon French property in the contingency of provision not being made for paying to the United States the indemnity stipulated by the treaty of 1831 during the present session of the French Chambers."

The sense entertained by the Senate of the importance of this report is manifested by the order of that body to print twenty thousand copies. Mr. Clay proposed five thousand.

Mr. Calhoun said he had heard the report read with the greatest pleasure. It contained the whole grounds which ought to be laid before the people. He should vote for the largest number. The resolution was unanimously adopted.

ATTEMPTED ASSASSINATION OF THE PRESIDENT.

A great commotion was created in the rotunda of the Capitol on the 30th of January, 1835, and had the result been the accomplishment of the apparent purpose, the day would have been signalized by a catastrophe of horror similar to that which enshrouded the city in gloom in the spring of 1865.

The funeral of Warren R. Davis, a member of Congress from South Carolina, had been attended in the hall of the House of Representatives by the President and his cabinet, who were now passing through the rotunda—were near the eastern door—to enter carriages to accompany the corpse to the burying-ground, when a person stepped from the crowd in front of the President and snapped a pistol at him, the percussion-cap of which exploded without igniting the powder. The would-be assassin was struck by some one near the President, but snapped a second pistol at him, the cap also exploding without igniting the charge.

The person attempting the life of the President was then seized and taken before Chief-Justice Cranch, and gave his name as Richard Lawrence. The pistols he had used were, upon examination, found to be well loaded. It appeared wonderful that the design had been baffled by the non-ignition, in both attempts, of the charge of the pistol by the cap, but most fortunate was it that the terrible catastrophe was prevented.

It turned out, however, that Lawrence was an Englishman and was insane.

EXECUTIVE PATRONAGE.

Early in the second session of the Twenty-third Congress, 6th of January, 1835, Mr. Calhoun introduced a resolution into the Senate, "That a select committee be appointed to inquire into the extent of Executive patronage, the causes of its great increase, and the expediency and practicability of its reduction," etc. As chairman of the committee, he made a long report on the 9th of February, which became the subject of a protracted and, at times, very sharp and spicy debate, especially between himself and Mr. Benton.

In opening the debate, Mr. Calhoun referred to the fact that this subject was introduced into the Senate eight years before, on the report of a select committee raised by the party then in opposition, who had pledged themselves, should they be elevated to power, to administer the government on the principles laid down in the report. The chairman of that committee was Mr. Benton, a member of the present committee. Mr. Calhoun quoted from Mr. Benton's report: "The President of the United States is the source of patronage. He presides over the entire system of Federal appointments, jobs, and contracts. He has power over the support of the individuals who administer the system. He makes and unmakes them, and may dismiss them as often as they disappoint his expectations. The principle will [in a short period] come to be open and avowed,—the President wants my vote, and I want his patronage; I will vote as he wishes, and he will give me the office I wish for."

That period, which Mr. Benton saw "in his mind's eye," soon came,—came with the advent of Jackson, when Mr. Marcy proclaimed that "to the victors belong the spoils of office,"—a doctrine which has ever since been acted on by all parties.

Mr. Benton, in this report, spoke of "the kingly prerogative of dismissing officers without the formality of a trial" having been yielded to the President, by which he "could create as many vacancies as he pleased, and at any moment he thought proper."

After quoting freely from this celebrated paper, Mr. Calhoun said, "It is impossible to read this report, which announces in such unqualified terms the excess and the abuse of patronage at that time [1826], without being struck with the deplorable change which a few short years have wrought in the character of our country.

. . . "We have grown insensible, callous," he said: "this power of removal was in the early years of our government almost unknown. It continued unknown till Mr. Jefferson's time. It had not been exercised at all by one of his predecessors,—Mr. Adams.

* * * * * * * *

"The practice of the administration [General Jackson's] of dismissing faithful officers on party grounds, and supplying their places with political partisans, has a tendency to produce all the results which I have attributed to it, and must ultimately convert the whole body of office-holders into corrupt sycophants and supple instruments of power. In making this assertion I have his [Mr. Benton's] own authority."

Mr. Benton replied, taking exception to the expression "corrupt and supple instruments of power," and to his being identified in some way with these: he declared it "a bold attack on truth;" thundering out the charge in the most vehement and angry manner.

This produced an exciting scene in the Senate. Mr. Benton was called to order, but the chair (Mr. Van Buren) decided that the words were not a breach of order. Upon this Mr. Webster appealed from the decision of the chair, and a debate on the question of order followed, which resulted in a reversal of the decision by the Senate. Mr. Benton was then permitted to proceed in order. His purpose, and the drift of his remarks, were to defend the administration from the charge of extravagance,—increasing (doubling) the public expenses over those of Mr. Adams's administration, which had been so loudly proclaimed "wasteful" and "extravagant" by himself, and to throw the responsibility for all expenditures under Jackson's administration on Congress.

Mr. Calhoun, in reply, reviewed with much causticity Mr. Benton's positions and palliations, and insisted that, as the administration had at all times, down to a very late period, a majority in both branches of Congress, it was responsible for all the appropriations and expenditures that had been made, especially as the President had freely exercised the veto power to prevent the passage of bills. It was not to be tolerated that those who expelled a former administration upon its alleged extravagance should now, when the administration thus brought into power proves to be doubly so, lay the blame on Congress, instead of taking it themselves. He would ask the Senator whether, when he drew up his report in 1826 and denounced the then administration in such severe and unqualified terms for their "*extravagance*," every item of expenditure at that time had not been authorized by Congress. He and those who are now in power have reaped the fruit by holding others responsible; so it is just that they should, in turn, be held responsible.

Mr. Calhoun proceeded to show that the administration had not made anything but party fealty a party question. A man might vote for or against internal improvement, for or against a tariff, for or against this or that expenditure, for or against a bank, without forfeiting his party character, provided always that he was a good Jackson man, submitted to party discipline, and sustained the party candidates for office. He said, "General Jackson bestowed the highest gift in his power on a Senator [Mr. Forsyth] who had openly, on this floor, in the very heat of the controversy, avowed himself a bank man, while other Senators who were openly opposed to the institution were denounced; thus furnishing a most striking illustration of the truth of what he had asserted, that *the only cohesive principle* which binds together the powerful party rallied under the name of General Jackson is *official patronage.* Their object is to get and hold office; and their leading political maxim, openly avowed on this floor by one of the former Senators from New York [Mr. Marcy], is, that '*to the victors belong the spoils of office;*' a sentiment reiterated at this session by an influential member of the House, who declares every man a hypocrite who does not avow it! *Can any one venture to say that our government is not undergoing a great and fatal change?* THE VERY ESSENCE OF A FREE GOVERNMENT CONSISTS IN CONSIDERING OFFICES AS PUBLIC TRUSTS, TO BE BESTOWED FOR THE GOOD OF THE COUNTRY, AND NOT FOR THE BENEFIT OF AN INDIVIDUAL OR A PARTY; AND THAT SYSTEM OF POLITICAL MORALS WHICH REGARDS OFFICES TO BE USED AND ENJOYED AS THEIR PROPER SPOILS, STRIKES A FATAL BLOW AT THE VERY VITALS OF FREE INSTITUTIONS."

Mr. Calhoun had accompanied his report by a bill, which was the subject of discussion, one section of which limited the power of the Executive in removals from office, and required him to give an account of his acts, and the reasons for those acts, to the Senate; a provision somewhat similar to the tenure-of-office bill passed by Congress during Andrew Johnson's administration, which became a law, his veto of it notwithstanding, and which was emasculated, or virtually repealed, by Congress at the opening of General Grant's administration.

Mr. Ewing, taking part in the debate, declared his most hearty approval of this provision of the bill: the first measure he had the honor to propose in the Senate, he said, was of this import, though it went further.

He laid down the proposition, and entered upon an argument to prove, that the Constitution does not vest in the President alone the power of permanently removing any officer who is appointed by the President by and with the advice and consent of the Senate.

Mr. Webster lamented that "the extent of the patronage springing from the power of appointment and removal of officers had already reached an alarming height. The principle of republican government is public virtue; and whatever tends to corrupt, debase, or weaken its force tends in the same degree to overthrow such government. The presumption that men in the performance of their political duties will be guided and influenced generally by an honest, intelligent judgment, and manly independence, lies at the foundation of all hope of maintaining a popular government. Personal, individual, or selfish motives influencing men on public questions affect the safety of the whole system. . . .

"The unlimited power to grant office and to take it away gives command over the hopes and fears of vast multitudes of men. It is generally true that *he who controls another man's means of living controls his will.* Where there are favors to be granted, there are usually enough to solicit them; and when favors, once granted, may be withdrawn at pleasure, there is, ordinarily, little security for personal independence of character. The consequence of this greed and rush and competition for offices is obvious,—*complaisance, indiscriminate support of Executive measures, pliant subserviency, and gross adulation.* All throng *and rush together to the altar of man-worship,* and offer sacrifices and pour out libations, till the thick fumes of their incense turn their own heads, and the head of him who is the object of their idolatry."

In regard to the constitutional question involved, Mr. Webster expressed the opinion that the power of appointment naturally and necessarily includes the power of removal, where no limitation is expressed nor any tenure but that at will is declared. The power of appointment being conferred on the President and Senate, he thought the power of removal went with it, and should have been regarded as a part of it. He thought, consequently, that the decision of 1789 was erroneous.

But this decision, having been so long acquiesced in as the settled construction of the Constitution, should be acted on accordingly. But he thought the legislature possesses the power to regulate the condition, duration, qualifications, and tenure of office, where the Constitution has made no express provision on the subject; and, further, that the incumbent shall remain in place till the President shall remove him for reasons to be stated to the Senate. He thought that this qualification would have some effect in arresting the evils which seriously threatened our government.

A PLEASANT "INTERPELLATION."

Incidents that broke in upon the grave routine of business or heated discussions of the Senate not unfrequently arose between Mr. Clay and Mr. Buchanan, sometimes creating much mirth, as on the present occasion.

Mr. Buchanan was *wall*-eyed, or cross-eyed; heavy, slow, and as destitute of humor as an undertaker; and upon him Mr. Clay delighted to play off his wit.

As Mr. Clay was addressing the Senate on the present occasion, he referred to, and spoke of, the *leaders* of the Democratic party, at the same time looking at Mr. Wright, between whom and himself sat Mr. Buchanan.

Mr. Buchanan rose and said, "he was very sorry the Senator from Kentucky was so often disposed to pay his respects to him."

Mr. Clay.—"I had no allusion to *you* when I spoke of the *leaders* of the administration, but to another honorable Senator," pointing to Mr. Wright.

Mr. Buchanan.—"When the Senator thus spoke he certainly looked at me."

Mr. Clay.—"No, Mr. President, I did not look at him: he was not in my mind; but," holding up and crossing his two forefingers, his eye twinkling with humor, he said, "it was the way *he* looked at *me*;" thus indicating, in a sportive way, Mr. Buchanan's defect of vision.

Mr. Buchanan was nonplussed, could make no reply, and, finding the laugh against him, sat down.

Mr. Buchanan, though, unlike Falstaff, destitute of wit, yet, like the fat knight, was the cause of wit in others, at least in Mr. Clay.

On another occasion, as Mr. Buchanan was defending himself against the charge of disloyalty during the War of 1812, he having been "an old Federalist," to prove his loyalty, stated that he entered a company of volunteers at the time the British attacked Baltimore, or at the time of the battle of North Point, and marched to Baltimore. "True," he said, "he was not in any engagement, as the British had retreated before he got there."

Mr. Clay.—"You marched to Baltimore, though?"

Mr. Buchanan.—"Yes."

Mr. Clay.—"Armed and equipped?"

Mr. Buchanan.—"Yes, armed and equipped."

Mr. Clay.—"But the British had retreated when you arrived?"

Mr. Buchanan.—"Yes."

Mr. Clay.—"Will the Senator from Pennsylvania be good enough to inform us whether the British retreated in consequence of his valiantly marching to the relief of Baltimore, or whether he marched to the relief of Baltimore in consequence of the British having already retreated?"

This colloquy, with its unlooked-for ending, was greatly enjoyed by the Senate and galleries, and put both in excellent humor.

Mr. Wright opposed Mr. Calhoun's bill and Mr. Clay's amendment, contending that the power of removal from office rested solely with the President.

Mr. White, of Tennessee, said that in 1826, as a member of the committee then raised on executive patronage, he came to the conclusion that it was dangerous to leave such power in the hands of the Executive, and through the chairman [Mr. Benton] expressed that opinion to the world. He entertained the same opinion now, and was prepared to reaffirm it. He was then in opposition to the administration; he was now a friend of the administration. "When we have *a pure and virtuous chief magistrate*," said Mr. White, "he will thank Congress to take from him every discretionary power which they can take with propriety. If ever it should be our misfortune to *have one of an opposite character, disposed to use all his powers for the benefit of himself, his relatives and friends, and for the purpose of perpetuating power in his and their hands, then society at large ought to thank us for stripping the Executive of this influence.*"

The bill was finally ordered to be engrossed for a third reading, by a vote of 26 to 15, and there it ended.

Time has by no means lessened the importance of this subject, which is at this moment (1872) under discussion by a commission, consisting of several eminent gentlemen appointed for that purpose by the President, with a view to devise and recommend some plan or system by which the great evils that have grown up in the civil service of the government may be remedied.

Those who live at the present day cannot but note with what prophetic accuracy some of the distinguished statesmen who took part in this debate, and the report of Mr. Benton, made *forty-six years ago*, depicted a condition of things which has become so familiar as to excite no special wonder among trained politicians, and is even justified by some whose political morals have been formed in the *Marcy school*, and who would perhaps say, as did the member of Congress from New York, quoted by Mr. Calhoun, that "he is a hypocrite who does not avow this dogma."

Of the excellency of this school of morals the country has lately (1871) had a striking illustration in the exposure of the operations of the Tammany politicians in New York.

But when and from whence arose the evils complained of,—this gangrene of the civil service, which, if not arrested, must infect with corruption and rottenness the whole foundation of our government and render it a by-word of scorn in the mouths of all honest men?

From the commencement of the government under the present Constitution, in 1789, down to the inauguration of General Jackson, in 1829,—forty years,—was a period of purity and honesty. It was administered with the sole view to the *public good;* men were appointed to office for their character, fitness, and integrity. This "period of political honesty, simplicity, and economy began with the supremely patriotic and honest administration of Washington,"—a model to all others, —"and ended with the cheap, simple, honest, and admirable administration of John Quincy Adams,"—not less pure, patriotic, and economical than that of Washington.

Then came General Jackson, the popular idol, with the vaunting cry of "*Retrenchment and Reform,*" and the unblushing charge against his predecessor that "the patronage of the government had been brought in conflict with the freedom of elections,"—a charge utterly groundless. Then commenced that system of "rewarding friends and punishing enemies," which has prevailed to a greater or less extent ever since, and has been one of the causes of the venality, corruption, and political prostitution that so widely prevail in the United States. Well might Mr. Calhoun, at one time one of the main pillars of the Jackson party, declare that the party was held together by "the cohesive power of public plunder."

It is a pertinent question to ask, Can the existing evils be remedied? Can we go back to the honest, unselfish ways of Washington, Madison, and J. Q. Adams? No. We might, perhaps, as well hope to go back to the more economical modes of living of our fathers and grandfathers. Corruption, extravagance, and laxity of morals are the inseparable concomitants of national wealth. If we seek and obtain the one, we must expect the others. But a wise, patriotic, firm, unselfish Executive can do much to restrain, if he cannot entirely eradicate, the evils complained of.

MISMANAGEMENT OF THE POST-OFFICE DEPARTMENT.—INTIMIDATION ATTEMPTED, BUT DISREGARDED AND DEFIED.—SOUTHERN MEN CATCH A TARTAR, AND BACK OUT.

The mismanagement of the Post-Office Department, under Mr. Barry, had become so notorious to Congress and the nation that during the first session of the Twenty-third Congress both the Senate and the House of Representatives took the matter in hand, and appointed special committees for the purpose of investigating the affairs of that department. They took the matter in hand; but the labor to be performed was so great, and the investigation so searching and thorough, that the committees were not able to make their reports until the second session of the same Congress.

In the House, a majority and a minority report were made; the latter very damaging to the Postmaster-General, as was also the very able and elaborate report of the majority of the Senate committee, drawn up by Mr. Ewing, of Ohio. The House minority report was prepared by Mr. Whittlesey, of Ohio.

ANECDOTE OF WILLIAM COST JOHNSON.

Mr. Barry had very warm personal and political friends in the House, who, not being disposed to allow his administration of the department to be criticised in a manner which the facts seemed to warrant, pretty broadly intimated that any attack upon him, or any severe animadversion upon his official acts, would be considered as personally offensive to them; and of course whoever after this intimation should have the hardihood to tread on the forbidden ground must expect to be called to an account.

I have spoken of William Cost Johnson, as the president of the Young Men's National Clay Convention held in Washington in May, 1832. He was now in Congress,—an able, ready speaker, a man of fine appearance and address, and one of the very last men, in the House or out of it, to be intimidated by any such warnings as had been given out. On the contrary, such intimations only aroused his spirit, and prompted him to test the sincerity and courage of those who would thus attempt to browbeat the House into silence. The House met at six o'clock P.M., February 24, for an evening session, and resolved itself into committee of the whole, for the purpose of taking up "the bill to establish certain post routes, and for other purposes." The bill having been under consideration for a short time, and sundry amendments having been offered, Mr. Johnson, who always occupied a seat in the front row and next to the principal aisle, rose, and, casting his eyes around, and looking significantly at Mr. Hawes, of Kentucky, who, with others, had attempted to intimidate the House, said, in a very distinct and deliberate manner, that he was opposed to the bill in every shape and form. He then paused for a minute or two, when, still looking at Mr. Hawes, he resumed: "Mr. Chairman, it has been broadly intimated by some gentlemen in this House that he who shall have the temerity to criticise the acts of the Postmaster-General must answer therefor elsewhere than in this hall. This I understand to be the purport, at least, of the remarks of some of the gentlemen on the other side of the House. Sir, I come from a portion of the country where the law of personal responsibility is recognized among gentlemen. I hold myself amenable to that law. I seek no personal conflict; but, sir, I shall never allow myself to be intimidated into its avoidance by menaces, come they from what quarter they may. As one of the representatives of Maryland, I intend to speak my sentiments here with perfect freedom; and now, in the face of those menaces which have been thrown out on this floor, and intending to be responsible for what I am about to say, I declare that the Post-Office Department is corrupt from head to foot, through and through, and I believe that the head of that department, William T. Barry, is as culpable as any officer under his control."

If a cannon had been fired in the hall it could not have created more surprise, commotion, and sensation than did this brief speech. A shot had been hurled dierctly into the covey, and there was great fluttering among them.

Mr. Hawes replied to Mr. Johnson. "If I understood the gentleman correctly," said Mr. Hawes, "he gave it as his opinion that the department was corrupt from the Postmaster down to the lowest officer in the service. Did I understand him correctly?"

Mr. Johnson.—"You did, sir."

Mr. Hawes proceeded in a deprecatory strain, and called on the gentleman from Maryland to give the grounds on which he had made the charge of corruption against the Postmaster, who, he asserted, was as honest and honorable as any man who had a seat on that floor.

Mr. Johnson did not doubt the sincerity of the gentleman from Kentucky when he asserted the honesty of the Postmaster, but at the same time he did not retract what he had said; on the contrary, he repeated, that he believed there was corruption from beginning to end, from head to foot, from the highest to the lowest officer in the department; though he did not mean to charge every one in the department, individually, with corruption. If his best and dearest friend had acted as the Postmaster had acted, he would, as the President should, have shaken him off as a viper whose touch brought pollution and death.

Great efforts were made to induce Mr. Johnson to qualify, soften, or explain away his broad and direct charge of corruption; but he declared he had made the charge, and he had spirit enough to stand to it, be the consequences what they might.

He was appealed to privately by personal friends from the Democratic side of the House to make some explanation that would save extreme measures. "No," was his reply; "I have no explanation to give; what I said I meant, and gentlemen may make the most of it."

While Mr. Johnson was as cool and serene as a frosty morning, the House was in a state of great excitement. It was obvious that there could be but one course pursued by those who had thrown out menaces: they must toe the mark,—nothing more nor less; Johnson could neither be intimidated nor persuaded; and he must therefore be challenged. But who was to challenge? This was answered by the son of Postmaster Barry sending a challenge, which was promptly accepted by Mr. Johnson, the duel to take place *immediately.* This was a stunner,—a precipitancy in settling the affair altogether unlooked for. It was suggested that the meeting be delayed for a few days. "Not an hour," was Mr. Johnson's reply. "The affair must be settled at once." Would he not consent that the challenge be withdrawn? To that he had nothing to say: the challenger had the power to withdraw it if he thought proper, whether he consented or not. The challenge was withdrawn, and never was renewed; the affair was ended. Johnson well knew that the best way to treat bullies is to outbully them. The Bobadils were thenceforward very tame and well-behaved members.

ABOLITION PETITIONS.

It was during the Twenty-third Congress, 1835, that the abolition of slavery, especially in the District of Columbia, may be said to have begun to move the public mind at the North. The first petitions presented to Congress for the abolition of slavery, at least the first to attract attention, were presented by Mr. Dickson, from the Canandaigua district, New York, who addressed the House in support of the prayer of the petitioners. Perhaps his speech, more than the petition he presented, served to stir up a feeling on the part of Southern men, and to cause other and numerous similar petitions to be gotten up at the North and sent to Congress. But from this time until the breaking out of the Rebellion in 1861, this subject did not cease to agitate Congress and the country. The South became alarmed; they considered their domestic affairs interfered with, their peace and safety endangered, and their rights under the Constitution invaded. The feeling thus excited was not only that of apprehension, but of intense anger, to which they gave vent in the debates that arose upon the presentation of this class of petitions,—debates, not upon the merits or demerits of slavery, or its consistency or inconsistency with Christianity or the moral law, for these they would not discuss, but upon the reception and disposition of the petitions.

The subject did not come again before the Twenty-third Congress; but the "irrepressible conflict" was begun, and we shall see much of it hereafter. The labors of the enemies of slavery, or "ABOLITIONISTS," had commenced, and by indefatigable men who believed they were serving God and the cause of humanity, and consequently it was with them a labor of conscience and duty, with which nothing should be allowed to interfere. Instead of petitions to Congress, they now sent large boxes of tracts, pamphlets, and various publications which the Southern people denominated "incendiary," to the post-office at Charleston, South Carolina, and other cities, to be distributed, as directed, to various persons.

This increased the complaints and inflammatory articles in the Southern papers. The publications thus sent were stopped in the post-office, and the postmasters addressed the head of the department, Amos Kendall, on the subject, who replied that though the law authorized the transmission of newspapers and pamphlets through the mail, yet the law was intended to promote the general good of the public, and not to injure any section; and intimated that, such being the effect of these publications at the South, postmasters would be justified in withholding them.

This transmission of "incendiary" publications through the mail caused great excitement, not only at the South, but in most of the sea-board cities at the North, especially New York, Boston, and Philadelphia, where public meetings were held on the subject and resolutions adopted tending to mollify the feelings of the South. The practice of sending such publications through the mail was strongly condemned, and resolutions adopted denying in emphatic language any right to interfere with slavery; that it was a subject which belonged exclusively to the State in which it existed. Such, in effect, was one of the resolutions adopted by a great meeting in Boston, in the proceedings of which many of the first citizens participated.

In Philadelphia the feeling ran high; and it being rumored that a box of these publications was on board of a steamer then about to depart for Charleston, a committee of citizens was appointed to ascertain the facts. They did so, found the box, opened it, and emptied its contents into the Delaware.

Each of the cities mentioned had, at that time, a valuable trade with the South, and the apprehension that this might be injuriously affected by the hostility then shown at the North against slavery, doubtless stimulated the action of those who manifested such earnest and lively opposition to the doings of the "Abolitionists;" though it must be admitted that at that time probably four-fifths, if not nineteen-twentieths, of the people of the non-slaveholding States, however opposed to slavery in the abstract, were equally opposed to any interference with it, not believing they had any right to meddle with it, and not thinking such interference calculated to preserve harmony or good feeling between the two portions of the country. Even Mr. Adams, the great champion of the right of petition, held this opinion.

NOMINATIONS FOR THE PRESIDENCY.

The election of a President to succeed General Jackson having to take place in the fall of 1836, the friends of the various aspirants took occasion to place their candidates before the people. The Legislature of Massachusetts presented her candidate, "the great constitutional expounder," Daniel Webster. Judge Hugh L. White, of Tennessee, was nominated by the Legislature of Alabama, and the nomination was approved generally by those opposed to Jackson at the South, including many who had formerly been warm supporters of the administration. Judge McLean and General Harrison were nominated in Ohio, and the latter by a convention calling itself "Democratic-Republican," at Harrisburg, Pennsylvania.

A NATIONAL CONVENTION of the Jackson, or, hereafter to be called, the *Democratic* party, was held at Baltimore on the 20th of May, 1836, for the purpose, not of selecting a candidate for the Presidency, but of nominating Martin Van Buren, *pro forma*; he having been for a long time fixed upon—if we may believe the reiterated assertions of Jackson men in Congress—by General Jackson as his successor.

Mr. Van Buren was never popular, and it required all his tactics and General Jackson's influence to unite the party in his support. He was strong only through party discipline and General Jackson's partiality. Without the known attachment of the President to him, and the equally known restiveness of the latter whenever his wish or *will* was thwarted, there can be little doubt that some other prominent Democrat would have been the nominee.

Judge White, a very prominent and original member of the Jackson party, the CATO of the United States, was a man of eminent abilities, honest and consistent in his political views, an able jurist, and an upright, estimable man, but opposed to the corrupting system of "rewarding friends and punishing enemies." This placed him out of the pale of the party at the North, where "the spoils" were everything desirable, but made him more popular at the South, which cared little for the minor offices of the government.

The unpopularity of the one, and the great respect and esteem felt for the other, rendered it necessary that the President should bring his influence to bear in favor of his pet, and he therefore addressed a letter to his friend the Rev. Samuel Gwin, of Nashville, in which, professing to stand aloof from the contest, he avoided saying anything against his old friend Judge White, but gave it as his opinion that it was the true policy of the friends of Republican principles to send delegates "fresh from the people" to a general convention for the purpose of making a nomination, etc.; and the inference to be drawn by the faithful was, that a nomination having been so made, it was the duty "of the friends of Republican principles" to support the nominee.

"DELEGATES FRESH FROM THE PEOPLE."

The press and public speakers soon rang the changes on this expression, which brought out the facts,—1st, that the forty-two delegates to the Baltimore Convention from the State of New York were *appointed* by a convention held at Albany, of which forty-eight were office-holders, eighteen of them postmasters, and twenty of the delegates thus appointed were office-holders; 2d, that a man named Edward Rucker, from Tennessee, was the only person from that State, and that he was self-appointed, chosen by nobody, representing nobody, yet representing in the convention the whole State! This created much sport and comment in the press, and gave rise to the expression "Ruckerizing," which was familiar in politics for many years; 3d, that many other members of the convention were self-appointed, representing no one but themselves, and acting in accordance with the wishes of no one in their respective States but the Federal office-holders. From these circumstances, and from the fact that a large number of the delegates were government employés, the convention was generally dubbed "the office-holders' convention." So far as it represented the true feeling or choice of the people of the United States, in regard to either of its nominees, it was a farce, if not a fraud.

In the Presidential campaign which followed there was no

enthusiasm: all was quiet. The numerous candidates in opposition to the Jackson nominee so divided the opposition as to preclude all hope for the success of either, and therefore little or no exertion was made to defeat Mr. Van Buren. Mr. Clay, seeing that it was quite impossible to unite all the elements of opposition upon a single candidate, very wisely refused to allow himself to be nominated.

EXPUNGING RESOLUTION.

On the last day of the Twenty-third Congress, in the Senate, on the motion of Mr. Clayton, of Delaware, was taken up for consideration the resolution some time before offered by Mr. Benton, to expunge from its journal the resolution adopted by the Senate on the 28th of March, 1834, condemnatory of the President for removing Mr. Duane and the public deposits. A discussion, partaking of great heat, party feeling, and as much of personality as decorum and the rules of the Senate would permit, ensued. Mr. White, of Tennessee, opposed the resolution offered by Mr. Benton, and moved to strike out "expunge" and insert "rescind, reverse, and to make null and void." Mr. Benton insisted on retaining the word "expunge." The word "rescind" was not strong enough. It was a *harmless* word, expressing no *marked disapprobation.* He wished to make use of a phraseology which would *strongly express* that the resolution ought never to have been put on the journal.

The vote being taken, amid much excitement, on a motion to strike out the words "ordered to be expunged from the journal," it was decided in the affirmative,—39 to 7.

Mr. Webster then said the vote, the great vote, which the Senate had just given accomplished all he had ever desired respecting this expunging resolution. He, however, moved to lay whatever was left of the resolution on the table, which was agreed to,—27 to 20.

But Mr. Benton, not discouraged by defeat, rose in a few minutes and again submitted the same resolution, which, he said, he desired should stand for the second week of the next session. Mr. Benton had at least the virtue of perseverance: he never gave up, even when defeated.

DEATH OF CHIEF-JUSTICE MARSHALL.

John Marshall died in Philadelphia in July, 1835, leaving vacant a seat the most important of any under the government,—an office more honorable, and requiring far superior mental powers and acquirements to fill, than that of President; an office in which he had become illustrious, and upon which he had conferred honor, by his profound learning as a jurist, his purity and simplicity of character, his ardent patriotism, his love of truth and justice, and his unaffected modesty.

He had occupied the elevated seat for thirty-five years, during a most eventful period, when it became the duty of the Supreme Court to settle the great questions arising out of the Constitution, concerning executive and legislative powers, the relative powers of the general government and those of the States, and innumerable others, and to declare what was constitutional and what was not.

Upon every subject with which he grappled he threw the light of a great intellect and brought to bear the most profound learning and logic, making clear the path he trod for others to follow. His name has become a household word with the American people, implying greatness, purity, honesty, and all the Christian virtues,—the simplicity of a child, the intellect of a Bacon, the greatness of a Mansfield. He was born on the 24th of September, 1755, and died on the 6th of July, 1835.

Mr. Roger B. Taney, late Attorney-General, and Secretary of the Treasury, who removed the public deposits from the Bank of the United States, was appointed on the 28th of December, 1835, to succeed Chief-Justice Marshall.

SURPLUS REVENUE.

Mr. Clay's bill (which had passed both branches of Congress by overwhelming majorities) to distribute the proceeds of the sales of public lands having been first retained till the next session, and then vetoed, and finally defeated, and it being apparent that there was to be—and, indeed, there already was —a large surplus of money in the treasury over and above the wants of the government, the Whigs introduced a proposition to distribute this surplus revenue to the States.

The bill, as it finally passed, provided that the share which fell to each State should be deposited with such State, subject to be called for by the general government whenever needed, and to be refunded by the State. The bill passed the Senate by 38 to 6, and the House by 155 to 38, and was reluctantly signed by the President.

Under this law, twenty-eight millions of dollars were distributed to the States, some of them, for a time, refusing to receive their allotted portion. No part of it has ever been returned; and, as the beggar said to Sir Walter Scott, who had given him half a crown, having nothing less, and told him to remember that he owed him two shillings, "Yes, your honor; and may your honor live till I pay it!" I would say, May the Union of these States never be broken until this money is refunded!

THE MANIA OF SPECULATION.

From the moment the United States Bank ceased to be the depository of the public moneys, the currency began to be deranged, exchanges high and irregular, the deposit or "pet banks" to discount freely, new State banks to spring rapidly into existence, and a superabundance of paper currency to be put into circulation. This, of course, affected prices of all kinds,—produce, merchandise, land, labor, etc., and created great activity and desire to speculate, to purchase lands, lots, and other property, which *seemed* to be constantly rising in value; the real fact, which the people could not then see, being that money, or that which passed as such, was falling in value from its superabundance.

The constant *apparent* rise in the value of lots and land stimulated further speculation. The new banks were desirous of putting their bills into circulation, and therefore discounted the notes of speculators freely. The "pet banks" had been charged by the Secretary of the Treasury to give liberal accommodations to the community, so as to prevent the withdrawal of the United States Bank circulation being seriously felt. They scarcely needed this hint to induce them to discount freely.

Hundreds and thousands, with the "money" thus easily acquired, rushed to the West, or wherever public lands could be obtained, and purchased largely. Other thousands—I might almost say millions—plunged deeply into other speculations, such as purchasing, and selling for advanced prices, city lots, wheat, corn, cotton,—everything, indeed, for sale, or in the market. Give what price one would, the article went up, up, up, and this produced a perfect rage for speculation. Everybody was getting rich.

But when the smash came, as come it must, and did, down went land, property of every kind, labor, and prices.

This was not unforeseen or unpredicted by the statesmen in Congress. In a debate on a resolution offered by Mr. Benton, that nothing but gold and silver ought to be received in payment for the public lands, he said "he was able to inform the Senate how it happened that the sales of the public lands had deceived all calculations, and run up from four to TWENTY-FIVE millions a year. It was thus: speculators went to banks, borrowed five, ten, twenty, fifty thousand dollars in paper, in small notes, usually under twenty dollars, and engaged to carry off these notes to a great distance, sometimes five hundred or a thousand miles, and there lay them out for public lands. Being land-office money, they would circulate in the country; many of these small notes would never return at all, and their loss would be clear gain to the bank; others would not return for a long time, and the bank would draw interest on them for years before they had to redeem them. Thus speculators, loaded with paper, would outbid settlers and cultivators who had no such accommodations from banks, and who had nothing but specie to give for lands, or the notes which were its equivalent."

THE MOON HOAX.

One of the most extraordinary pieces of deception ever played off upon a community was perpetrated in New York in August, 1835, with complete success. It was known that Sir John Herschel, the leading astronomer of his day, had been for a considerable time at the Cape of Good Hope, for the purpose of making astronomical observations and discoveries, and that he was supplied for this purpose with a very large telescope. People were therefore prepared, or would not be surprised, to hear of very important, and even extraordinary, discoveries made by him.

But they *were* surprised, delighted, astounded, thrown into ecstasies, by a long, minute, and dazzling account which appeared in the "New York Sun," a penny paper, one morning, and continued for several days, of the wonderful and interesting discoveries made by that eminent astronomer, in the moon.

Hoax though it was, it was so ingeniously got up, had such an odor of science, and so much *vraisemblance*, or appearance of truth, that not only common people, uneducated and unscientific, were taken in, but editors and scientific men were completely deceived.

In the first place, the title of the hoax, or satire, was well calculated to blind those not very sharp-sighted: it was thus:

"GREAT ASTRONOMICAL DISCOVERIES lately made by Sir John Herschel, LL.D., etc., at the Cape of Good Hope." And it was announced that it was "first published in the 'New York Sun,' from the supplement to the 'Edinburgh Journal of Science.'"

A very few pronounced it a hoax, but the multitude believed it an account of veritable but extraordinary discoveries. It absorbed conversation; it was the one topic of wonder and remark. The question *would* arise, Is it, *can* it be true? And the answer generally given was, Why, it must be; nobody could invent such wonderful discoveries.

One of the New York daily papers noticed it thus:

"STUPENDOUS DISCOVERIES IN ASTRONOMY.—We have read, with unspeakable emotions of pleasure and astonishment, an article from the last number of the 'Edinburgh Scientific Journal,' containing an account of the recent discoveries of Sir John Herschel at the Cape of Good Hope," etc.

Another New York paper said, "No article, we believe, has appeared for years that will command so general a perusal and publication. Sir John has added a stock of knowledge to the present age that will immortalize his name and place it high on the page of Science."

From another paper:

"DISCOVERIES IN THE MOON.—We commence to-day the publication of an interesting article, which is stated to have been copied from the 'Edinburgh Journal of Science,' and which made its first appearance here in a cotemporary journal of this city. It appears to carry intrinsic evidence of being an authentic document. We have seen no allusion to the article in the last English papers; but it is known that Sir John Herschel has been stationed at the Cape of Good Hope for some time, under the patronage of the British government, in making astronomical observations, for which purpose he was furnished with instruments of extraordinary power. It was also announced a month or two since, through the German papers, that the great astronomer at Vienna had received information from Mr. Herschel himself that he had made highly important discoveries, which would in due time be communicated to the world. These circumstances induce us to give place to an article which, if genuine, will be of the utmost importance to the cause of science."

But "the fun of it was," that before the publication of the whole story—it was very long, filling eight or ten close columns in some papers—it leaked out, and began to get through people's heads, that the public had been most completely taken in; in truth, fairly hoaxed. It was amusing, then, to hear from every one the declaration that "he *knew* it was a hoax from the first; that *he* had never been deceived for a moment; nobody had ever believed it,—it was a palpable fiction on its face;" and many such asseverations.

I was then editor and proprietor of a daily paper—the "Commercial Herald"—in Philadelphia, and although I was at first one of the victims of this clever, ingenious, and extraordinary fiction, it so happened that I did not commit myself as to my belief of its truthfulness; nor did I feel ashamed, or mortified, at having been "taken in." It was so cleverly done, and I had such multitudes of companions, that I could afford to laugh as everybody did.

The hoax was written by Richard Adams Locke (who died in 1871), then editor of the "Sun," to which it gave great *éclat* and a very large circulation. It gave him, moreover, for many years, great celebrity; and even to the present day he is well remembered by those who were then old enough to participate in the affairs of life. I shall, without giving this famous *quiz* too much space, endeavor to convey some idea of it by making a few short extracts.

Mr. Locke began by giving some account of "great astronomical discoveries," more or less true or fictitious, to prepare the mind for his account of wonderful discoveries never made, and finally of the "prodigious lens" procured by Dr. Herschel to enable him to explore the heavenly fields of space and to examine the moon from his station at the Cape of Good Hope. This monster lens, he said, weighed fourteen thousand eight hundred and twenty-six pounds, or nearly seven tons, and its magnifying power was estimated at forty-two thousand times. After describing some of the topographical discoveries, he proceeds thus:

"Having continued this close inspection nearly two hours, during which we passed over a wide tract of country, chiefly of a rugged and apparently volcanic character, . . . the lenses being removed, and the effulgence of our unutterably glorious reflectors left undiminished, we found, in accordance with our calculations, that our field of view comprehended about twenty-five miles of the lunar surface, with the distinctness both of outline and detail which could be procured of a terrestrial object at the distance of two and a half miles. . . . Presently a train of scenery met our eye, of features so entirely novel that Dr. Herschel signaled for the lowest convenient gradation of movement. It was a lofty chain of obelisk-shaped, or very slender, pyramids, standing in irregular groups, each composed of about thirty or forty spires, every one of which was perfectly square, and as accurately truncated as the finest specimens of Cornish crystal. They were of a faint lilac hue, and very resplendent. . . . He (Dr. H.) pronounced them quartz formations, of probably the wine-colored amethyst species, and promised us, from these and other proofs which he had obtained of the powerful action of the laws of crystallization in this planet, a rich field of mineralogical study. On introducing a lens, his conjecture was fully confirmed; they were monstrous amethysts, of a delicate claret color, glowing in the intensest light of the sun! They varied in height from sixty to ninety feet, though we saw several of a more incredible altitude."

He then describes some curious animals they discovered in some beautiful valleys, their playfulness, agility, and exquisite beauty; also various kinds of birds,—two or three long-tailed birds which were judged to be golden and blue pheasants! They also discovered on the shores of a sea countless multitudes of univalve shell-fish! But this "fish story" staggered the most credulous; and a good many absolutely and positively declared, as the Indian did to the missionary about Jonah's being in the whale's belly, that they would not believe "the fish story;" and some even went so far as to declare that it was all a lie.

Mr. Locke goes on and on with his glowing account of these astounding discoveries. One "was a pure quartz rock, about three miles in circumference, towering in naked majesty from the blue deep: it glowed in the sun almost like a sapphire." Then they discovered flocks of lunar sheep, of an extraordinary character, as indeed everything was.

But did not these wonderful discoveries bring forth "the man in the moon"? Certainly, or some lunar creature which must take his place. The account goes on, after several days' narrative, thus: "But we had not far to seek for inhabitants of this 'Vale of the Triads.' . . . We saw several detached assemblies of beings whom we instantly recognized to be of the same species as our winged friends of the Ruby Coliseum near Lake Langrenus [an account of whom, or which, had been given some time before]. Nearly all the individuals in these groups were of a larger stature than the former specimens, less dark in color, and in *every respect* an improved variety of the race. [This is evidently a hit at the negro.] They were chiefly engaged in eating a large yellow fruit, like a gourd, sections of which they dexterously divided with their fingers and ate with rather uncouth voracity, throwing away the rind."

What a wonderful lens that "nearly seven tons" lens must have been, to enable Dr. Herschel to discern the fingers of those winged creatures, and to see how they ate their fruit and threw away the rind!

"The most attractive of all the animals discovered was a tall, white stag, with lofty spreading antlers black as ebony. We several times saw this elegant creature trot up to the seated parties of semi-human beings and browse on the herbage close beside them. . . . This universal state of amity among all classes of lunar creatures gave us the most refined pleasure."

Such, briefly, was "the Moon Hoax," which excited as much interest, and caused as much talk and wonderment, for a time, as did the "falling stars" when first seen in all their splendor and glory.

FIRST SESSION OF THE TWENTY-FOURTH CONGRESS.—ABOLITION PETITIONS.

A great portion of the time of both Houses of the Twenty-fourth Congress was consumed in debate upon the reception of petitions for the abolition of slavery and the slave-trade in the District of Columbia, and upon the subject of suppressing incendiary publications or preventing their being transported in the mail. Mr. Calhoun introduced a bill upon the latter subject, which underwent the usual amount of discussion, though the speeches upon this subject, and upon the proposition, by Mr. Calhoun, in the Senate, to reject all petitions for the abolition of slavery in the District of Columbia, were far more temperate and dispassionate than those in the House.

But the more violently the Southern members opposed the reception of petitions, the more rapidly they poured in, and with their increase the feeling of Southern men rose against abolition, or the interference of the North with their rights. They supposed that by refusing to receive petitions they could stop them: as well might they have attempted to stop the flow of Niagara.

Mr. Adams declared that he was opposed to granting the prayer of the petitioners, and advocated their reference to a committee, to be instructed to report the reasons why the prayer of the petitioners ought not to be granted. Had this course been taken, and himself placed at the head of the committee, he would have made an able report in accordance with the views he expressed, and then petitions would have been referred without debate,—debate being, as he declared, what he wished to prevent, its tendency being to excite angry feelings between the two parts of the country.

But Southern men would not agree to this wise and prudent course; on the contrary, they struck at the right of petition, and in doing so found Mr. Adams an indomitable champion of this right to the day of his death, and in the end they themselves brought about that which they so strenuously, passionately, and furiously strove to prevent. Had Southern members refrained from debate on the reception of these petitions, let them come in unopposed and be referred silently to a committee,—the tomb of the Capulets,—there to remain undisturbed, it cannot be doubted that they would soon have ceased, and the angry feeling between the South and the North would have been avoided. But Providence had decreed that slavery in this country must be extinguished, and those who clung to it were made the instruments of its destruction by Him who causeth the wrath of man to work out His designs. They hammered the rivets of the chain which bound their slaves till it broke and the slaves went free.

UNFRIENDLY RELATIONS WITH FRANCE.

Our relations with France were still of an unfriendly character. France owed us money,—five millions of dollars,—which she had stipulated to pay, and was ready to pay upon certain conditions. The President had used language which she construed into a threat: he had recommended reprisals upon her commerce unless the money should be promptly paid. Her national pride was touched: she would not act under an implied threat, but was ready to comply with her stipulations if assured that no threat was intended. All she desired was to protect her honor, and in regard to that she was, as she ever had been, highly sensitive.

But General Jackson was as stubborn as France was proud;

and so the two nations stood, when the President sent a special message to the Senate on the subject of these relations, evincing anything but amicable feelings or a conciliatory spirit. Its tone was, indeed, menacing, and calculated to irritate, not to soothe. One of its recommendations, or rather its specific recommendation, was "*to prohibit the introduction of French products into this country.*" The "Globe" broke out in raptures at "the high, patriotic stand the President had assumed," and Mr. Buchanan could not refrain from speaking in the Senate in glowing terms of its manly tone, and expressing the great satisfaction it gave him. Others of the Jackson party followed in equally high praise of the message.

On the other hand, Mr. Calhoun, Mr. Webster, Mr. Clay, and others strongly reprobated its unfriendly and menacing tone, as uncalled for, impolitic, and calculated to embroil us with a foreign nation not disposed to be unfriendly.

Mr. Calhoun spoke in his usual emphatic manner in condemnation of the message, deeming it most unwise and tending to involve us in an unnecessary conflict. Never did he listen, he said, to a document with more melancholy feelings, with a single exception,—the war message from the same quarter, a few years before, against one of the sovereign members of this Confederacy.

He feared that the condition in which the country is now placed has been the result of a deliberate and systematic policy. The cause of the difference between the two nations was too trivial to terminate in war. He would not assert that the Executive has deliberately aimed at war from the commencement, but he would say that from the beginning of the controversy to the present moment the course the President has pursued has been precisely the one calculated to terminate in a conflict between the two nations.

Fortunately, the government of Great Britain, at this moment, tendered its mediation for the adjustment of the dispute, which the President in a special message, on the 8th of February, informed Congress he had accepted.

STIRRING SCENE IN THE HOUSE OF REPRESENTATIVES.

On the last night of the last session of the Twenty-third Congress an amendment was inserted, in the House, to the Fortification bill, appropriating three millions of dollars to be used at the discretion of the President.* This item was rejected by the Senate, after much heated debate, and in the contest between the two Houses in regard to it the bill itself failed,—the hour of twelve o'clock P.M. of the 3d of March having arrived before the bill could be, or was, reported to the House by the committee of conference, and many members believing that as a legislative body Congress was defunct.

The failure of the bill, considering the unfriendly relations existing between the United States and France, and the unprepared condition of our coast defenses, created a good deal of feeling, called forth much censure, and elicited crimination and recrimination between the two branches, each charging the failure of the bill upon the other.

On the 22d of January, Mr. Cambreling rose in the House to reply to some criticisms upon his action in regard to that bill on the occasion mentioned. He was charged with the responsibility of defeating the bill; his object, as was alleged, being to throw the odium of its defeat upon the Senate.

The subject being thus brought up, Mr. Adams rose and submitted a resolution for the appointment of a special committee to inquire into the causes of the loss of the Fortification bill at the last session. It was well known that he intended to seize the first opportunity to reply to Mr. Webster's speech in the Senate on the night and the occasion referred to, to settle some old accounts.

Whether such motives prompted him or not, his speech was filled with invective.

In the commencement of his remarks, Mr. Adams referred to the proceedings of the Senate on the last night of the last session, and he was twice called to order by the Speaker. Mr. Adams then said he would endeavor to keep himself within the rules of the House. He would transfer the *place* where these

* To prepare for war with France.

things (which he was commenting on) occurred to the office of the "National Intelligencer," and asked if the gentleman from Virginia (General Mercer), who had also called him to order, had any objection to that.

Mr. Mercer said he objected to *quibbling*. Mr. Adams proceeded to reply to allegations made elsewhere, that the failure of the Fortification bill was owing to the fault of the House.

He said it was admitted that the failure of the bill was caused by the introduction of a section in which three millions of dollars were appropriated. Upon this subject an issue had been taken in the "National Intelligencer" (meaning the Senate), which involved not merely the President of the United States but the House of Representatives. Mr. Adams proceeded in a strain of vehemence, which created great feeling and caused him to be called frequently to order; great confusion, noise, and disorder reigning in the hall.

In giving the history of the introduction of the three-million section into the bill, and in assigning a cause for it, he said that in the multitude of reproaches as to the unconstitutionality of the proceedings, both of the Executive and House of Representatives, at the last session, one of the great charges was that the House inserted this appropriation without a recommendation from the Executive. This was the great basis upon which was founded that burst of patriotic indignation and eloquence which would rather have seen an "enemy battering down the walls of this Capitol" [words used by Mr. Webster] than have agreed to this appropriation for the defense of the country. "Sir," said Mr. Adams, "only one step more was necessary, and an easy step it was, for men who would refuse an appropriation, even in the terms and under the specifications in which that was proposed, if the enemy were at the gates of the Capitol. I say there was only *one* step more, and that a natural and easy one,—to join the enemy in battering down these walls."

Upon the utterance of these words in Mr. Adams's dramatic manner and with great vehemence, the Jackson men in the House broke into a wild shout of applause,—sprang to their feet, clapped their hands, and screamed with exultation.

The Speaker (Mr. Polk), for some time, in vain attempted to

restore order. In rebuke of the House, he said he had never witnessed anything of this kind before.

Mr. Mercer said that nothing like it had ever before occurred; it was wholly unprecedented; and he hoped he should never witness a like scene again.

Order being restored, Mr. Adams proceeded, and in due time completed his extraordinary harangue. The shaft thrown with such force and temper was aimed at Mr. Webster: hence the exultation of the Jackson men.

THE SCENE CONTINUED.—MR. WISE'S EXTRAORDINARY SPEECH.

When Mr. Adams resumed his seat, Mr. Wise (of Virginia) rose and stated that he had not expected to address the House that day: he was in preparation for this discussion, but it had come up unexpectedly; but, as it had arisen, he would, though not prepared as he desired to be, avail himself of the occasion and deliver what he had to say upon it. The question was, "Who is responsible for the failure of the Fortification bill of the last session?"

Mr. Wise proceeded, and frequently referred to members by name, and was as frequently called to order by the Speaker. He went into a history of the Fortification bill at the last session, his aim evidently being to fasten the responsibility of its failure upon Mr. Cambreling, chairman of the committee of ways and means, who had charge of it. In giving this history, he continued to speak of members by name, and was on every such occasion called to order by the Speaker. This produced much irritation and intemperate language, Mr. Wise being somewhat choleric, irascible, and free-spoken. He claimed that he read the names of members from the journal of the last Congress, which he had a right to do, though they were members of the present Congress, and he challenged the right of the Speaker to interrupt him.

Mr. Wise proceeded for some time in giving this history, and all the circumstances attending the progress and failure of the bill, and also of the termination of the session, and then said, "Such was the termination of the last Congress; and I do say, sir, it was one of the most disgraceful scenes I ever witnessed;

it was unbecoming barbarians and savages, much more the representatives of a civilized nation! Sleepy, tired, drunk!"

Mr. Bynum.—"Is the gentleman in order when speaking thus of the last Congress?"

Mr. Wise.—"I do not pretend to say, Mr. Speaker, that all Congress was drunk, or one-half, or one-third, or one-tenth of the members were drunk; but I know that some were; and so it was that, what with manœuvring, being tired, opposed to some measures, sleepy, and drunk, no quorum could be had unless it had suited certain individuals.

"I have given the facts upon the journal; but there are other important facts, facts unwritten. Sir, it is said the bill failed in the House. That is not true. It failed before it got to the House from the conference-room. It dropped like a spent ball before it quite got here; it dropped near the door. Sir, there are two statements about the matter; they may be conjectural. I put it to the gentleman [Mr. Cambreling], Did no 'busybody' whisper aught in his ear as he was on his way to report to the House? Did no one tempt him to strangle the bantling in his care? Was there no 'magician' near? No d—l and his imps? Did no member of the committee receive a billet-doux after he resumed his seat? . . . What prevented the report being made? Sir, there were spirits haunting the Capitol that awfu' night; there were strange whispering chattering elfs,—ghosts, as I am told,—I did not see them,—blue devils and imps! Is it true? Was there any dealing with the 'infernals' that night? Tell us, I pray you; tell us, and let the curse fall on the necromancers,—not on the victims of the horrid spell."

Mr. Wise proceeded in this strain of violent invective, bringing charges against Mr. Cambreling and Mr. Polk (now Speaker), and finally, having made a specific charge against the latter, exclaimed, in a bold, accusative tone, "Is it true? Yes or no? Guilty or not guilty? I call on the chairman of the committee of ways and means of the last Congress [Mr. Polk] to answer."

Great confusion and agitation followed, Mr. Wise being repeatedly called to order by members, and many of the

Speaker's friends objecting to his answering. He, however, preferred doing so, and gave an account of what took place, in which there was nothing unusual, nothing which needed explanation. Mr. Polk said he was really unable to conceive how this could be a matter of any sort of importance.

Mr. Wise occupied parts of two days in delivering this wild, ranting harangue,—Randolph-like, taking a wide field of excursion, and firing right and left, though not at random; now throwing an arrow into Mr. Adams, who, he declared, had always had the bad fortune to prostrate his own friends, now sending a shaft into the Executive and the ruling party, accusing both of attempts to coerce Congress.

Mr. Cambreling, in replying to him, said he should not astonish the House with indecorum, and hoped he should never be tempted on any occasion, even by the wild rant of disappointed ambition, to forget his own self-respect or his regard for the dignity of the House so far as to treat any gentleman with disrespect.

Mr. Wise had asked if there was no *magician* near (meaning Mr. Van Buren). In reply, Mr. Cambreling said, the Vice-President and Secretary of State were in the House and about leaving when the committee of conference returned to it. He had a few words of conversation with the Secretary, but not a syllable passed between him and the Vice-President. And so the "magician," "devil and his imps," "blue devils," "infernals," and all the evil spirits which had been conjured up by a fervid imagination, were at once dispelled and resolved into "thin air," or flesh and blood, in the shape of Mr. Van Buren and Mr. Forsyth.

THE SCENE CONTINUED. — MR. HARDIN'S, MR. REED'S, AND MR. EVANS'S REPLIES TO MR. ADAMS.

At the close of Mr. Wise's speech, Mr. Hardin, of Kentucky, took the floor to reply to the speech of Mr. Adams, so denunciatory of Mr. Webster and the Whigs of the Senate who refused to vote for the three-million section of the Fortification bill.

Mr. Hardin was a "rough-and-ready" debater, accustomed

to "the stump" in Kentucky, and trained by conflicts with opponents of more wit than worth, more common sense than common-school education, more pugnacity than polish. He was known by the sobriquet of "Meat-axe Hardin."

Mr. Hardin ironically expressed his admiration at the courage of the chairman of the committee of ways and means (Mr. Cambreling), who some days before intimated that he had higher game than the gentleman from Virginia (Mr. Wise) in view, alluding to Mr. Webster; and when the gentleman rose yesterday, he said, he looked for a battle of the giants. He then drew something of a contrast between the chairman of the committee on finance in the Senate (Mr. Webster) and the chairman of the committee of ways and means in the House (Mr. Cambreling), to the great amusement of the House.

Mr. Hardin soon paid his respects to Mr. Adams, the loud-voiced Sempronius, whose "voice was still for war;" quoting Sempronius's speech. The gentleman had been eight years Secretary of State under Mr. Monroe, and four years President, during all which time the French refused to indemnify us for our losses. Was he then so full of fight? Yet now he declares that those who voted against the appropriation of three millions at the last session had but one step more to take, and that was to open the gates of the Capitol to the enemy, and then join them.

The gentleman would remember that the modest Lucius replied to Sempronius, "My thoughts, I must confess, are turned on peace," and that in the sequel Sempronius deserted to Cæsar, but Lucius remained faithful to Cato, and fought it out like a man.

Mr. Hardin asked who were the men whom Mr. Adams had attacked and denounced as traitors? They were his old friends and political supporters, who stood by him in former times and faced the battle and the breeze; who, on account of their supporting him, have been proscribed by the government and party in power: and now the very man for whom they are proscribed turns against them and joins the ranks of their enemies!

Mr. Evans (of Maine) followed in the discussion, and in the course of his remarks paid his respects to Mr. Adams. "The gentleman," he said, "when called to order for violating a rule of the House which interdicts any allusion in one branch to the doings in the other, said he would transfer the location of the place where these things happened, from the Senate to the 'National Intelligencer,' and then, quoting with literal fidelity expressions used in a debate in the Senate, he proceeded to comment upon them in a tone which I forbear to characterize. On the following day the gentleman interrupted the remarks, pungent and conclusive as they were, of the honorable member from Virginia [Mr. Wise], 'to explain.' In what he had said the day before, he alluded to no individual whatever; he had no person in his mind; he only 'personified a sentiment;' and to that personification he addressed himself. Such was the explanation. Now, sir, I must be permitted to say, if he was not replying to what had been said in the Senate,—if he had no reference to particular members of it,—in his own language, 'all that eloquence was gratuitous, and all that indignation wastefully squandered away;' and, I may add, the time of this House was also wastefully squandered away. He either had reference, and pointed reference, too, to a distinguished member of that body, or he had not. If he had, then he violated the rules of the House. If he had not, then was his speech an effusion of unmeaning bombast, aimed at nothing, proving nothing but the ill-suppressed feelings which prompted it. The great business of the nation must stop to allow the gentleman to run a tilt against 'the personification of a sentiment,' and the House exhibits the disgraceful spectacle of boisterous applause at his fancied success in overthrowing 'a personified sentiment.'"

Mr. Evans closed his scathing philippic by saying that he (Mr. Adams) had become the object of commiseration to his friends and of derision to his enemies, and to both he would leave him.

Certainly his friends felt deep regret at the course he had taken. For a time his old friends were estranged; but the bad feelings thus created gradually wore away, and former relations were restored.

UNITED STATES BANK.

Application was made to the Legislature of Pennsylvania for a State charter, which, after much opposition from the Jackson men, was granted, and the bill was signed by Governor Ritner, on the 8th of February, 1836. The bank gave a large bonus for its charter, a portion of which constituted and was the commencement of a common-school fund for the State, and was, moreover, the origin of the present excellent common-school system of Pennsylvania, which has done, and is doing, so much for the State.

For this great blessing the children and youth of that State owe eternal gratitude to THADDEUS STEVENS, at that time a member of the Legislature, who insisted upon a portion of the bonus the bank was to pay being thus disposed of, and who carried through the Legislature, against great and fierce opposition, the bill, drawn by himself, creating the common-school system now in existence.

It has been the great luminary whose rays have penetrated and enlightened the dark places, for a long time obstinately shut against light. School-houses now dot every part of the State, even those formerly benighted regions where a schoolmaster was held to be a rogue or a vagrant, and if he did not immediately disappear would have stood a fair chance to be "hung with his pen and ink-horn about his neck;" where it was unsafe to "talk of a noun, and a verb, and such abominable words, and people made their mark, like honest, plain-dealing men."

REBELLION AND REVOLUTION IN TEXAS.

Much excitement was created in every part of the United States, but especially in Georgia, Alabama, and some other Southern States, and in Pennsylvania, by accounts from Texas, first of the march of an army, headed by Santa Anna, into Texas, and then of battles; of the massacre of Colonels Fannin and Ward and the troops under their command.

The first battle fought was that of the Alamo, in which these two officers and their troops, numbering about four hundred, were defeated and taken prisoners by an immensely superior force. In surrendering as prisoners of war, they stipulated to retain their arms, but without ammunition. The battle had been a desperate one, about four hundred Mexicans having been killed.

After the battle they were marched to Goliad, where they were retained as prisoners. On the eighth day after reaching Goliad, they were marched out a short distance from the fort, on the pretense that they were to go on a buffalo-hunt, halted, ordered to ground arms, throw down their blankets, and face to the right about. In this position they were fired upon, and nearly every man killed!

Colonels Fannin and Ward were from Georgia, as were many of their men, who had gone out to aid the Texans in their struggle for independence. There were men with them, and with General Houston, their leader, from almost every State,—several from Philadelphia: hence the deep and intense interest felt in these transactions; but they were such as could not fail to shock the feelings of every one by their horrid barbarity.

Colonel Crockett had gone out to join the Texans, and was one of the victims of the bloody massacre at the Alamo. "He was found within the Alamo, lying on his back, his bowie-knife in his hand, a dead Mexican lying across his body, and twenty-two more lying pell-mell before him." He had evidently maintained a desperate fight to the last, and had sold his life dearly.

Shortly after these tragic scenes had occurred, Santa Anna with his whole army attacked the small force under General Houston, at San Jacinto, and a desperate and bloody battle, lasting two days, 20th and 21st of April, 1836, followed, which resulted in the total rout and almost entire destruction of the Mexican army, and the escape to a wood, and final capture, in the fork of a live-oak-tree, of their commander. The watch-word of this fierce and sanguinary battle, "Remember the Alamo," fired the hearts and nerved the arms of this little band of heroes, who, at least in part, avenged the massacre of their brothers, and paid the cowardly, savage Mexicans for their treachery.

It was with no little difficulty that General Houston could

protect Santa Anna from the fury of his justly incensed officers and men, who demanded his life as a forfeit for his treacherous brutality to Fannin and Ward and their men.

General Houston, however, made a treaty with him, which the Mexican government repudiated. But the Texans had gained their independence; the Mexicans having had all the experience they desired of their fighting qualities at San Jacinto, where the victory was a rout and a slaughter, no quarter being given, and only those saved their lives who could escape by swift flight into the woods and swamps.

MIRABEAU B. LAMAR.

Among those who fought with such desperate valor at San Jacinto, no one so distinguished himself for daring courage, for dashing assaults and furious attacks upon the Mexicans, as he whose name stands above. Mr. Lamar went to Texas as a literary, not as a military, adventurer; but, being there at the time Santa Anna entered Texas, and fired by the Alamo and Goliad massacres, he joined the army as a volunteer private upon the eve of the great conflict, and fought, as a private, on horseback, on the first day of the battle. But such was the valor and ardor he displayed, and so greatly did he distinguish himself, that he was placed, by acclamation, in command of the mounted men on the morning of the second day; and well did he fulfill the expectations of his command. He was everywhere in the thickest of the fight, and it was said by eye-witnesses that his sword swept off Mexican heads as a man would cut off heads of wheat, dashing through the field and cutting right and left. At every sweep of his weapon he would yell out, "ALAMO!" "FANNIN!" "WARD!" inspiring his men with his own fiery spirit, dashing through the ranks of the Mexicans like a tornado of fire, and, finally, pursuing and slaughtering them in their flight. He too was a Georgian.

Mirabeau Bonaparte Lamar: I knew him intimately; a nobler, braver, more generous, unselfish heart never beat in human breast. He would shed his blood, if necessary, unhesitatingly, for his friend; and as readily would he take that of an enemy to revenge an insult or a reflection upon his honor or courage. He had the spirit of chivalry in him, and was as true a knight as ever shivered lance or wore his lady's favor.

General Lamar—as he became—was subsequently elected President of Texas; but he had less taste for public affairs than for literature,—courted the Muses when he should, as a politician, have courted the people; disliked business of all kinds, to which he could never give his mind. He came into the world at a wrong period; he was born for a knight-errant, and should have lived in the Middle Ages.

SEMINOLE WAR.

The Seminole Indians in Florida began committing depredations, burning houses and destroying plantations, in the fall of 1835. These depredations were continued, and became so frequent and flagrant that the people had to flee from the section of the State about the lakes and the head-waters of the St. John's River. Troops were sent to protect them and drive the Indians back; but they could do but little. The Indians would dash out of the swamps and morasses, commit depredations, and disappear where it was impossible to pursue them. The district they occupied was what was called "the Everglades," which it was not safe for any white man to attempt to penetrate. General Clinch, General Gaines, and General Scott were successively in command of the troops there, and some battles were fought, with varied results, but with little effect in repressing the Indians. General Call, Governor of Florida, succeeded General Scott in command of the army there, and he was succeeded by General Jessup, perhaps others, who found more hard work to be done, more obstacles and perplexities to be encountered and vigilance required, than laurels to be won.

The Indians were insignificant in numbers, but full of strategy, courage, and perseverance. There could be little glory won by defeating them, and yet it seemed impossible to conquer them. The war continued for several years, to the great annoyance of the people and expense to the nation. The names of some of the Seminole chiefs are still familiar as household words to us. Among these were Osceola, a very superior man and true hero, Billy Bowiegs, Wild Cat, Micanopy, and Alligator.

THE SPECIE CIRCULAR.

I have spoken of the mania of speculation and the inflated condition of the currency following the removal of the public deposits from the United States Bank to "the pet banks," as the State banks selected for deposit were generally called.

Gold, which it had been predicted would "flow up the Mississippi River and glisten through the interstices of the long silken purses of every substantial farmer," obstinately refused to fulfill the prediction. Prices had become inflated, especially of breadstuffs, meat, rents, and, indeed, all the necessaries of life; and this produced great discontent among mechanics and the laboring classes generally, the formation of many trades-unions, and frequent "strikes" for higher wages. Great complaints were made of frauds, favoritism, speculations, and monopolies in the purchase of public lands. Capitalists and companies, who could command bank credit, went largely into the purchase of public lands, interfering injuriously with actual settlers, who had only money enough to purchase what they wished to cultivate: these speculators buying large tracts and holding them at high prices prevented settlement.

Shortly previous to the close of the first session of the Twenty-fourth Congress, Mr. Benton submitted a resolution in the Senate, declaring that nothing but gold and silver should be received in payment for public lands; which was rejected. But what the Senate refused to do was done by the Executive immediately after its adjournment, July 11, 1836, and upon the suggestion and inspiration of "Old Bullion," as Mr. Benton was called. He states that he was consulted and assisted in drawing up the circular known as "the Specie Circular," which was nominally issued by the Secretary of the Treasury, Mr. Woodbury, but was prepared at the White House.

The "circular" set forth that, in consequence of complaints which had been made of frauds, speculations, and monopolies in the purchase of the public lands, and the aid which was said to have been given to effect these objects by excessive bank credits, and dangerous, if not partial, facilities given by the banks, etc., it was ordered that from and after the 15th of August, then next (the circular bore date July 11), nothing but gold and silver, and in proper cases Virginia land-scrip, should be received in payment for public lands. An actual settler, or a bona fide resident of the State in which the land-sales were made, was, however, permitted to pay, as heretofore, in bank-bills.

This was a tremendous bomb thrown without warning into the business transactions of the country. It broke the bubble of inflation, which the government's own measures had created, and produced a sudden collapse.

The banks at once took the alarm, held on with a tightening grasp to the specie in their vaults, called in, as rapidly as they could, their loans, and refused further accommodations. Every man indebted to a bank was pressed for payment, and the pressure became universal. Another "panic" had been brought about by what was termed another "experiment" upon the currency. A great revulsion took place, property was sacrificed, and of course prices went rapidly down. The annual sales of public land, which formerly amounted to from two to four millions of dollars, under the late state of things had run up to twenty-five millions of dollars, and a surplus of revenue had accumulated in the deposit banks of some twenty-five or thirty millions, which was shortly to be distributed to the States under Mr. Clay's bill, now a law, commonly called the Distribution act.

In discussing the subject of the Treasury circular in the Senate, Mr. Ewing said he had, in a former speech, explained the manner in which the public funds, under the present deposit system, were made to pay for the public lands, performing a circuit from the deposit banks to the speculator, from him to the land-office, and from the land-office to the deposit banks again, thus operating the exchange of the public lands by millions of acres to large purchasers for mere credit.

One effect of this circular, he said, had been to banish gold and silver. These are never seen at the West; and a five-dollar bill cannot be changed into specie in a ride of thirty miles.

The wealthy speculator from Boston, New York, Philadelphia, or elsewhere, finds this circular no obstacle in his way, as he can easily make an arrangement with any number of men, inhabitants of the State in which he wishes to purchase lands, to purchase in their names,—in the name of each one three hundred and twenty acres. He uses no specie, yet gets all the land he wants; while others, of less capital and less genius, have to lug specie some hundreds of miles, which no sooner performs its office by paying for land than it goes back again to the East.

Mr. Ewing's resolutions to repeal the Treasury specie circular underwent discussion in both houses of Congress during the last session of the Twenty-fourth Congress, occupying a considerable portion of the time.

By the Whigs and the business-men of the country generally it was considered a very mischievous measure, pregnant with evil consequences to the country, and productive of no good. That it produced the serious consequences I have mentioned, and attributed to it by the speakers in Congress who advocated its repeal, can hardly be questioned; but a state of things pervaded the country which was a monstrous evil,—the superabundance of bank-paper, the great facility of obtaining it, the entire absence of silver and gold, the mania of speculation, and the enormously high prices of everything purchasable.

The object of the circular was to cure this evil; to restore the circulation of the country to its normal condition by driving out the superabundant bank-paper and replacing it with specie.

The remedy, however, was, for a time, worse than the disease. It undertook to cure this too suddenly,—all at once,—and the effect was what we have seen. Prices were brought down with a tremendous jar.

The bill repealing it passed in the House, 143 to 59; and in the Senate, 41 to 5. It was quite probable, from this vote, that had the President sent the bill back with his veto it would have been passed, his reasons to the contrary notwithstanding. He did not, therefore, return it, but put it in his pocket, and sent his reasons for not signing it to the "Globe," where they were published. The bill not having been sent to him ten days before the close of the session, he could retain it till after the close of the session without its becoming a law. This was called the "Pocket Veto."

A SCENE IN THE HOUSE OF REPRESENTATIVES.

The "scene" I am about to describe was the precursor of many others which occurred in subsequent years, each more or less dramatic, but all exciting and disreputable.

On the 6th of February (1837), after sundry petitions had been presented by different members for the abolition of slavery and the slave-trade in the District of Columbia,—several by Mr. Adams,—he presented a petition from nine women of Fredericksburg, Virginia, praying Congress to put a stop to the slave-trade in the District of Columbia. One of these petitions, Mr. Adams said, seemed so strange to him that he did not feel perfect security that it was genuine. He then said he held in his hand a paper on which, before he presented it, he desired to have the decision of the Speaker. It was a petition from twenty-two persons declaring themselves to be slaves. He wished to know whether the Speaker considered such a petition as coming within the order of the House.

The Speaker said he could not tell until its contents were in his possession.

Mr. Adams said if the paper were sent to the Clerk it would be in possession of the House; if sent to the Speaker, he could see its contents. He wished to do nothing but in submission to the rules of the House. It had occurred to him that the paper was not what it purported to be. He would send it to the Chair.

Objection was made. The Speaker (Mr. Polk) said the circumstances of the case were so extraordinary that he would take the sense of the House on the course to be pursued. He then stated to the House the circumstances as above related, and said he desired the sense of the House.

Mr. Haynes, of Georgia, was astonished that the gentleman from Massachusetts should offer such a paper. If he were to object to receiving it, it might be giving it more attention than it deserved.

Several Southern members now expressed their astonishment and indignation, in fitting terms, that any one should present a petition which on its face appeared to come from slaves. After much of this, Mr. Waddy Thompson, of South Carolina, offered a resolution declaring that the Hon. John Quincy Adams, by attempting to introduce a petition purporting on its face to be from slaves, had been guilty of a gross disrespect to this House, and that he be instantly brought to the bar to receive the severe censure of the Speaker.

Mr. Thompson said he felt infinite pain in being forced by an imperious sense of duty to present this resolution. He spoke of the age of Mr. Adams, and of the stations he had filled; but when age is used to throw poisoned arrows it ceases to be sacred. The act of the gentleman from Massachusetts was an insult to a large portion of the members of the House. "Does the gentleman know that there are laws in the slave States, and here, for the punishment of those who excite insurrection? I can tell him there are such things as grand juries; and we may yet see an incendiary brought to condign punishment." Mr. Thompson proceeded in this strain, amid great manifestation of feeling in the House, for some time, when

Mr. Haynes moved to amend Mr. Thompson's resolution by striking out all after the word *Resolved*, and inserting—

"That John Quincy Adams, etc., has rendered himself justly liable to the severest censure of this House, and is censured accordingly, for having attempted to present to the House the petition of slaves."

The House was now in a high state of commotion; Southern members were like a disturbed hive of bees,—restless, excited, angry, denunciatory.

Mr. Granger, of New York, addressed the House, endeavoring to calm its passions and soothe the irritation of the South, but with little effect. He concluded by expressing his regret at the occurrence of the morning, and his opinion that the gentleman from Massachusetts, so far from rendering the right of petition more sacred, had done what was calculated to render it a mere bauble to be played with. This did not mollify the South.

Mr. Lewis, of Alabama, then offered the following resolution, which Mr. Thompson accepted as a modification of his:

"*Resolved*, That John Quincy Adams, by his attempt to introduce into this House a petition from slaves for the abolition of slavery in the District of Columbia, committed an outrage on the rights and feelings of a large portion of the people of this Union, a flagrant contempt on the dignity of this House, and, by extending to slaves the privilege only belonging to freemen, directly invites the slave population to insurrection; and that the said member be forthwith called to the bar of the House to be censured by the Speaker."

Further vehement debate, or rather declamation, followed.

Mr. Adams now said he had remained mute amid the charges of crimes and misdemeanors that had been brought against him, and he supposed that if brought to the bar of the House he should be struck mute by the previous question before he had an opportunity to say a word in his own defense. He had not presented the petition, but merely asked of the Speaker whether he considered the paper he described, and which he held in his hand, included within the general order of the House that all petitions, memorials, resolutions, and papers relating to or upon the subject of slavery should be laid on the table. He intended to take the decision of the Speaker before he went one step towards presenting, or offering to present, that petition. He said, in reference to the resolution of Mr. Lewis, that it stated what was not the fact, namely, that it was for the abolition of slavery,—when, in truth, it was for *his own expulsion!* He should not present the petition until the decision of the House was announced.

Mr. Adams further said it was well known to all the members that from the day he entered the House to this time he had invariably declared his opinion adverse to the abolition of slavery in the District of Columbia. But he had maintained the right of petition. There is no absolute monarch on earth who is not compelled by the constitution of his country to receive the petitions of his people. The Sultan of Constantinople cannot walk the streets and refuse to receive petitions from the meanest and vilest in the land. Objections had been made to the petition of the nine women on the ground that they were prostitutes. In reply to this, he asked, Does our law require that before presenting a petition you shall look into it and see whether it comes from the virtuous, the great, the mighty?

He said he was still waiting the decision of the Speaker. If the House thought proper to receive the petition, he should present it.

Further acrimonious declamation followed, and additional resolutions, modifying those before the House, were submitted and discussed, the House being in an uproar until the close of the day. On the meeting of the House on the 7th, the unfinished business came up. Mr. Drumgoole, of Virginia, offered a resolution in substance declaring that by what he had done (reciting it) Mr. Adams "*had given color to an idea*" that slaves have the right of petition, etc., and that the said John Quincy Adams receive the censure of the House. More violent speeches were then made by sundry members.

Mr. Robertson, of Virginia, was the only Southern man, and Mr. Graves, of Kentucky, the only Southwestern man, who in any manner exculpated Mr. Adams. Mr. Robertson said the gentleman had cleared himself of any supposed contempt by disclaiming any intentional disrespect. But it may be said that he is not censured for asking the question of the Speaker, which he did, but because that question *gives color to the idea* that slaves may petition, etc. Absurd and offensive as such an idea is, he had yet to learn that members of Congress may be proceeded against criminally for intimating or uttering opinions here which a majority may consider heretical.

Mr. Graves thought that the adoption of a resolution of censure on the venerable gentleman from Massachusetts, taken in connection with the severe censure which Southern gentlemen, in this debate, have cast on those deluded citizens of the North who have sent their petitions to us, would be the most unwise step that could be taken by that body. No community could be driven, and no denunciations would convince them that they were in error.

Mr. Lincoln, of Massachusetts, at length, stirred by the torrent of invective that was so freely cast upon his colleague and the North, rose in defense of both,—the first Northern man, except Mr. Granger, who had participated in the general *mêlée*. He said that such was the reverence due to the age of his colleague, such the respect paid to his character and the remembrance of his public services, so high the confidence in his integrity and the purity of his motives, so beloved and honored was he at home, and so known to fame abroad, that, whatever the action of the House upon these resolutions, there are those, and they are not a few, here and elsewhere, who will deeply sympathize with him in the trial to which he is now informally subjected. He declared that he planted himself by his side on the principles for which he was contending, though he needed not his aid, being abundantly able to defend and sustain himself.

Mr. Thompson, of South Carolina, again came into the field, full of zeal for the South and of acrimony towards the North. He declared that slaves had no right to petition. They were *property*, not *persons;* they had no political rights, and therefore Congress has no power in regard to them, and no right to receive their petitions.

Replying to Mr. Lincoln, he said, "The gentleman has given us another eulogy upon these amiable fiends,—these most respectable *assassins* [the petitioners of the North]. As a class, they are fools or knaves; and there is no escape from the alternative."

Mr. Thompson went on in a long speech in a similar strain of acrimonious vilification of the North, but especially of Massachusetts, raking the history of the past to find acts which cast odium upon her people, from the time the Pilgrims landed at Plymouth down to the present day.

It was his avowed intention to wound; he declared in the outset that he should not bate his blows. Nor did he.

But there were sons of the North, and of Massachusetts, present, who could deal blows too,—who could strike as hard and hit as tender points as Mr. Waddy Thompson, as he soon found to his cost. Her champion now appeared.

Mr. Cushing, of Massachusetts, said the sentiments uttered by his colleague, Mr. Lincoln, did honor to his head and heart. They met his cordial concurrence: to no resolution of censure, based on the matters now before them, to no rebuke, express or implied, to no action of the House that shall touch his colleague (Mr. Adams) with so much as the uttermost edge of the shadow of indignity, would he give his assent.

Referring to the speech of Mr. Thompson, he said that, having gained the floor, he should feel that he was a recreant craven if he could permit any personal consideration to repress the feelings which had been excited by the stormy progress of this question, and the menace, defiance, and crimination which had been thrown at the people of the North.

Like his colleague (Mr. Lincoln), he, too, could say he was from the frigid North. But we from the North could pour forth declamation as little to the purpose as others do, if it comported with our notions of good taste or good sense. They might be less irritable than those with whom they were associated; but they were accustomed to think that in questions like the present, involving the first principles of civil liberty and the dearest rights of mankind, passionate invective, rash menace, and random exclamation are poor substitutes for reason and argument. He had been keenly sensible to the wrongs heaped upon the North in this debate, and he meant to vindicate the rights of his constituents and the fame of his forefathers. He did not wonder at the sensitiveness of Southern members in regard to the general question of slavery. It was indeed a great and grave question, and should be treated with calm gravity. He asked in all sincerity if they supposed that angry attacks on the freedom of opinion, of speech, of the press, of petition, of debate, are likely to check the spread in the United States of that disapprobation of slavery which is but another form of the love of liberty. Gentlemen who pursue the course proposed towards his colleague, and who suffer their feelings to hurry them into transports of violence here, greatly misjudge in the measures they adopt if they would allay the fever of abolition.

But it is not necessary to give an abstract of the whole of this caustic speech, in which Mr. Cushing, after defending Massachusetts from the charges brought against her, carried the war into the domains of her assailants, bringing crimination for crimination, charge for charge, and obloquy for obloquy, showing that the North could give as well as receive blows.

With Mr. Cushing's speech ended the second day spent on this business. The next, the 8th, was devoted to counting the votes for President and Vice-President.

On the 9th the subject was resumed, and another day spent in clamorous, violent declamation, in altering, modifying, and taking the votes on the resolutions before the House, and in listening to Mr. Adams in his own defense. The House would now have laid the mistake on the table, having become tired of it, if not disgusted with it; but Mr. Adams objected, and desired to be heard. Of this defense it is hardly necessary, at this day, to speak; yet a few words. Mr. Adams stated that it had not yet been decided whether he might present the petition or not; which was the real question before the House. He spoke of the various resolutions which came pouring down upon him, and the speeches which fell so thickly,—calling him infamous, and other hard names. From one quarter of the House he heard the cries, "Expel him! expel him!" All reminded him of the expression of Dame Quickly, "Oh, day and night, but these are bitter words!" He referred to Mr. Drumgoole's resolution charging him with "*giving color to an idea*," for which it was proposed to censure him! He commented with bitter and scathing force upon the menace of Mr. Thompson that there were such things as grand juries, etc. He wished to know if there were others who held that a member of Congress was amenable to a grand jury for what he might say or do in that hall! And he wished the people to know who uttered such a sentiment. If a member of the Legislature of South Carolina is made amenable not only to the Legislature, but to grand and petit juries, he thanked God he was not a citizen of that State.

His remarks created great agitation.

He said he could not make his defense in any system or order, such was the variety and disorder of charges against him. When he took up one idea, before he could *give color to the idea* it had already changed its form and *color*. If he were to plead guilty, what is the offense? He was unable to shape his defense, not knowing of what he had been guilty. But he begged to say that he should deem it to be the heaviest calamity which had ever befallen him in the course of a life checkered with many vicissitudes, if a vote of censure from that House should pass upon his name. He had been foremost in defending its honor and dignity on more than one occasion. Were these instances of contempt? And now was he to be brought to the bar for a contempt of the House for doing that which was done in the most respectful manner?—for asking a question of the Speaker? consulting him first on the admissibility of a petition?

In conclusion: If the House had suffered the petition to be laid on the table, with the multitude of petitions there buried in oblivion, no one would have heard of it more. He appealed to the House and to the nation that he was not answerable for this loss of time.

The House then voted on the resolutions before it:

First, "That any member who shall hereafter present any petition from the slaves of this Union ought to be considered as regardless of the feelings of the House, the rights of the Southern States, and unfriendly to the Union." Yeas 92, nays 105.

Second, "That the Hon. John Quincy Adams having solemnly disclaimed all design of doing anything disrespectful to the House in the inquiry made of the Speaker, etc., therefore all further proceedings in regard to his conduct do now cease." Yeas 21, nays 137,—Mr. Adams's friends voting in the negative, with a view to give him an opportunity to be heard, of which he availed himself. It is not necessary to give even a synopsis of his defense or remarks: we may be sure he did not spare his assailants.

Subsequently, resolutions were offered, discussed, and variously altered, which finally passed. The first resolution was preceded by a preamble declaring that, Mr. Adams having solemnly disclaimed all design of doing anything disrespectful to the House in the inquiry made of the Speaker, etc., therefore—

"1. *Resolved*, That this House cannot receive said petition without disregarding its own dignity, the rights of a large class of citizens of the South and West, and the Constitution of the United States." Yeas 160, nays 35.

"2. *Resolved,* That slaves do not possess the right of petition secured to the citizens of the United States by the Constitution." Yeas 162, nays 18.

This *scene* commenced on Monday, February 6, and closed with the passage of these resolutions, on Saturday, the 11th: a week of violent altercations, embittered sectional animosity, fierce attacks, angry charges, and the repelling of these by the assailed with a spirit less fiery but not less resolute than that of their assailants. The storm had exhausted itself chiefly in wind, which did little damage to any one, save that it had the effect to increase greatly the feeling against slavery at the North, and thus to injure the South. The speeches and proceedings in this conflict occupy many columns of the "National Intelligencer."

In this memorable onslaught upon Mr. Adams, the Southern Hotspurs, who were so eager to fire at him, let their guns off, so to speak, at half-cock. They did not wait to see what the petition was which he did *not* offer, and which he only made an inquiry about of the Speaker, but assumed that it must be for the abolition of slavery: they were taken aback, and became laughing-stocks, when he informed them that it was for just what they were proposing to do, namely, to expel him from the House. They were several times, like a pack of hounds, "at fault," but still kept baying away. Mr. Dixon H. Lewis, one of the clearest-headed men of the party, endeavored to restrain the intemperate ardor of some of the less sagacious Southern members when he saw them start off in a wrong direction, and to give them the true scent by his resolution; but even he was "at fault," and became perplexed. And then came Mr. Drumgoole, an experienced parliamentarian, and the shrewdest tactician on that side of the House, with a resolution charging Mr. Adams with "giving color to an idea;" which he most scathingly ridiculed. Mr. Lewis was a man of great weight,—to wit, some five hundred pounds,—a mountain of flesh and fat; but he had brains too, which also gave him weight of a different kind. No ordinary chair could hold him, and one had to be manufactured expressly for him.

It will be seen that in this famous *émeute,* though the tide seemed at first to be overwhelmingly against Mr. Adams, in the end he came off with flying colors, the South being glad to escape the biting sarcasms and virulent rhetoric of "the old man eloquent" by wisely letting him alone. Besides, they found they had made themselves ridiculous, and were glad to get out of the scrape.

A GLOOMY DAY, AND A DEED OF DARKNESS IN THE SENATE.

I have, in its proper place, mentioned that on the last day of the second session of the Twenty-third Congress, March 3, 1835, the resolution introduced by Mr. Benton to expunge from the Senate journal the resolution passed by the Senate on the 28th of March, 1834, censuring the President for removing the deposits from the United States Bank, was, after the words "ordered to be expunged" were stricken out, laid on the table. As there mentioned, Mr. Benton immediately gave notice that he should again offer the resolution to expunge, etc., at the next session of Congress; and in accordance with said notice he again, on the 26th of December, 1836, offered the same resolution.

After the resolution was emasculated and laid on the table by the Senate, on the 3d of March, 1835, vigorous efforts were made by the administration not only to secure a Democratic majority in the Senate, but to get State Legislatures to instruct their Senators, especially those who had opposed it, to vote for it. The Legislature of Virginia thus instructed her Senators; but John Tyler, refusing to act upon such instructions, resigned, and W. C. Rives was elected in his place. By this means a majority in the Senate for this famous resolution was secured, and it was resolved by its friends that it should be passed.

It was called up on the 12th of January, by Mr. Benton, who supported it in an elaborate, carefully-prepared speech, chiefly eulogistic of General Jackson and his administration, the measures of which during his eight years' service in the Presidential office he reviewed and commended as wise, prudent, and statesmanlike, claiming that the country under his rule had enjoyed, and was now enjoying, a high degree of prosperity. "Gold," he said, "after a disappearance of thirty years, is restored to our country;" and, negativing the various charges of the opponents of the administration, made from time to time, he alleged that "domestic industry is *not* paralyzed; confidence is *not* destroyed; workmen are *not* mendicants for bread or employment; credit is *not* extinguished; prices have *not* sunk; grass is *not* growing in the streets of populous cities; the wharves are *not* lumbered with decaying vessels; columns of curses rising from the bosoms of a ruined and agonized people are *not* ascending to heaven against the destroyer of a nation's felicity and prosperity. On the contrary, the *reverse* of all this is true."

Of General Jackson he said, "Great is the influence, great the power, greater than any man ever before possessed in our America, which he has acquired over the public mind. The mind instinctively dwells on his vast and unprecedented popularity."

He closed his remarks with the following memorable exordium:

"And now, sir, I finish the task which, three years ago, I imposed on myself. *Solitary and alone, and amidst the jeers and taunts of my opponents, I put this ball in motion.* The people have taken it up and rolled it forward, and I am not anything but a unit in the vast mass which now propels it. In the name of that mass I speak. I demand the execution of the edict of the people; I demand the expurgation of that sentence which the voice of a few Senators, and the power of the confederate, the Bank of the United States, has caused to be placed on the journal of the Senate, and which the voice of millions of freemen has ordered to be expunged from it."*

* Colonel Benton could have found a precedent for *expunging* the journal of a legislative body. The Stamp Act of England had deeply stirred the people of the Colonies, especially in Massachusetts and Virginia, both of which remonstrated against it. But this had no effect. The subject afterwards coming up for discussion in the House of Burgesses of Virginia, May, 1765, Patrick Henry, "alone, unadvised, and unassisted," prepared and offered five resolutions, in substance declaring that "we, Englishmen, living in America, have all the rights of Englishmen living in England; that every attempt to invest such power [of taxation] in any person or persons whatever, other than the General Assembly [of the Colony], has a manifest tendency to destroy British and American freedom."

Mr. Henry supported his resolutions in that fervid and eloquent speech which acquired historic fame, and in which, upon the cry of "Treason!" he uttered

Mr. Crittenden, of Kentucky, next addressed the Senate, on the same day, in opposition to the resolution, and Mr. Dana, of Maine, next day, 13th, in support of it. Mr. Preston, of South Carolina, followed, in a strain of eloquence inspired by his deep feeling of aversion to this whole proceeding. Referring to Virginia, his native State, having instructed her Senators to vote for expunging, he said he mourned from the bottom of his heart the instructions under which the Senator (Mr. Rives) felt himself constrained to vote for this extraordinary resolution.

Mr. Rives replied, but his remarks were never reported.

Mr. Moore, of Alabama, reminded his colleague, Colonel William R. King, that when this subject was last up his colleague had agreed with him, and even himself moved to strike out the words "ordered to be expunged." His colleague and himself then followed the lead of that stern and inflexible patriot (Judge White, of Tennessee) who now opposed this resolution.

It was thus shown, what the record also exhibited, that Colonel King, of Alabama, was one of those whom the discipline of party compelled to face to the right about, take the back track, and wheel into line.

Mr. Southard, of New Jersey, was desirous to speak, and, it being late, moved that the Senate adjourn; but, the motion failing, he declined speaking at so late an hour. But Mr. Calhoun, who had sat all day in his seat, scarcely moving, an attentive listener, an expression of unusual gravity pervading his sallow countenance, scarcely exchanging a word with any one, but communing with his own thoughts, now slowly rose, in the dim twilight, and, standing a minute or two, as if to collect himself, spoke in a calm, deliberate, and impressive manner. Every ear was open, and every eye intent upon the speaker, who might have been taken for one of the prophets of old,

the bold defiance, "If that is treason, make the most of it." Under the effect of his glowing patriotism and burning eloquence, his resolutions were carried.

But the Tories, who then were the leading men and men of power, became alarmed, and, after a violent struggle, succeeded in *expunging* Mr. Henry's patriotic resolutions. Colonel Benton did not quote this.

such was his venerable and picturesque appearance, heightened by his full, bushy head of hair, his long gray locks hanging wildly down his neck and over his shoulders, his deep-sunken but still penetrating eye lighted up with the fires within.

"Sir," he began, "there are some questions so plain that they cannot be argued; nothing can make them more plain; and this is one. No one not blinded by party zeal can possibly be insensible that the measure proposed is a violation of the Constitution. I know perfectly well that gentlemen have no liberty to vote otherwise than they will. They are coerced by an exterior power. They try, indeed, to comfort their consciences by saying that it is the voice of the people. It is no such thing. We all know how these legislative returns have been obtained. It is by dictation from the White House. The voice of the PEOPLE! I see before me Senators who could not swallow that resolution when it was first introduced: has it changed its nature since? Not at all. But executive power has interposed. Talk to me of the voice of the people! It is the combination of patronage and power which coerces this body to a palpable violation of the Constitution.

* * * * * * * *

"But why do I waste my breath? I know it is all utterly vain. The day is gone; night approaches, and night is suitable to the dark deed meditated. The act must be performed; and it is an act which will tell on the political history of this country forever. . . . The act originates in pure, unmixed, personal idolatry. It is the melancholy evidence of a broken spirit, ready to bow down at the feet of power. The removal of the deposits was an act such as might have been perpetrated in the days of Pompey or Cæsar, but an act like this could never have been consummated by a Roman Senate until the times of Caligula and Nero."

Mr. Calhoun's short, compact sentences, uttered in a sharp, incisive manner, with scarcely a single gesture of the hand or movement of the body, except as he turned to look at Senators on whose course he was commenting, fell like sledge-hammer blows upon heads bowed in very shame at what they were about to do under compulsion.

The subject did not come up in the Senate on Saturday, the 14th. But so vigorous had been the opposition to the passage of the resolution, and so odious with the intelligent portion of the country was the idea of *expunging* the records of the Senate, that its leading advocates were not without some anxiety in regard to their ability to carry it through; and Mr. Benton relates how Senators were drilled preparatory to voting. "They were called together," he informs us, "at night, at the then famous restaurant of Boulanger, giving the assemblage the air of a convivial entertainment: it continued," he says, "till midnight, and required all the moderation, tact, and skill of the prime movers to obtain and maintain the union upon details, on the success of which the fate of the measure depended." But the form of the resolution and the process of expurgation were finally, under the influence of good wine, oysters, and terrapin, some coaxing and some threatening, agreed to, "each one severally pledging himself to it," and that there should be no adjournment of the Senate after it was called up until it was passed, and that it should be called up on Monday morning, January 16th, the caucus being held on Saturday night, the 14th.

On Monday morning, therefore, it having become generally known that the expunging resolution was to be taken up, discussed, and passed on that day, or before the Senate adjourned, the galleries were crammed at a very early hour, the circular gallery being reserved for, and filled by, ladies. The subject created intense interest.

The resolution was called up by Mr. Benton, after the morning hour, and the discussion proceeded during the whole day, the interest deepening as the hours wore away. Mr. Clayton and Mr. Bayard, of Delaware, Mr. Kent, of Maryland, Judge White, of Tennessee, Mr. Ewing, of Ohio, and Mr. Clay, were among those who spoke this day in opposition to, and Mr. Buchanan and one or two others in favor of, the resolution. The spectators in the galleries held tenaciously to their seats during the whole day and till twelve o'clock at night.

After the day was far spent and the shades of night came on, Judge White, the life-long friend of Andrew Jackson, addressed the Senate. His tall and emaciated form, his venerable appearance, his long, white, flowing locks thrown back from his forehead, made him an object of peculiar interest and profound respect. Every one, except the expurgators, felt that no measure could be right which such an impersonation of truth and sincerity opposed, and in thus opposing was reluctantly compelled, by an imperious sense of duty, to array himself against an old friend. But his voice was unheeded; and so would have been the voice of the archangel Gabriel, had he descended from heaven and addressed the Senate.

The debate went on till very late at night, the crowd in the galleries and lobbies becoming densely packed, and every inch of the Senate floor being occupied by members of the House and by ladies who had been admitted by the courtesy of the Senate. The scene was grand, impressive, and imposing: it was even solemn. It seemed as if some terrible rite was to be performed, some bloody sacrifice about to be made upon the altar of Moloch.

A pause in the debates occurring, and a dead silence prevailing, all eyes were turned to Mr. Clay, who was the great leader of the opposition, and had not yet spoken. Slowly his tall form rose. There was a gentle bustle, as if all were striving to get a good view of him. He waited a minute or two, and the Senate became still as death. Upon no occasion in his life, probably, did he feel more deeply the importance of the subject to be discussed, or the solemnity of the occasion. It was another great battle between him and his implacable enemy Andrew Jackson, —one of a series which began in 1825 and ended only with the death of his indomitable foe.

Mr. Clay appeared unusually grave. He at first spoke in a subdued tone; yet such was the peculiarly clear, silvery, sonorous quality of his voice that every word could be distinctly heard by every one in the chamber.

He commenced by saying that, considering that he was the mover of the resolution of March, 1834, and the consequent relation in which he stood to the majority of the Senate by whose vote it was adopted, he felt it to be his duty to say something on this expunging resolution. He referred to the action of the Senate at the close of the last Congress, in laying the resolution of expurgation on the table. That, he had supposed, was the final disposition of it. But since then successful efforts had been made to change the political character of the Senate, by the use of such means as were at the command of those in power, and it was now the design of the advocates of this measure to bring it to an absolute conclusion.

After taking a retrospect of the causes which had led to the passage of his resolution, and speaking of what was now proposed to be done to wipe out that just condemnation of the President's unwarrantable act of removing the public deposits, Mr. Clay said, "I put it to the calm and deliberate consideration of the majority if they are ready to pronounce for all time that, whoever may be President, the Senate shall not *dare* to remonstrate against any Executive usurpation whatever. For one, I will not."

* * * * * * * *

Of the President he said, "In one hand he holds the purse, and in the other brandishes the sword, of the country. Myriads of dependants and partisans, scattered over the land, are ever ready to sing hosannas to him and to laud to the skies whatever he does. He has swept over the government during the last eight years like a tropical tornado. . . . What object of his ambition is unsatisfied? When disabled from age any longer to hold the sceptre of power, he designates his successor, and transmits it to his favorite. What more does he want? Must we blot, deface, and mutilate the records of the country to punish the presumptuousness of expressing an opinion contrary to his own? . . . Is it your design to stigmatize us? You cannot.

'Ne'er yet did base dishonor blur our name.'

"Standing securely upon our conscious rectitude, and bearing aloft the shield of the Constitution, your puny efforts are impotent, and we defy all your power. Put the majority of 1834 in one scale, and that by which this expunging resolution is to be carried in the other, and let truth and justice in heaven above and on earth below, and liberty and patriotism, decide the preponderance."

This challenge was uttered in a tone of proud, lofty, and

indomitable defiance, and with an air of conscious, undeniable superiority.

"Black lines!" exclaimed Mr. Clay. "Sir, let the Secretary preserve the pen with which he may inscribe them. . . . And hereafter, when we shall lose the form of our free institutions, some future monarch, in gratitude to those by whose means he has been enabled upon the ruins of civil liberty to erect a throne, and to commemorate this expunging resolution, may institute a new order of knighthood, under the appropriate name of 'THE KNIGHTS OF THE BLACK LINES.'

"But why should I detain the Senate? The decree has gone forth. The deed is to be done,—that foul deed which all the multitudinous seas' will 'never wash clean from their hands.' Proceed, then: do the noble work before you; and when you have perpetrated it, go home to the people and tell them what a glorious work you have performed!"

Mr. Clay was never more impressive than on this occasion; never bore himself more loftily, and never had greater occasion to feel the towering eminence he occupied over the expungers, whom he looked *down* upon. Mr. Benton admits that his speech "was grand and affecting."

The expungers had the numbers; but the talent, the eloquence, the moral power, "not an unequal match for numbers," were arrayed against them; and against them, also, were the sympathies of four-fifths of those present, and nearly the whole intelligent, educated portion of the people.

Mr. Buchanan, the most faithful of partisans, the most ready and willing to put his shoulder to the wheel when the party needed help, followed Mr. Clay in a speech of an hour and a half in support of the expunging resolution. He considered the question before the Senate most grave and solemn. It was in fact, if not in form, the trial of the Senate for having unjustly and unconstitutionally tried and condemned the President. He then asked who was the President of the United States, and answered the question by a glowing eulogy of General Andrew Jackson.* He then reviewed Mr. Clay's charges against the President in connection with the doings of the Bank of the

* Which General Jackson would never reciprocate.

United States, the re-chartering of the bank, and the vetoing of the bill by "the old Roman;" accused the bank of entering the arena of politics for the purpose of defending itself and attacking the President, and arraigned it for the policy it had pursued financially, which provoked the President to remove from its vaults the public deposits. This was a blow from which it never recovered. It was the club of Hercules with which he slew the Hydra. For this the President was not only justified, but deserved the eternal gratitude of his country. For this the Senate had condemned him; and this condemnation was now about to be expunged from the Senate's journal.

Mr. Bayard took the floor after Mr. Buchanan. He did not intend to inquire into the motives which moved gentlemen to support this resolution. The motives of every man are his individual property. He could not say that the act which is now required to be done is a sacrifice to the Moloch of party spirit. He could not say that it is homage to an idol, nor could he say that it is intended to smooth the mane and calm the roar of the lion. Mr. Bayard then went into a review of the whole subject, and examined also the general character of the administration; remarking that "one of the strongest objections he had to the course of the present administration was its constant effort to array the different portions of society against each other, and its habit of appealing for support to the worst passions and prejudices of our nature."

The debate was further continued by Mr. Hendricks against, and by Mr. Strange in favor of, the expunging resolution: the latter in a long speech.

Mr. Ewing, of Ohio, whose mental powers well corresponded with his physical proportions, closed the debate, speaking for an hour or more with great force.

Mr. Ewing said he envied not the triumph of him who had pressed forward this resolution against the opinions and feelings and consciences of those whom he had found means to *compel* to its support, which he had urged on with passions fierce, vindictive, furious; still less did he envy the condition of those who were *compelled* to bow their necks to the yoke and to go onward, against all those feelings and motives which should direct the actions of an enlightened and conscientious legislator. "Why," continued he, "do I see around me so many pale faces and downcast eyes? Do remorse and repentance go hand in hand with the deed? They are truly objects of pity and commiseration. But the scene is passing, and soon will be passed, and its actors must and will be judged by posterity: to that posterity, who will judge us when we and our opponents—all within the sound of my voice—shall sleep in our graves, we solemnly, but confidently, appeal."

Another pause and profound silence ensued: the clock had struck the hour of eleven, and time moved on. There was an inquiring look from the expungers, especially towards the Senator from Massachusetts. Mr. Webster sat for a few minutes looking around to see whether any other Senator would rise. As none did, he rose, with a paper in his hand. "Midnight," says Mr. Benton, "was approaching. The dense masses which filled every inch of room in the lobbies and galleries remained immovable. The floor of the Senate was crammed with privileged persons; it seemed as if all Congress was there." Every eye was now turned on Mr. Webster. His dark visage seemed to assume a deeper hue. His deep-toned voice became almost sepulchral. He spoke low, but distinctly. He said that argument was exhausted; more was useless. The deed was to be done, and execution was near at hand: midnight was approaching, fitting hour for such a deed. As the rules of the Senate did not permit a Senator to enter a protest upon the journals, he had prepared a protest against this whole proceeding for himself and colleague, which he should now read. Having read this PROTEST, his duty, he said, was now performed, and took his seat.

And now, the vote having been taken,—24 to 19,—the deed was to be done.

The Secretary brought in the record-book of the Senate. But, to avoid witnessing this desecration of the journal, those Senators who had opposed the proceeding left the chamber. Opening the journal at the page which contained the resolution to be expunged, the Secretary, in the presence of such members as remained, proceeded to draw black lines entirely around the resolution, and to write across it the words, "Expunged by order of the Senate, this 16th day of January, 1837."

No sooner had this been done than a loud, sudden, and continued hiss broke forth from various parts of the galleries. The pent-up feeling of the people found vent in the only form in which they could express their indignation.

It was, of course, a violation of the rules of the Senate and of decorum; but such was the intensity of the emotion of disgust that it would *out*, in spite of all rules.

And now came another scene. The Vice-President very properly checked the hissing, and the Sergeant-at-arms received orders to clear the galleries and arrest any one who had violated the rules. A Senator, in great passion, cried out, "The Bank ruffians are here! Arrest them! seize them! bring them before the Senate! let them be punished!" or words as nearly like these as can be recollected.

A gentleman by the name of William Lloyd, of Ohio, was arrested by the Sergeant-at-arms, and was brought before the Senate; but there was no proof that he had been guilty of violating the rules of that body, and he was finally discharged.

The names of those who voted for the expunging process were published in the Whig papers, in large, full-faced capital letters, and with heavy black lines drawn around them, as "THE KNIGHTS OF THE BLACK LINES." For awhile they occupied "a bad eminence," but Time, which has buried the names, if not the memory, of some of the expungers in oblivion, has also nearly obliterated from the memory of man the act itself. Though every actor in that extraordinary scene has gone to his long home, the record they mutilated on that gloomy night still remains to tell the story of its desecration to this and all future generations.

By the expunging of this resolution censuring General Jackson he completely triumphed over his opponents, as he had always done through life. It must have been gratifying to him to have this censure wiped out by the Senate, just as he was about to close his *reign* and retire to the Hermitage for the remainder of his days. That he felt exultant is shown by his giving a grand dinner, in a day or two, to the expungers and their wives. Mr. Benton—"Old Bullion," as he was usually called—says "his gratification was extreme. Being too weak to sit at the table, he only met the company, placed *the head expunger* in his chair, and withdrew to his sick-chamber." Thus was Mr. Benton honored for the part he had taken.

The feelings of the better portion of the people of the United States—of all except the "whole hog" Jackson men—on this occasion are forcibly expressed in the following letter, addressed to Mr. Clay by Chancellor Kent, of New York, very soon after the transaction:

"NEW YORK, February 20, 1837.

"MY DEAR SIR,—I hope I shall not be deemed too obtrusive, but I cannot refrain from declaring my admiration of the speech delivered by you in the Senate, in January last, on the expunging resolution. My sympathies and judgment and confidence and patriotism and grief and indignation are with you in every point; and if I was in Washington I would go directly up to you and give your hand the hearty shake of sympathetic feeling. You have vindicated the resolution of 1834 with irresistible force, and damned the other to everlasting fame. If you, and such men as you, who are storming despotic and servile meanness in the Senatorial hall, have no other recompense, it may possibly give you some consolation to be assured that you are receiving the silent admiration and gratitude of thousands, and by none with more hearty pulsation than by

"Your most respectful and obedient servant,

"JAMES KENT."

The state of the country, politically, at this time; the blind devotion of a great portion of the people to General Jackson; the belief that he could do no wrong, or that, if he did, it was with honest intentions, and therefore not to be censured; the complete ascendency of the Executive; his usurpations of power; his ebullitions of temper and restiveness when his will was in the least checked, thwarted, or questioned; the absolute and abject fear in which his political friends stood of him; the rigid requirement of the *party* of unquestioning submission to whatever were its behests; the implicit obedience exacted from all executive officers, from the highest to the lowest; the unhesitating dismissal of all who did not promptly obey; the denunciation and proscription of all who did not conform to the prevailing creed, or who attempted to maintain an independent opinion; the bestowal of liberal, and even profuse, rewards upon the most faithful and subservient,—all this was calculated to dishearten honest, independent, patriotic statesmen, and drive them into retirement. No wonder the most eminent felt despondent, and almost despaired of the republic. A letter written by Mr. Clay at this time to his friend Francis Brooke strongly expresses this sad feeling. He says,—

"Mr. Webster retires positively; Mr. Ewing is ousted; and Leigh and Clayton and Mangum and Porter are gone. What good can I do, what mischief avert, by remaining?" . . .

Mr. Clay and Mr. Webster both intended to withdraw from public life, discouraged and disheartened and sickened and calumniated and abused as they were. But the friends of both, and of the country, remonstrated, and implored them to remain, and not to give up the ship. Fortunately, they reconsidered their resolution, and remained.

Happily for the country, this state of things was drawing to a close. The constitutional term of him whose *will* was the law of his partisans and, when they were in the majority in both branches of Congress, of the whole country, was about to expire; and though his successor might be ambitious to "tread in the footsteps of his illustrious predecessor," his stride fell far short of those enormous "footsteps;" and though the sceptre so powerfully and mercilessly wielded by his predecessor might pass into his hands, they were powerless to wield it. Fortunately for the country, the JACKSON DYNASTY could not be perpetuated by a Van Buren.

GENERAL JACKSON RETURNS TO THE HERMITAGE.—A SKETCH OF HIM.—HIS DEATH.

Up to this time General Jackson has been the principal figure in these reminiscences. But his second Presidential term closed on the 3d day of March, 1837, and, after attending the inauguration of his successor, whom he himself had made such, he left Washington for his residence, the Hermitage, near Nashville, never again to revisit the national capital.

For good or for evil, or a mixture of both, his record was made, and not liable to be *expunged*. By that posterity will judge him more impartially than we can, who lived during his time, took part in public affairs, or at least a lively interest in the various political questions which then divided parties, and judge of public men and measures as they were seen from a partisan stand-point.

General Jackson was a remarkable man: remarkable, first, for an indomitable *will;* remarkable, second, for his sagacity in judging men, his clear insight into human character and the motives which actuate men; remarkable, in the third place, for his great moral and physical courage; remarkable, in the fourth place, that he never took a backward step. Whatever he fully determined to do, he persevered in until it was accomplished, stand who would in his way. It was flatteringly said by his admiring friends that he was "an old Roman," and that he was "born to command." Much as there was of obsequiousness in these expressions, which did not fail to reach his ears, there was still more of truth. It cannot be denied that "he was bountifully endowed by Providence with those high gifts which qualified him to lead, both as a soldier and a statesman;" and he had many of the noble qualities which we usually attribute to the "old Roman." He was restive of restraint, contradiction, opposition, or censure, and looked upon all who indulged in either as personal enemies; and, having a large share of combativeness, he was pretty sure to throw down the gage of battle to all such. But to his trusted friends his kindness and gentleness, his affability and frankness, were unbounded.

That he was patriotic, no one can doubt. That all the measures he adopted he believed to be for the best interests of the country, I do not doubt; though his strong feelings of hostility to Mr. Clay, and his antagonism to the opposition, often blinded his judgment and induced him to adopt and persevere in measures which were highly injurious to the country; his enmities being as powerful in moving him as his desire to promote the public interests, sometimes perhaps even more so,—as, for instance, in the war he waged against the United States Bank, and in uttering, perseveringly, charges of bargain and corruption against Messrs. Adams and Clay, but especially the latter, after he had failed to prove anything of the kind.

That some, perhaps many, of his measures which were strongly opposed by the Whigs were wise and beneficial to the country the test of time has proven,—one of these being what was called the "Sub-Treasury," or "Independent Treasury," still in existence.

General Jackson's popularity was most extraordinary; especially with the less informed,—"the unsophisticated classes" of people,—with whom he was, indeed, an idol. It was a common remark, and sometimes the boast of his supporters, that "his popularity could stand anything;" and there was in it more truth than boasting. No matter what he did, with the classes I have mentioned, he "could do no wrong." They believed him honest and patriotic; that he was the friend of the *people*, battling for them against corruption and extravagance, and opposed only by dishonest politicians. They loved him as their friend, and admired him as all admire heroic characters,—men of "iron will" and courage, who grapple with and overcome all opposing obstacles. He seemed to have an intuitive knowledge of the people,—how to move them and to win their confidence, as was evinced in his Dauphin County letter, and in his communication to the Legislature of Tennessee resigning his seat in the Senate. His power over his party was absolute, and enabled him to crush any one who manifested a disposition to act independently, or who failed to support any one of his measures; and this was done so promptly, remorselessly, and effectually as to strike terror into others. The discipline of his party was the discipline of his army,—the head only must command, all below implicitly obey, and every deserter be shot. No doubt the effect of this discipline was to give strength and unity to the party. It was no uncommon thing for members of the party, in conversation with gentlemen opposed to them, to condemn earnestly a government measure and yet to vote faithfully for it. And the explanation was that though they deemed it wrong and injurious to the country, yet to vote against their party or an Executive measure would be committing political suicide.

General Jackson's whole Presidential term of eight years was an unceasing conflict with Henry Clay, the Bank of the United States,—or, more accurately speaking, Nicholas Biddle,—and John C. Calhoun; each and all of whom he overcame, attaining every object he aimed at, even the election of a successor designated by himself, and the expunging from the records of the Senate of the resolution of censure introduced by Mr. Clay, supported by Mr. Webster and Mr. Calhoun, and passed by the Senate, so obnoxious to him.

This was his crowning triumph, and one nearest his heart, if we except the election of his favorite, Mr. Van Buren, as his successor. These triumphs were due to the facts I have mentioned,—his great skill in controlling public opinion and winning popular favor; his disciplining and governing his party; his bold and daring measures; his having around him men unsurpassed for shrewdness and ability as political managers and writers, and the implicit fidelity and devotion with which they executed his known wishes. The able pens of Benton, William B. Lewis, Amos Kendall, Blair, and Eaton were ever ready and ever active. The "Globe" was a power, and gave the cue in regard to all political matters to the Jackson press in every part of the United States. It was fierce and merciless in its assaults upon prominent individuals, especially Mr. Clay, and any one upon whom General Jackson's wrath had fallen, as in the case of Mr. Calhoun. With the venerable Judge White, one of the purest and most respected men in the nation, between whom and himself a life-long friendship had existed, he did not hesitate to fall out, because, instead of supporting his favorite, Mr. Van Buren, for President, he became a candidate himself; and, as a punishment for his disloyalty, the Legislature of Tennessee adopted such resolutions of instruction as they knew the Judge could not obey, and, as an alternative, would resign his seat in the Senate.

In conclusion, it may be said that every principle which General Jackson announced before his election as President —namely, that of destroying "the monster, *party*," by selecting members of the cabinet from both parties indiscriminately, that of holding the office of President for one term only, that of the non-appointment of members of Congress to office during the term for which they were elected and for two years thereafter, and that of not seeking the office of President—was, after his election, cast aside and utterly disregarded.

On retiring, he followed the example of General Washington, and issued an address to the people of the United States, which probably not one in a thousand of the people now living ever saw or heard of. Born on the 15th day of March, 1767, he died on the 8th day of June, 1845.

Parton, in his "Life of Jackson," has thus truthfully and skillfully analyzed and depicted him:

"No man will ever be able quite to comprehend Andrew Jackson who has not personally known a Scotch-Irishman. More than he was anything else, he was a North-of-Irelander. A tenacious, pugnacious race; honest, yet capable of dissimulation; often angry, but most prudent when most furious; endowed by nature with the gift of extracting from every affair and every relation all the strife it can be made to yield; at home and among dependants, all tenderness and generosity; to opponents, violent, ungenerous, prone to believe the very worst of them; a race that means to tell the truth, but, when excited by anger or warped by prejudice, incapable of either telling, or remembering, or knowing the truth; not taking kindly to culture, but able to achieve wonderful things without it; a strange blending of the best and the worst qualities of two races. Jackson had these traits in an exaggerated degree: as Irish as though he were not Scotch; as Scotch as though he were not Irish."

"The border warfare of the Revolution," says Parton, "whirled him hither and thither; made him fierce and exacting; accustomed him to regard an opponent as a foe. They who are not for us are against us, and they who are against us are to be put to death, was the Carolina doctrine during the later years of the war." And it was Jackson's doctrine ever after. It was the doctrine enunciated in his first inaugural address; and the doctrine on which "the spoils system," announced by Marcy in the Senate, was based.

END OF VOL. I.

www.ingramcontent.com/pod-product-compliance
Lightning Source LLC
LaVergne TN
LVHW010159110826
845151LV00002B/561

* 9 7 8 1 4 2 5 5 3 6 3 3 6 *